Dollars, Diamonds, Destiny & Death

This book is dedicated
to my fellow spiritual seeker Doris Duke.
I'll always remember the very special time
we spent together.

—Nischintya Dasa

Dollars, Diamonds, Destiny & Death

Nischintya Dasa &
Joseph P. Higgins

VEDIC CULTURAL ASSOCIATION PUBLISHING

Honolulu • Los Angeles • Chicago

Dollars, Diamonds, Destiny & Death

Front cover artwork by Amrita devi dasi Griesser
Doris Duke's passport photo/J.B. Duke portrait: original art-
work by Gunamai devi dasi
Cover design and concept by True Faust/Bimala devi dasi

Endpapers Front: "The Beach House"—Doris Duke's casual
name for her five-acre oceanfront estate located on the island
of Oahu, Hawaii. Built in 1935, the estate is formally known
as Shangri-La. Original artwork by Amrita devi dasi Griesser.

Endpapers Back: "The Cottage"—Doris' casual name for her
ten-acre oceanfront estate located in Newport, Rhode Island.
Its formal name is Rough Point. Original artwork by Amrita
devi dasi Griesser.

Vedic Cultural Association, Inc.
3765 Watseka Avenue, Suite 5
Los Angeles, CA 90034

Special Limited Edition
First Printing, 2000: 3,000 copies

ISBN 1-928869-01-7

Printed in Hong Kong

Contents

• • • • • • • •

Preface

• • • • • • •

Doris Duke.

Who's Doris Duke?

If you asked me that question prior to 1989, I would have answered: "I don't know. Who is she?" Most of my generation never heard of the woman. In fact, when I tell people I was Doris Duke's astrologer, they'll ask: "You were Doris Day's astrologer?" or "You were Patty Duke's astrologer?" All I knew before I met the lady was that she was a tobacco heiress and an elderly recluse.

I was not aware of just how famous the woman had been when she was growing up. I did not realize that the lady had globetrotted decades before the jet age. I was not privy to the numerous public, private, and certainly scandalous affairs the twice-married woman enjoyed in her younger days, though I would have been familiar with many of the men's names.

Doris Duke. Who was she?

She was soon to be my client, a friend, a confidant. Someone I would grow to love and care about. Someone I could joke with. Someone much more interesting than anything that had been printed about her.

Dollars, Diamonds, Destiny & Death

Before I begin my remembrance of Doris Duke, it might be helpful to bring her vast wealth into perspective. As an astrologer to the rich and famous, I had previous millionaire and multi-millionaire clients. In many ways, they're just like you and me.

Granted, they own larger homes, drive fancier cars, hire servants to wait upon them and travel first class, staying at all the best five-star hotels. Yet their lives are pretty much the same as ours—just bigger and better.

But Doris Duke's life was "Life Styles of the Rich and Famous" times ten. She had lavish estates in Hawaii, Beverly Hills, New Jersey and Rhode Island, as well as a penthouse on Park Avenue in New York City. She traveled the world in her private $25 million 737 jet. In fact, to paraphrase former business manager Patrick Mahn and Tom Valentine in their book *Daddy's Duchess,* pound for pound, dollar for dollar, asset for asset, there was no one richer in this world than Doris Duke.

She was a multi-*billionaire*. Each and every billion she possessed equaled the net worth of a thousand millionaires. If you picked up a dollar bill a second and worked forty hours a week, it would take you 134 years to become a billionaire. Laid end to end, that currency would wrap around the world almost four times.

It's a helluva lot of money, ain't it?

What kind of life style do you think she led? What kind of problems could a multi-billionaire possibly have? What did Doris Duke *do* each day? I mean, the lady didn't have to work. Was she happy? Was she sad? Was she nuts? Was she paranoid? What was Doris Duke *really* like?

I could only guess. But I found out.

And that's my story.

Nischintya Dasa
October 1997

Introduction

• • • • • • • •

This is not a biography in the strict sense of the word, though Doris authorized me to write one about her. It is, rather, a remembrance of the good and bad times I shared for a few years with a unique, close friend.

Before I begin this special memoir, I would like to give a brief—and I do mean brief—synopsis of what Doris Duke did before I met her in 1990.

A Doris Duke Chronology:

1912   Doris Duke is born on November 22. She is dubbed "the richest baby in the world" by the press. Her father, James Buchanan "Buck" Duke, 55, the ninth richest man in the U.S., founded the American Tobacco Company in 1890. Her mother, Nanaline "Nana" Lee Holt Inman Duke, 43, is a Southern widow and Buck's second wife. Nana's son by her first marriage, Walker Inman, 17, lives with them in a newly-constructed, Fifth Avenue mansion in New York City.

1921   Jenny Renaud, a French-born private instructor, is hired as a tutor and governess for Doris. The woman remained with her charge for 13 years. She is the closest female figure in Doris' early life, a surrogate mother-figure.

1922   Doris is enrolled in the exclusive Brearley School. Among her classmates are Dottie Mahana (Doris' best friend and a corn products heiress), Betsy Jennings (whose mother was an Auchincloss, the very elite of NY High Society), Marion Snowden (later known as Princess Rospigliosi), and Barbara "Babs" Hutton (of Woolworth fame). Buck Duke awards Trinity College a $1 million grant.

1923   Angier "Angie" Buchanan Duke, son of Benjamin "Ben" Newton Duke, a first cousin of Doris, is killed in a boating accident on Labor Day. With his sudden and unexpected death, Buck and Ben Duke begin to prepare Doris, at ten years of age, for her future role as head of the family business.

1924   Walker Inman becomes *persona non grata* in the Duke household due to conflicts between him and his stepfather. Buck Duke donates a $40 million endowment to Trinity College, which will subsequently change its name to Duke University. The Doris Duke Trust is created along with the Duke Family Foundation.

1925   Buck Duke dies after a lingering illness on October 10; Doris, his only child, is six weeks shy of her 13th birthday. She becomes heiress to a fortune of $100 million. Her father's Will stipulated that it be given to her in three equal installments: on her 21st, 25th and 30th birthdays.

1927   Fourteen-year old Doris files a lawsuit against her mother for sole ownership of the three Duke properties. The courts rule in her favor; Nana is given permanent residency at the New York and Rhode Island mansions. Nana enrolls Doris in Fermata School.

1929   In January, Ben Duke passes away. Doris meets her future first husband, James "Jimmy" Henry Roberts Cromwell, in Bar Harbor, Maine. She is 16. In June, Doris leaves Fermata; by December, she officially quits the school.

1930   In May, Doris Duke and a select handful of American debutantes are presented to the King and Queen of England at St. James Court. Later that year she makes her social debut in American high society.

1935 Doris and Jimmy are married on February 16; the bride is 22, the groom 38. Walker Inman gives his sister away in the private ceremony held at the New York mansion. The newlyweds begin their "around the world" honeymoon cruise. Doris meets Mahatma Gandhi in India. She starts affairs with both Duke Kahanamoku, the Olympic swimming champion, and his brother Sam, the local sheriff. Doris is the first "white woman" to become a "surfer queen." While in Hawaii, Doris begins construction of the Shangri-La estate, the first home in Hawaii to cost more than $1 million.

1936 Doris becomes romantically involved with Alec "Bobbie" Cunningham-Reid, a British Member of Parliament while simultaneously hobnobbing with known Nazis.

1939 Doris flies between Europe and Hawaii to be with her three lovers: Duke, Sam, and Bobbie. She finds time to enjoy a tryst with a Hollywood legend, Errol Flynn.

1939 Doris undergoes an abortion at Queen's Hospital in New York City.

1940 Doris gives birth to her only daughter, Arden, on July 11. The infant dies the following day. Doris chooses to separate from husband Jimmy.

1941 Doris samples the sexual charms of Errol Flynn for a second time.

1942 In September, Jimmy files for a limited divorce from Doris in New Jersey. In October, Doris counters with a divorce action of her own in Nevada. The Reno court rules in her favor by December, however, the decision is not recognized by the New Jersey court until two years later.

1944 Doris works for the United Seaman's Service in Egypt at a salary of $1 a year. This is one of the happiest times in her life.

1945 Doris is appointed to the OSS, the forerunner of

the CIA, in January. Her code name is "Daisy" (based upon the character Daisy Mae Yokum in the Li'l Abner comic strip). She tours with Eleanor Roosevelt in Italy. Doris works there for the International News Service in Rome as a journalist and war correspondent, interviewing Benito Mussolini's widow. While doing a story on General George S. Patton, Doris and the war hero spend a four-day dalliance together in a chateau near the Russian border. On her return home from Europe, Doris purchases a well-endowed, Dominican playboy and polo player Profirio "Rubi" Rubirosa from his wife, French movie star Danielle Darrieux, for $1 million.

1947   Doris marries her second husband, Rubi, on September 1. CIA agents, acting as attorneys for Doris, "convince" the groom to sign a prenuptial agreement, hinting that if he refused, Miss Duke would be a widow before the honeymoon. Rubi faints after the exchange of vows. He is 39, she 34.

1948   Rubi and Doris divorce, though they continue to see one another.

1950   Doris meets author Louis Bromfield. With his encouragement, she begins a major, ecological renovation of Duke Farms. Doris donates her New York Fifth Avenue mansion to NYU's Institute of Fine Arts. Nanaline is moved to the Stanhope Hotel.

1951   Doris' half-brother, Walker, marries Georgia Polin in March.

1952   Her nephew, Walker Inman, Jr., is born. Nana Veary, a famous Hawaiian spiritualist, befriends Doris. The two women begin the first of many worldwide trips seeking "The Truth."

1953   Doris starts a relationship with jazz pianist, Joseph "Joey" Armand Castro.

1954   Walker Inman passes away.

1956   Louis Bromfield dies.

1962   Her mother, Nanaline, passes away on April 12. She leaves the bulk of her estate to Doris.

Introduction

1964 By court order, Joey, who claims to have been married to Doris, is banished from all Duke residences.

1965 Doris befriends Eduardo "Eddie" Tirella, an interior decorator and Hollywood art designer. Ex-husband Rubi is killed in a car crash on July 5.

1966 Doris establishes the Preservation Society of Newport County. Eddie dies in a mysterious automobile accident at Newport on the night of October 2; Doris is behind the wheel at the time.

1972 Long a fan of Black Gospel music, Doris sings with Reverend Lawrence Roberts and the Angelic Gospel Choir in Harlem, much to the consternation of her security people.

1985 Doris meets Charlene Gail "Chandi" Heffner, a Hare Krishna devotee.

1986 Doris offers refuge and assistance for ousted Philippine heads of state Ferdinand and Imelda Marcos.

1988 The Marcoses are indicted on racketeering charges in New York Federal Court. Doris posts $5.3 million bond for her Filipino friends. On November 10, Doris officially adopts 35-year-old Chandi.

1989 Ferdinand Marcos dies from a serious illness before his trial would be heard in court; Doris lends the former First Lady moral, legal and financial support, as well as use of her private jet.

CHAPTER 1

Chandi Duke Heffner— Heir Apparent

• • • • • • • •

I met Doris Duke through my association with her adopted daughter, Chandi Duke Heffner.

Both of us personally knew our Spiritual Master, A. C. Bhaktivedanta Swami (Srila Prabhupada). Chandi's husband had been one of his first disciples. Eventually, she tired of the spiritual scene on the Big Island of Hawaii and took off on her own. Chandi left behind a large number of Hare Krishna people who were glad to see her go. Many devotees thought she was a real pain and hated her guts.

Despite Chandi's formidable—almost ruthless—reputation, I wouldn't categorize her as an evil woman. She is a very high-strung, sensitive individual. Not only could Chandi lose her temper over trivial matters, but she would take insignificant things seriously. Chandi was one of those people you couldn't joke about in a good-natured, innocent manner. To her, this type of humor was a personal affront. Any droll remarks wore heavy on her heart. Most people shrug off these types of immodest, yet humorous, barbs of witticism—not Chandi.

Her local, infamous nature notwithstanding, Chandi and I got along pretty well. We shared some good times together. The two of us had another Hare Krishna friend in common:

Pushkar. He was one of the artists at the temple, talented and sarcastic. At the time when I was the temple president in Honolulu, Pushkar was invited to visit Chandi at Shangri-La, Doris' estate at nearby Black Point.

Though he never got the chance to meet Doris, Pushkar tripped out on all the magnificent artwork and the awe-inspiring architecture. With his Fine Arts background, he was able to appreciate the grandeur of Miss Duke's palatial surroundings.

Chandi had been given a 300-acre horse farm on the Big Island. Doris paid over one million dollars for the property. Her ranch is about 3,000 feet or higher in elevation. It's located on the side of the island which is plagued by constant cold and frequent rain. Most of the time, the weather is not pleasant. The area offers few amenities.

In one of her rare, generous moods, Chandi allowed me and Pushkar to visit her private retreat. We flew on Doris' recently-purchased, personal, $25 million 737 jet. The trip was made without Miss Duke. A lady friend of Chandi's, who was a pilot for one of the major airlines, came around to check out this state-of-the-art plane; she was impressed.

Chandi is very paranoid of having her picture taken. She once blew up at a temple devotee with a camera at a Feast Day banquet. Yet, I have a photo from that trip—one of the few that she has ever consented to have taken. We are standing in the rear of the plane. Chandi is in jeans, barefoot, carrying an oxygen tank; whenever she flew, Chandi always took along her own personal air supply. On long flights, breathing pure oxygen helped her deal with jet lag. Apparently—that day—Chandi appears to have been in a good mood.

When we returned after our brief stay, I thought to myself: "Who the hell would want to live there?" But Chandi loved it.

Doris was into Indian mysticism and mythology. Chandi convinced her that she should have a complete set of Srila Prabhupada's fifty-volume encyclopedia at each of her residences in the United States. Well, four of the five estates—Chandi never got around to buying a set for Doris' penthouse in New York City.

I was a distributor for numerous publications written by our Spiritual Master. Chandi had difficulty obtaining some of these texts, both in Hawaii and Los Angeles. I usually had a large quantity on hand, so Chandi would order from me. Not only could I supply her with the editions she wanted, I was also able to sell them for less than what the original booksellers charged. Although the young woman now had access to vast amounts of money, Chandi always wanted the best deal she could cut when buying them. She constantly haggled on the prices: "Can't you do a little better?"

Chandi purchased the four encyclopedia sets from me—all at a substantial discount from the wholesale price. Every now and then, she would come and visit, picking up her books or ordering new ones. She even bought a few East Indian drums for Doris.

Whenever Chandi stopped by, she brought along her bodyguard and boyfriend, James Burns. Sometimes, because I wasn't that far from Shangri-La, I delivered her purchases. On two of those occasions, I glimpsed Miss Duke on the grounds. The first time, she was with Johnny Gomez, the *majordomo*. During the second trip, Bernard Lafferty was helping Doris out of the pool. Chandi seemed nervous; I think she was afraid that the butler would bring Miss Duke over to where we were.

Chandi never introduced me to Doris on either of these visits. In fact, she never had Miss Duke meet any of her friends. Chandi was very protective, and guarded her second mother against any outsiders. Doris may have been her own private piggy bank, but there was more to their relationship than just the money. I think she really loved Doris.

During all my wheelings and dealings with Chandi, I was approached by some producer friends of mine. They were involved in putting together television shows which featured some of the local color. Their programs ran on Hawaiian Public Access Television.

They wanted me to do a "How To" show about astrology. I was reluctant to participate because I was concerned about the quality of the program. I felt that the production wouldn't be quite up to the standards I wanted. My friends had an extremely limited budget, which prohibited any major—and sometimes necessary—editing.

They finally convinced me to do it. I was pleased with the result but, deep down, knew that with the proper funding and facilities, the show could have been much better.

"Island Astrologer" was a basic introduction to Vedic Astrology. I commented about how and why it was different from Western Astrology, instructing the viewers in the use of a telescope. In Vedic Astrology, the stars and planets are in their true positions astronomically; that correlation is not present in Western Astrology.

To illustrate how long this Eastern astrological system had been around, I brought with me a few of my palm leaf scrolls. The ones I own are only hundreds of years old. The originals which depict the symbols, instructions and terminology have been preserved on scrolls dating back thousands of years.

After taping, the show aired. Either the station received a good response, or the executives liked it and they didn't have any other suitable programming, because this show was constantly run—an endless barrage of repeated broadcasts. I thought it was overkill. Little did I know how wrong I was.

One day, in Shangri-La, James Burns was flipping through the television channels and came across my program. He let the other security members in on the fact that he knew this studio celebrity: "Hey, that's the guy Chandi gets all the books from."

James called up Chandi, who was eating lunch with Doris, and informed her: "Nischintya's on TV." So, while they finished their meal, Miss Duke and Chandi watched the rest of the show.

Afterward, Doris told her: "I want him to be my astrologer." Miss Duke was aware that Chandi knew me.

The next day, I got a call from her. "Nischintya, I need you to do some charts for me. That is, Doris would like you to do her horoscope."

"Okay, fine. Great."

"How much will this cost?" On the program, I mentioned that Ronald and Nancy Reagan had paid their astrologer $3,000 for a consultation. Ever frugal, Chandi was still trying to save money.

At that time, I used to charge $555 for either a reading or for an entire set of Srila Prabhupada's books. If a person paid me to do a chart, I would give them a complimentary book collection; if someone bought a complete, fifty-volume publication, I would do a free chart as part of the deal.

"Look, Chandi, you bought four sets of books, so you've got four readings coming—no charge."

"Really?"

"Yeah."

"Okay," she pondered, "I want you to do a chart for Doris, another for me, one for Imelda Marcos.... The last reading will be for James."

"Fine. You're entitled."

I don't think Chandi was quite keen on the idea of me doing a chart for Miss Duke, but because Doris was always adamant about things, she had little choice. It also helped that she had the readings coming to her at no cost.

She gave me the natal information I needed for both her and Doris. The two of us arranged a day and time for me to do Doris' chart. Before I hung up, I asked Chandi: "What do I call her?"

"You call her 'Miss Duke.' Everyone does."

"Okay. Do I curtsy?"

Chandi started laughing. "No, no, of course not."

Another thought struck me. I wondered if I was going to have to get dressed up for the appointment. I prefer very informal clothing. I didn't even own a suit. Hadn't worn one in over fifteen years. "Do I have to wear anything special?"

"No, we're pretty casual here. You don't have to worry about that. Whatever you decide on will be fine."

Boy, was I relieved. "Great. See you then."

One of my policies when it comes to doing a person's chart is that they come to me. I don't drive. If they prefer that I do the reading at their place, I insist they either pay for a cab or send their own driver.

I didn't live that far from Shangri-La. Chandi sent Johnny Gomez to pick me up. He arrived in a station wagon. I was a little disappointed that it wasn't a limousine. I wore a combination casual Hawaiian and Hare Krishna outfit.

We drove down Kalakaua Avenue through one of Honolulu's poshest neighborhoods, through the swarms of international tourists, past the luxury hotels to Diamond Head Road.

The Duke Estate is enclosed within thick, towering walls. It's almost like a fortress. You just can't walk into the place. The security guards do not wear dress uniforms. Most of them are natives. They patrol the perimeter and scout the area clad in casual, Hawaiian clothes. No guns—but then, these are big guys, as formidable as the front entrance.

Johnny stopped the auto and talked on the car phone: "Here we are. We're coming."

The enormous gate opened. We proceeded on to the main house. At Black Point, Doris had acquired five-and-a-half acres of land. Not even the Kahala Hilton in Hawaii owns the land it is built on; the property is leased. Kahala in Honolulu is home to some of the most expensive real estate in the world. And Doris possessed a sizable chunk of it.

The road leading to the mansion was lined with tall banyan trees laden with figs. As we pulled up to the regal main house, it reminded me of scenes from the television show

"Life Styles of the Rich and Famous." Only better. Much, much better. I was ushered in through this massive door; the ornate, imposing entry was flanked by a pair of gigantic stone camels. Inside I met the butler, Bernard Lafferty. He was dressed in formal attire but sported both an earring and a pony tail. No—contrary to rumors—he wasn't barefoot.

"Oh, Miss Duke has been waiting for you." Bernard brought me down to where I was going to meet Doris.

CHAPTER 2

The Duke and I

• • • • • • •

Chandi furnished me with the date and place information I required to do Doris' chart, however, there was a discrepancy as to the hour of birth. Nanaline, Miss Duke's mother, had told her one time, and a psychic insisted she had been born at a different hour.

In order to accurately lay out the horoscope, I had to do what is called a "chart rectification." Interpolating from the earliest moment to the latest time of birth, I mapped out twenty possible charts. I managed to narrow it down to two choices. One of them had to be The One.

Most people who know something about astrology would have picked the second one [Second House orientation] that said: "money, money, money." But the first chart seemed more Doris Duke. It still read "money," but it also emphasized notoriety, talent and good business acumen. The chart reflected a life that wasn't dominated by wealth, though it revealed the history of a person who started with a lot of money and made even more over the years.

Doris' horoscope was similar to that of a rich, influential prince from India, centuries earlier. Both revealed a person who inherited a large amount of money, making even more over the years. Miss Duke's chart was unlike that of her contemporary, Barbara Hutton, who started out with a fortune and ended up with very little at the end.

I made the decision to work from the former chart. I didn't do it based upon events in her life, because I hardly knew anything about Doris. I said to myself: "No, this one is gonna be hers. Miss Duke is not going to be a Libra-rising, but a Scorpio-rising." The majority of Scorpio-rising people have a "certain forceful energy" or "a fierce look" to them.

While I waited to meet Miss Duke, I was nervous. I've done charts for all sorts of people—movie stars, celebrities, rich people—but I'd never done a reading for such an illustrious client before. I had heard—and it wasn't just from Chandi or Puskar—that Doris Duke was one of the wealthiest women in the world.

Not only did I know she had fame and fortune, but from my astrological insights I also had another image of this remarkable woman—she's kinda far out. Much of what I uncovered reminded me of myself in earlier, wilder and carefree times. I wondered if this would be true about Miss Duke.

Bernard helped Miss Duke down the few steps into the room. She was walking very slowly. I knew she was an elderly lady, but I've known people in their eighties and nineties who put me to shame. Miss Duke was not in good shape. Even though she wore casual attire, her fashion choices reflected both elegance and good taste. Bernard made the introductions and we shook hands.

Doris had this "fierce look in her eyes," very typical of a Scorpio-rising person. "Where would you like to go to do this?" I asked, observing how huge her place was.

"Let's go outside on the patio, there."

"Outside" overlooked the ocean. Beautiful beach. Gorgeous landscapes. We were surrounded by all this lush, tropical foliage and exotic, Eastern architecture. I remember feeling good. It had rained earlier and a mist was still in the air. Off to one side, a rainbow stretched across the waves. I knew that this meeting was an auspicious occasion.

As a Vedic Astrologer, whenever I see a rainbow before I'm about to do something or when I'm discussing an important matter, I know it to be a good omen. I felt that our encounter was going to turn into something really special.

I also realized this wasn't going to be the only time I would spend with Doris Duke. Even before I met her I knew that I was destined to be her personal astrologer.

I got out my books and papers. "You know, Miss Duke, when Chandi first asked me to do this chart, I thought you were just some old biddy recluse. But from your chart, I can tell you're actually a complete party animal."

That broke the ice. Doris warmed to me.

When I do a reading, some of the time I cite from one or more of my books. I do more talking than quoting, though. It's not very exciting for people when you just read stuff to them. They can do that on their own. I throw in bits and pieces for a purpose. I show my clients that I'm not making up things or just rambling off the top of my head.

Much of what I tell people *has* been delineated in a number of the standard texts. But the astrologers, who wrote these particular books, have had more time to articulate and express their thoughts. When I do it on the spot, I'm not always able to put the words in such a flowery language as they have done. Over the years, my clients have told me: "Well, you may not be the most pleasant person to talk to, but at least you're honest." In a word: brash.

Many people have this stereotypical concept of an astrologer: someone very serious, with long, gray hair, glasses, casting a heavy aura of mysticism. I'm usually a disappointment for them in the physical sense. But I make up for it with my personality. More than a few patrons have commented: "You're the most entertaining astrologer I've ever met. When you do a chart, it's like a party."

Before I explained the horoscope to Doris, I alleviated her fears. "I realize you're a famous person, Miss Duke, and that this is a private—very intimate—confidential reading. Don't worry about any of this getting out during your lifetime. I once studied to be a Catholic priest. Please understand our meeting is just as sacred to me as if it were taking place in the Confessional."

Then I threw up my arms and admitted: "Of course, if I'm tortured—or someone even threatens to torture me—I'm going to give you up in a minute."

Doris loved that. She smiled.

"Then again," I further stated, "if I was offered a pile of money—and I mean one or two hundred million dollars—I'd probably talk, too. Just being honest. I'd give you a cut."

We shared a good laugh. I was being both candid and outrageous—that is, myself—and Doris appreciated me because of my bluntness and candor. To her, I was someone real and a refreshing departure from all the "yes"-men she had to deal with over the decades.

Doris believed she could trust me. I never betrayed her faith in me nor my responsibility to her. Other people—not only employees and servants—had to sign a document stating they would never say or reveal anything about her. Every person she hired had a confidentiality clause in their contracts. Not only could they lose their jobs for such a breach, but they could be sued by Miss Duke.

Doris never forced the issue with me. As far as I know, this is the only authorized biography of Doris Duke. I have witnesses to that effect. She said that I could write about her. And I informed Doris that I would. I mentioned several times about writing a book and making a movie about her.

If she had not wanted me to do any of this, Doris would have had me sign a paper the first day I met her. I believe that Miss Duke figured I would give her a fair portrayal. I would show sides of her that nobody had seen; but I would also reveal the bad as well as the good. Everyone has a dark side. Doris was no exception. Neither am I.

Some of the world's greatest heroes have regretted certain spiteful or selfish decisions, which tarnish their otherwise unblemished reputations. And even the most horrendous blackguards have done some good deeds that endear them to someone at one time or another.

We finally got down to the reading. I had to ask a few intimate questions to make sure I had the proper chart. At that time, she didn't give me any particular details but merely confirmed my inquiry. Her responses were short and to the point: "That's true!" or "Yes, it happened."

"Good," I replied. "We're on track here. Miss Duke, you are a Scorpio-rising with four planets in the First House." When I mentioned that such individuals have this "fierce look in their eyes," she stared at me with a puzzled look on her face.

"Oh, really?" She almost laughed, smiling to herself. Doris got a real kick out of that bit of information.

I showed Doris her horoscope, pointing out the different Houses, the planets, the Deities, and the Zodiac signs, and explained the significance of their relative positions to one another.

When we came to one section of her chart [Rahu in the Fifth House], I commented: "This will produce an abortion, a miscarriage, a stillbirth, or a child who dies very soon after being born."

Doris' eyes became watery. She nodded. I had no idea then that the woman was recalling the birth of her only biological daughter, Arden, who died the day after she was born.

Toward the end of our discussion, I concluded: "This is not the chart of someone who just inherits vast amounts of money, but one that indicates a person who is very adept at making more." [Strong Second and Eleventh Houses]

"No, no, no." Doris trivialized the observation. "I don't really. . . . I'm just Dolly Ditz."

I looked Miss Duke square in the eye, then joked with her. "I know you pretend that you have no idea what's being done with your money, but you probably know exactly where every penny of it is. I'll bet you're very on top of how all of your financial resources are invested. You've been gifted with a rather shrewd business acumen." [Lord of the Second in the First House]

Doris still denied it, or rather, she wouldn't admit it. Not to me. Not to anyone. But she knew. And she knew that I knew.

"Even though your particular chart indicates great prosperity," I continued, "this is not the same as good fortune. Wealth is the physical cash, assets or property—and evidently, you possess that.

"But your actual sense of good fortune is not very strong. [Lord of the Ninth House was placed in the Sixth—very weak] Other people, usually those who may not be rich, they feel very good about life. They're certain that God has blessed them. They feel fortunate. But not you, Miss Duke..."

And that's when Doris came up with the saying I will always remember: "As much as it's been a blessing..." She swept her arms about, indicating the exotic grandeur and magnificent splendor that surrounded us. "It's been a curse."

When Doris said the word "curse," I felt that this person had suffered more than anybody I'd met in my life. I could feel a psychic impression. My heart hurt, in a physical sense, when she spoke that word.

"As much as it's been a blessing, it's been a curse."

I recall how sorry I was for her. Doris and I didn't get into her troubled circumstances much during our first meeting. Later, after listening to her stories, I understood. But in that emotive moment, out on the terrace in Shangri-La, I experienced a small part of the pain and suffering money had brought Miss Duke.

I consulted with one of my texts. "You've had more than one marriage. The first one was with someone older. It wasn't a very happy time for you?"

Doris shook her head.

"Yet," I said, "the relationship you had with your father, on the other hand, was exceptionally good. He was your life and soul."

"Yeah."

"But not longevity, huh?"

"Uh-uh."

Doris was in her late seventies when I met her. She still loved her father. Though Buck Duke had passed away before Doris had turned thirteen, that length of time had no meaning for the woman. It was almost as if her dad had passed away only recently.

"Your mother," I pointed out, shaking my head, "not very good at all?"

"I hated my mother," Doris confessed. "I couldn't stand her. It was terrible. We never got along."

Doris was no longer bitter or resentful toward her mother. Neither did she hate her first husband, Jimmy Cromwell. At this stage in her life, she was not in the mood for holding grudges. She may not have sent flowers when they died, but Doris had forgiven them for all the pain they had caused her.

"It seems like there was some surrogate mother, though?"

"Yes, my father hired a governess. She was more like a nanny, really. I had such a good time with her. Jenny was so much fun."

Doris was impressed. She could see that I hadn't done any research on her. Other than the information in her chart, I knew nothing about her past or what had gone on in her life.

When I usually do a person's chart, I try to have as little— if any—background information. I would rather get a feel for the individual while I do the reading. Sometimes I receive psychic impressions or karma connections. Intuition and empathy also come into the picture.

I find it more difficult to have an understanding of a client if I know them. I'm too focused on who they are supposed to be. I can't tap into their energy flows as easily as I can when I'm with strangers.

At some point, it started raining again, heavy this time. We went back inside. As I had progressed with the reading, more was revealed. I had the distinct impression that Doris was someone I had known from at least one past life, perhaps more.

Doris and I went from doing her chart in the first hour to "talking story" for several more after that. We discussed what was going on in our lives, hers as well as mine. We were like two bosom buddies who hadn't seen each other for years.

Every now and then, Doris and I returned to review what was in her horoscope.

"Are all your homes like this, Miss Duke?"

"Well, this one...and the two I have in Newport and Somerville. Why?"

"It's in your chart." [Venus in the Second House in Sagittarius]

"Oh?"

"These symbols refer to someone who lives in a palatial building or will try to make their house as ornate as possible."

"You'll have to visit my farm in New Jersey. I think you'd like it there."

We started talking about the famous people Doris had met over the years. First, she mentioned the celebrities: Errol Flynn, Elizabeth Taylor, Aretha Franklin, B. B. King, to name a few. Next, Doris commented about the politicians and heads of state she knew, both past and present: King George V of England, the late Ferdinand Marcos of the Philippines—and his widow, Imelda—Ronald Reagan, Eleanor Roosevelt, Henry Kissinger and Mahatma Gandhi.

When she mentioned Gandhi, the conversation took a mystical turn. Doris was a "Seeker of Truth." She made numerous, international, spiritual journeys. On one of them, she met and talked with Mahatma Gandhi.

"I was impressed," she said. Though Doris was reluctant to elaborate, the woman felt that he was a sincere, virtuous person. The experience changed her, though she didn't decide to model her life after his. "It was a rewarding meeting," she noted.

"The Maharishi," Doris continued, "teaches the same philosophy, though I think now these modern religious leaders are getting more into the potential financial rewards."

"Yeah, most of them just want to get rich."

"I heard that he and his followers sell *mantras* to the public."

"We don't."

"No?"

"The Hare Krishnas give them away."

"Interesting."

"Of course, we usually ask for a donation."

Doris smiled at my insinuation.

"I may not charge my customers at the Vedic Cultural Association for any *mantras*, but I do charge them for the books."

Doris laughed.

"Your chart indicates that a few of your past lives have been spent either as a spiritual seeker or a healer. You have a definite religious connection."

"Really?"

We continued to loosen and lose ourselves in the timelessness of a comfortable conversation. Then I remembered.... I had promised my wife, Karina, that I would try to be home before ten o'clock. When it got around nine, I told Doris: "I should be going now. It's been pleasant."

"No, no. Please. Stay for dinner."

I hedged a bit, but Doris was not going to be denied.

"Good vegetarian food," she plugged. Chandi had mentioned to Doris about me being a strict vegetarian.

I thought, "What the hell!" and stayed for supper.

Doris hadn't lied; it was excellent food. Chandi joined us. We made small talk during dinner.

Doris referred to a remark I had made much earlier. Nothing escaped her. The woman's wit was sharp. "Do you still believe that I'm a 'complete party animal,' Nischintya?"

"Definitely."

"You don't think I'm crazy or just being eccentric?"

"There's only one difference between crazy people and those who are eccentric."

"What's that?"

"The money."

Doris got a kick out of that comment.

"It's kinda like, if you thought you were Napoleon—only you've got the money to hire an army to prove it—nobody's going to argue the point with you. That makes you eccentric. But other people, without the big bucks to back up their claims, they're just nuts."

Doris and I enjoyed a good laugh together.

When I was getting ready to leave, I mentioned to Doris that I would probably see her tomorrow when I did Chandi's chart. She gave me a slip of paper; the private, unlisted number to Shangri-La was handwritten on it.

"Call me before you come over." She smiled at me. "Just to make sure I'm here."

We said our good-byes. Before she retired to her bedroom, Doris palmed Chandi an envelope.

"Here are those checks you wanted."

Chandi showed me to the door, where Johnny Gomez was waiting to drive me home. She handed me one of the checks.

"Doris wants you to have this." And Chandi reluctantly added: "She wants you to be her personal astrologer."

I looked at the check. It was made out for $3,000.

Even though the reading had been paid for, the lady would not accept it as a complimentary service. And there was no way that Doris Duke was going to pay her astrologer any less than what the President had paid his.

CHAPTER 3

My Name Is Doris

· · · · · · · ·

In her younger years, Miss Duke had been a spiritual seeker.
She still was. Doris was well-versed and experienced in metaphysical and religious topics. I decided that when I visited her
the next day, I would bring her a special good luck charm from
the Los Angeles Temple.

Atop the altars in Hindu temples are statues of the Deities.
Priests, devotees and pilgrims adorn these sacred effigies with
jewelry and clothing. In former ages, such outfits and orna-
mentation consisted of gold, silver and precious gems. Many
collections of such wear were worth millions of dollars.

My Spiritual Master, Srila Prabhupada, cautioned his disciples in the United States: "Do not use real jewels, because
they will only attract thieves. In fact, some of our own devotees may steal such things, if the gems are genuine. So, please
use costume jewelry."

In the temple, as the imitation finery would become old
and worn out, we would replace it with new decorations. The
discarded trinkets are eventually given away as spiritual talis-
mans or religious lucky pieces. From among the cast-off
jewelry, I selected an appropriate brooch.

Remember, Doris Duke was a worldwide collector of art

and precious gems. Though she wore very little herself, the lady appreciated valuable jewelry. She acquired diamonds, rubies, emeralds and sapphires. You name it, she owned it. Doris had also purchased pieces from Czar Nicholas II's Faberge collection, some mid-Eastern sultan's treasury, as well as priceless royal diadems, earrings, necklaces, and bracelets.

Here I was, about to bring some worthless bauble—according to material calculations—to one of the wealthiest women in the world. But I knew Doris would understand.

Before I went to bed, I was reading one of my Spiritual Master's books. I came across a picture of a *gandharva*, a heavenly musician, who had been cursed and transformed into a crocodile as punishment. The eyes of this ancient reptile reminded me of "that fierce look" in Doris' eyes when I first met her.

I experienced a "vision" that night.

I hate telling people: "I had a vision." They start looking at me like I'm weird, or worse, that it's time for the Funny Farm. Sometimes, it really is a vision. On certain occasions, the present gives way to the past, and I'm reliving a moment from a previous existence. Some events are much more obscure; the incident is more like what Rasputin of Russia used to say: "I picture the scene in my mind, but it's the same as if I saw it in front of me."

This vision concerned Doris and one of her past-life existences. I made notes so that I could tell Miss Duke about it when next I saw her.

The following morning, when I called to arrange for my ride to Shangri-La, I talked to Doris: "I marked up one of my astrology books for you. I highlighted the pertinent sections that relate to your horoscope, Miss Duke."

"I told you, my name is Doris."

I recalled that Chandi had instructed me to call her "Miss Duke" while I was doing her chart. But early on during the reading, Miss Duke insisted: "You can call me Doris. My name is Doris." At that point, I knew I wasn't one of the paid help anymore. I was a friend. That moment still remains one of my fondest memories of my billionaire companion.

Doris Duke wasn't someone who easily decided that you could be her friend, however, certain individuals were "in." With me, I think it had more to do with our strong past-life connections. I believe that's why the two of us hit it off so well.

For me and Doris, it was like we were instantly best friends. Just add water and the relationship was there. I'm sure that whenever Doris met someone, she wondered about the person's motives or was concerned about a possible hidden agenda.

The second day, I did Chandi's chart. What fascinated me during our brief session was that she wasn't really into the reading. It seemed as if she didn't care, or that she was only having me do this because it was already paid for and she had it coming.

Chandi's mind was focused on financial matters. I could see that. When I do horoscopes for some people, I'm pointedly perceptive about what's going on in their mind. The image may not last long, but it is strong and basic.

I made a notation on her chart. Chandi asked me what it meant. "Oh, this refers to a problem or injuries to the knees," I replied.

"Really?" Her interest perked up. Chandi inched the hem of her dress up, exposing her knees. "Look at this." On the one knee stretched a huge, nasty-looking, surgical scar.

I concluded the reading with a startling prediction/revelation: "You know, Chandi, this is the chart of someone who can gain a fortune in a split second. It's also the chart of a person who can lose a fortune in a split second. And perhaps, not even just once or twice. Especially considering the period you're about to enter.

"You must return to your spiritual roots," I warned her. "Contemplate your motivation for the things you're doing."

"Yeah, I've already lost an entire fortune," she confessed. "I don't really care about money that much." Chandi launched into an elaborate, biographic spiel: She was from a really wealthy family. They had been disgraced when Chandi had "turned on, tuned in, and dropped out" with the revolutionary crowd. When she became a Hare Krishna, her parents had disowned her and written her out of their Will.

Her story wasn't quite the truth. Chandi had been born into well-off circumstances. Her parents were upper middle class. Her sister, Claudia, had married a successful businessman, Nelson Peltz, who made a fortune.

As far as I could see, Chandi was very much into what money really was. She wouldn't understand what I had told her that day until much later.

My relationship with Chandi soured as my friendship with Doris improved. She was still pleasant, but it was like someone who has to be friendly to you. I got the impression that Chandi wasn't too happy that Doris had found a new friend. The fact that Doris and I got on so well disturbed her. She no longer possessed an exclusive. I don't think she hated me. It was more like the young woman was reluctant to share Doris with me.

Chandi had been my original connection to Miss Duke. Because Doris wanted my company, my relationship with her was no longer dependent upon my friendship with Chandi.

As the weeks passed, her attitude toward me changed. I remember running into her once or twice while visiting. Chandi had come to tell Doris that she was flying to the Big Island or that she was going to take care of some horses on the North Shore. Chandi didn't say anything wrong—it was just a vibe I got, like "What's he doing here?"

After doing the chart for Chandi, Doris and I got together. First, I gave her the highlighted astrological text I had marked up. Then, I showed her the book with the crocodile. I mentioned the vision and its connection to that "fierce look in her eyes."

"I can see where you could get that impression," she commented.

Doris flipped through the book. I told her she could borrow it. "Tell me more, Nischintya."

In a previous incarnation, Doris lived on the heavenly planes. She alternated between being a *gandharva*, a celestial musician, and existing as one of the *apsaras*, the sacred dancing girls of the gods.

Doris was excited with my discovery. I had made her day. I didn't know of her interest in music and dancing at the time.

I find that when I delve into someone's past lives, many times the individual will play both roles, such as being an "Indian" one time and the "Cowboy" the next. Others switch off between the sexes, being both male and female over time.

During this former life, Doris did something wrong, or perhaps, she had offended some deity. The Celestial Court cursed her, exiling her to earth. Our planet lies on the middle planes, between the heavens and the hellish regions.

Doris, though, still had enough karma to enjoy her life here and live like a goddess. I reminded her: "Look around you. You're still surrounded by opulence, only now you experience it in a mortal shell."

In the months ahead, I would constantly razz Doris about her situation. "Just think of it, Doris. You wanted to be a dancer or a musician or a comedienne. Instead, you got stuck being a billionaire. Life is tough, huh?"

Later that day, I presented Doris with the brooch that had been worn by the temple deities. "Hey, Doris, I've got something for you. Look, it's not real diamonds or anything…"

Doris grabbed the trinket from my hand. "I know. I know. The vibrations." And she immediately pinned it on.

During the years that I knew Doris, I would regularly see her wearing the brooch. This lady, who had access to Tiffany's, Harry Winston, etc., was proudly displaying the costume jewelry pin that I had given her.

When Doris had snatched the bauble from me, I experienced a flashback. Not quite *déjà vu*. At the time, I was not prone to those things. I was an astrologer then, not a psychic.

The present faded and I was reliving the past. I was a little boy, and Doris was my mother. She was a very powerful woman. A monarch or head of state. People would live or die depending on her whims. I was giving her some stupid, little trinket as a present. And my insignificant gesture meant more to her than any of her subjects adding to the royal coffers or her fellow royal rulers bestowing her with the most expensive gifts in the world.

I felt the whole energy of the incident engulf me. I started to cry. It was a very personal, emotional moment. I had already determined to decline Miss Duke's offer of employment. That past-life recurrence merely confirmed my decision.

I broke the disappointing news to Miss Duke. "You know, Doris, I can't really have a business relationship with you. I know you wanted a personal astrologer on retainer, but I don't think it will work out."

She was displeased by this turn of events. I had to give her the whole picture, so she would understand my reasons.

"Don't get me wrong. I guarantee you that any astrologer on this planet would be happy as a pig in shit to know that he's just landed Doris Duke as a client."

Doris started laughing.

"Believe me, Doris, this is like 'my ship has come in,' but I can't do it. Not with you. You and I, we've been connected in a number of past lives.

"How 'bout...we're friends. You need some astrological work done, I do it. And you treat me—you take care of me from time to time. When I drop by, I know your hospitality will be really nice."

I explained to Doris how, in the past, the great kings of Asia gave their Brahmin counselors food and shelter in return for their services. Those monarchs received the best possible advice for the least possible expenditure.

She liked my proposed arrangement. I think Doris also felt the same kind of bond.

"You're always welcome here, Nischintya."

For the next month, until Doris and Chandi left for the East Coast, I came over as often as I wished, in addition to those times when Doris needed my services. Some astrology stuff was done, but it was more like two chums catching up on things.

Within weeks, she and I were good, close friends.

CHAPTER 4

Saving Imelda Marcos

• • • • • • • •

The servants and staff in every Duke estate were never allowed to refer to any guest by their first name. Doris would always call me Nischintya; so, they always called me: "Mr. Nischintya." I always got a kick out of that. Mr. Nischintya. Makes you feel important. Like one of the rich and famous.

Every time I would visit, the proper etiquette was observed. None of the hired help would break the tradition or formality. It didn't matter if I was on the phone or riding in one of Doris' cars. Everyone knew I was Miss Duke's guest, and they *treated* me like Miss Duke's guest.

Nice, huh? I'm all in favor of tradition and formality—but only when you're on the receiving end.

Later, when I became more friendly with her entourage, it was "Mr. Nischintya" in front of Doris, and when I was just hanging out with them, they would call me "Nischintya."

Miss Duke knew my legal name but respected my "reborn" status as an initiate into ancient India's brahminical culture.

During the month before Doris left Hawaii, we got together many times. As far as I could tell, she was drawn to characters who reminded her of her father, James Buchanan Duke. Doris was in ecstasy when she discovered that my birth-given first name was James. She asked me what my full name was.

"James Edward Higgins, III."

"I like that." She rolled it off her tongue, savoring the sound of the words. "Sounds impressive and official. Reminds me of my first cousin's name, Ambassador Angier Biddle Duke."

The birth dates between me, Doris and her father had meaning. I pointed it out to Doris: "You were born November 22, 1912. My birthday is December 22nd, but forty years and thirty days after yours. Your father's day of birth was the 23rd of December."

Doris loved life's little coincidences.

Over the years that I knew Miss Duke, she always called me Nischintya. She only jokingly referred to me as James or Mr. Higgins. In the book which I highlighted when I did her chart, Doris wrote down my name and phone number so she could get a hold of me. It says "Nischintya" not James.

I didn't just call *her*. Doris phoned *me* many times. I even gave her the number at the temple, so she could reach me there if necessary. The devotees were always nervous and panicked whenever she called: "Nischintya! Nischintya, Doris Duke is on the phone! She wants to talk to you." They were always hyper about it. Most of them were afraid to talk to her; all of them were terrified that they might say the wrong thing.

Whenever Doris required astrological help or just wanted to talk with her new-found friend, she would track me down until she found me. Miss Duke was most persistent. She also made sure that I would be able to contact her. Before Doris left for the East Coast, she gave me the number where she could be reached in New Jersey. At some point, Doris gave me each of the private numbers of her other residences. It wasn't that she listed them all for me; over time, I acquired all the phone numbers.

As our bond of friendship grew stronger, certain people told me I should tell Doris I was her father reincarnated. These subversive individuals would regularly try to get me to propose some business deal to her. They wanted Miss Duke to buy something ridiculous, or were seeking an angle or a scam to con her out of money.

I couldn't do that to Doris. We had many different relationships in past lives, but being her father wasn't one of them. I may have reminded her of her dad, but I wasn't him—past or present. I always gave those unscrupulous, former acquaintances the same response: "Gimme a break. The lady's my friend. Why should I give her some bullshit story like that? I care about her."

Doris cared about me, too.

* * * * *

I have asthma. Many times when I'm in Hawaii, I suffer. Most people wonder how I could have a respiratory problem breathing some of the freshest air in the world. The air may be clean and devoid of any man-made pollution, but it is filled with natural irritants. Mold and pollen can pose a peril to any person's health, especially if they have any breathing disorders or ailments.

When plants are damp from a morning rain or if it's a day with high humidity, I can suffer an attack. Also, when I eat too much at night, a full stomach can really aggravate my condition.

One night, when I was having dinner with Doris, I must have overindulged. Believe me, Miss Duke could afford good cooks. Because of a high pollen and mold count that day, in addition to having stuffed myself, I started wheezing a bit. Not a full-blown attack, but enough to cause me discomfort.

Doris noticed. "Oh, you have asthma." She was very sympathetic. Either Doris knew someone with the same affliction, or she had suffered with it when she was younger, because the woman knew how I felt. That's when I found out about her unique healing ability.

"Here, let me." Doris placed her hands on my chest and started giving me *reiki*.

To simplify it, *reiki* is basically similar to what Christians call "the laying on of hands." By using your hands, and employing *mantras* [chants] and *yantras* [invisible drawings], it connects you with the universal healing energy. Within the cosmos there exists this beneficial bio-force which is all around us. Reiki allows you to tap into this metaphysical, recuperative power.

It doesn't take anything out of a person to do *reiki*. This is not like giving a massage or draining your life-force. Your body acts as a conduit. The energy flows through you. You channel it through your body, your hands directing the dynamic vitality into the other person. You are not the one doing the actual healing. You're merely focusing the energy toward the one who needs it.

To perform *reiki*, you keep your fingers and hands together, cupping them slightly as they are placed on the person in pain. Your hands will sometimes be inclined toward certain spots. You move them around until it "feels just right."

At some point, both will know that "you're done" and that the treatment isn't needed any longer. An entire *reiki* session usually lasts about forty-five minutes. There are numerous positions, but it's not necessary to go through them all or take that much time.

Doris was remarkable. Her efforts relieved my breathing difficulties. I was amazed. And grateful.

Reiki is not a cure-all, nor are you miraculously healed as if by a television evangelist. It is a temporary, but refreshing, relief. The practice is beneficial for both parties.

Doris loved doing this service for her friends. She actually prided herself in this ability. Giving *reiki* was good for her. Doris always felt better—mentally, if not physically—after doing a session.

Not too many knew that Miss Duke was a healer. Most

people would not have believed it possible. Doris very seldom showed her generous nature. And when she did, it was usually anonymous.

One of the ways that Chandi had ingratiated herself with Doris was because of her knee surgery. After the operation she was still in pain. Doris regularly performed *reiki* on Chandi's knee to ease the discomfort and reduce her suffering.

Believe me, Doris possessed this power of healing with her hands. She had this gift from a past life when she was a monarch in Europe. There were kings and queens in medieval times that used to heal their subjects. Sometimes, all the afflicted needed to do was touch their royal masters or their clothes. Doris still retained that power in her present incarnation.

Normally, you are required to go through a particular study and initiation process, as Miss Duke had done, but she was impatient in many matters. She taught me how to do *reiki,* so I could help heal her knees. Doris would say: "Oh, just do it." No preliminaries, no rituals.

When you discuss *reiki* with people, the majority of them shake their heads, muttering: "Yeah, right." I could write a whole chapter about the things that Doris did for me that were practically miraculous. She even told me about certain exercises that I could do to help me breathe when I had an asthma attack. And they worked. The fact is, Doris helped me.

And in return, I would help her.

* * * * *

One of the duties that Doris was interested in having me do, besides being her astrologer, was to be her wizard. I would concoct potions and lotions to help improve her health, make her more beautiful, or just allow the woman to feel better. Those are some of the other services I perform as a *shaman.*

Though I'm not a herbalist, I know how to prepare elixirs. I also have an intuitive understanding or grasp of certain remedies that people can utilize to help them relieve specific ailments. Many persons who heed my advice have had their medical problems clear up.

I've never urged any of my "patients" to get rid of their present physician. I merely give them dietary suggestions or organic alternatives to help with particular chronic disorders.

I recall one incident where this individual had a skin condition. The woman had been to numerous specialists and spent tons of money on prescription drugs. Nothing helped. I did a preliminary diagnosis and told her: "You're probably allergic to milk. Either cut milk out of your diet or take lactase before you eat; this will help you digest dairy products properly."

The person had to have been thinking: "I've been to all sorts of doctors, and this guy, who doesn't have any medical degree or pharmaceutical background, is telling me what the problem is?!" But the lady took my advice. She cut milk from her diet for two weeks and the whole skin condition cleared up.

Doris wasn't in too good of health when I met here in March of 1990. Because of this, I didn't expose her right away to any "heavy duty" natural and organic medicines. Until her strength improved, I only prescribed some simple remedial substances.

I proposed some changes to her diet and even brought her special Indian meals. One time, I brought Karina along. We were celebrating a feast at the Honolulu Temple, and I had set aside many of the more delectable portions of the banquet for Doris.

Doris sampled each of the dishes. She ate a healthy amount, commenting about how good the food was. Doris, who had an obsession with fashion, also checked out Karina. My wife was decked out in a colorful, Indian, silk sari complete with rings, bells, bangles and bracelets. Doris didn't miss a trick. I hadn't noticed it, but Karina later pointed out how much Doris had been observing her during dinner.

Saving Imelda Marcos

That evening, Doris invited me and Karina to stay with her in New Jersey: "Look, Nischintya, I'm going to my estate on the East Coast. Why don't you come visit me at Duke Farms? I'll set up a little cottage for you and Karina. And you can come and go as you want."

* * * * *

Chandi had her own set of Deities. She took them with her whenever she and Doris traveled. She usually had them dressed and wearing jewelry. Chandi also made daily offerings of flowers and incense to the statues.

As Doris and Chandi prepared to leave Hawaii, Chandi was bundling up her Deities. She neglected to pack the one of Lord Narasinghadeva—the God of Protection—Who's half-man, half-lion. Very ferocious. Very formidable. His statue was sitting on a table behind a vase. Alone. Naked. No clothing, no jewels.

"What about Lord Narasinghadeva, Chandi? Are you going to leave—"

"You take Him, Nischintya. Take Him, take Him," she pleaded. "You take care of the Diety. You keep Him."

"Hey, Doris," I pondered, "this Deity can help Imelda. I'll use Him in the ritual."

"Really?"

"Sure. When I'm in Los Angeles, before I come visit, I'll do the *Narasinghadeva Puja*."

Doris had wanted me to help her and Chandi's friend, Imelda Marcos, the former First Lady of the Philippines. She and her late husband, Ferdinand, had been exiled from the Asian country and accused of embezzling billions of dollars from the funds given to their nation by the United States.

Doris was excited that I would do the ceremony to assist Imelda. Normally, the fee for such a *puja* would be a few hundred dollars, however, I was not about to charge Doris, especially after she and Chandi had given me this Deity.

Doris had loaned Imelda over $5 million to help with court costs and legal fees. She sought my *shaman* services to perform a *puja*, so her friend could win the judicial battle going on in New York City. Doris requested that I do Imelda's horoscope, to see what was upcoming in her future.

I've done these rituals before, a few of them for lawyer friends so they could win their court cases. It was not an unusual nor unreasonable request.

I never did an actual one-on-one, person-to-person reading for Imelda Marcos. Doris had me write down the chart and my predictions for her.

I wondered why Doris wanted me to do all this work for Imelda but never allowed me to meet the woman. During the few weeks that I had known Doris, I had gotten bipolar vibes concerning their relationship. Some days, it seemed as though the two of them were best friends; other times, Doris couldn't give a damn about Imelda.

I thought maybe Doris was jealous. She hated to share anything, whether it was Chandi with James, or me with my wife, Karina. Was Doris thinking: "This is my astrologer and you can't have him, Imelda?" I couldn't fathom what the big deal was about me not seeing Imelda.

A psychic friend of mine pointed out to me: "Doris knows something about Imelda; it concerns her dark side. She is just trying to protect you. Leave it at that. Don't push the issue."

I had to put the whole matter on the back burner, because I was in the midst of a moral dilemma. I had second thoughts about performing the religious ritual. When Doris first asked me to do the *puja*, I hadn't done Imelda's chart. Even before I met Miss Duke, I had heard stories about Imelda on the news broadcasts and read articles about her in the newspapers. All the information about this woman seemed to be negative.

I was reluctant to assist because I had been thinking: "Why should I help someone who's hurt so many of her people and may have been a conspirator in all these terrible crimes?" But then I thought about my reputation. I regularly tell people when I do their charts: "Don't worry, I don't prejudge." I had bragged about it constantly and used it as one of my selling points, yet I had condemned this woman even before doing her reading.

I pondered the issue and finally made a decision. Someone had asked me for assistance and I should help. I shouldn't make a judgment call, even if what's been said about her is true. Though I resolved to perform the ceremony, I felt that I could never be a close friend of Imelda's. It showed in her chart. Had Doris introduced us, I might have been able to hang out with Imelda, here and there, but nothing else.

Imelda Marcos had purchased her own residence in Hawaii. She visited Shangri-La regularly, however, Imelda was never there when I stopped by. The situation kind of reminded me of how Chandi would never let me meet Doris when I made my book deliveries weeks earlier. Doris made sure our paths never crossed.

Before Ferdinand Marcos had passed away, Doris called upon him numerous times. She would perform *reiki* over the dying man. I imagine that her healing ability was one of the reasons why Ferdinand held on to life for so long.

CHAPTER 5

Alfred B. Ford, Landlord

• • • • • • • •

I performed the *Narasinghadeva Puja* in May of 1990, when Karina and I stayed in Los Angeles. We were going to be in California for a few weeks. After that, she and I planned a stopover in Florida, prior to our "vacation" with Doris in New Jersey.

When I do a chart for a client, as I mentioned previously, I highlight one of my astrology books and give it to the person. I did this for both Doris and Chandi. When I'm paid extra, I will write out specific notes for their convenience.

For Doris, I wanted to do something special. I felt I should give the woman her money's worth. After all, she had given me a $3,000 tip and offered me a monthly retainer.

During those few weeks in Hawaii, I had become fascinated by the woman and her changing lifestyles. Friends of mine were able to locate an out-of-print biography on Miss Duke, *Daddy's Duchess*, written by a former business associate, Patrick Mahn, and Tom Valentine, a ghostwriter. This book confirmed all my suspicions about Doris being a "complete party animal."

Under my supervision, Karina did the research. She consulted with dozens of astrological books and prepared a lengthy draft, which I edited. When everything was to my liking, publisher friends of mine checked the spelling and formatted the document. We printed out the thirty-page report on the computer and bound it with special covers. I wanted this presentation to be both distinctive and impressive, worthy of a woman of Miss Duke's status.

* * * * *

The reason for our layover in Florida was so I could visit another devotee friend and wealthy client, Alfred B. Ford. The great-grandson of Henry Ford, the automobile tycoon, he is a multi-millionaire in his own right. His mother, a granddaughter of Henry, is regularly listed in *Forbes* as one of the four hundred richest people in America.

Alfred became a Hare Krishna around 1972, near the time that I also converted. In 1974, he bought the Coelho estate in Nuuanu Valley. This two-acre property boasted a large house surrounded by lush, tropical grounds. He purchased it for Srila Prabhupada. This became the Honolulu Temple for the Hare Krishna sect on the Island of Oahu.

Alfred Ford was initiated by our Spiritual Master in 1975. He was given the name Ambarish. (I called him Ambo for short.) Srila Prabhupada told Ford his name was that of a great king and a great devotee. I showed Ambarish how to put on the *dhoti*, the bottom garment that male devotees wear. This part of the outfit looks like "balloon pants," but it's actually one long piece of cloth. Orange indicates being single; the white denotes married status. That was my first association with Alfred Ford.

I got a kick out of Ambarish. Despite being this rich and powerful business magnate—who just donated this huge estate—he was a regular guy. Ambarish was not on any ego trip. He's actually a pretty humble, modest man.

He and I got along very well, right from the beginning.

Alfred B. Ford, Landlord

Later on I became really close friends with him.

Ambarish later married an Indian lady, Svaha. She was trained as a doctor in Australia, her home country. The mother of two children, Svaha became a homemaker.

Fourteen years later, in either 1988 or 1989, I was in Florida visiting a mutual acquaintance. When Ambarish heard that I was in town, he wanted me to stop by. My reputation as an astrologer and *shaman* had preceded me. Ambarish is really into the whole scene. Tarot cards. Psychic stuff. Astrological readings. He talked with our friend: "Ask Nischintya if he can do my chart."

We made arrangements. The day that I did his reading, he asked me how much it was. My standard rate was $555, but I reflected on the past dozen-plus years before I answered him.

"Considering, Ambo, that I've been living in and out of your house—the Honolulu Temple—for the last thirteen or fourteen years, I can't charge you. Believe me, I've gotten my money's worth out of this deal."

Ambarish smiled and shook his head at my explanation. He still gave me a $108 donation. In Vedic tradition, one hundred and eight is an auspicious number.

While I did his chart, we talked. Despite our friendship, I was able to make "a connection." This was probably due to the years we hadn't seen each other. I made several personal references and more than a few, very intimate observations.

Ambarish was stunned by my insight. "Oh my God, it's like you're seeing me naked," he admitted. I was really able to tune in to where he was at, what was going on, and what had happened in his life.

"It's all right," I reassured him. "I don't judge anybody. Believe me, Ambo, I've done worse."

The day after, he invited me to his daughter's birthday party—one of only three people (outside of his immediate family) who received this special invitation.

Dollars, Diamonds, Destiny & Death

* * * * *

Before our return visit to the Fords in Florida, Ambarish and his family were going on a cruise. I recommended that he purchase an emerald for astrological reasons.

"Now, don't buy the first damn emerald you see, " I warned him. "Better to get something small and eye-clean than something large and dirty. Look at it carefully. Make sure that it's a good one. No spots or discoloration. You're Alfred B. Ford; you can afford the best. Take my word for it."

So what did he do? At the beginning of his ocean voyage, Ambarish bought the first emerald he saw. And it's a slightly flawed gem. Things started going badly for him and his family and continued for the rest of the journey. His wife insisted that he take off the ring and put it away.

See what happens when you don't take your astrologer's advice?

Karina and I flew to Miami. I was on a roll. First, I was going to visit the Fords. Then, I was going to stay with the Dukes. Nischintya Dasa, a humble astrologer, hobnobbing with American High Society. With my new wife by my side, I was doing horoscopes for the Rich and Famous.

I was definitely feeling good.

Though we were going to Florida for pleasure, I also had some business with Alfred Ford. For both financial and legal reasons, Ambarish rented the temple property to the devotees for a dollar a year. Pretty reasonable rent. Anywhere.

Since 1974, the Hare Krishnas had not fulfilled their part of the lease. I was there to pay the back rent on the estate. I gave Alfred Ford twenty dollars; that would cover us through 1993.

"This way, Ambo," I told him, "if anybody in the organization gives me a hard time, I'll be able to point out that I paid the rent on the temple for twenty years."

"Yeah, you deserve a little respect, Nischintya."

We laughed about the situation.

I had a photo taken to commemorate the business transaction but, unfortunately, forgot to get a receipt. Since the temple has a long-term lease, the next time I see Alfred Ford, I will not only pay him the $10 balance, but have the man write a proper receipt for my records. Once that's done, I will have paid the entire rent for the Honolulu Temple's thirty-year contract.

After the official function was out of the way, we caught up on things. He showed me his imperfect jewel. I shook my head, reminding him of my instructions. Ambarish recounted all the bad luck he had during his trip.

"I should have listened to you."

"Why did you buy it?" I asked, disappointed.

Ambarish shrugged his shoulders.

"You can use it for religious purposes—*pujas*, chanting, praying to the Deities—but I wouldn't recommend wearing it when you go out."

Ambarish handed me the ring. "Take it! Take it!"

He just gave this $3,000 emerald to me. I was very appreciative, and so overwhelmed by his generosity that I neglected to consider the flawed jewel's short-circuiting power.

* * * * *

Karina and I were staying at this really nice hotel on Biscayne Bay. Her mother had given us some half-price coupons. The hotel was close to the Miami Temple and the Ford residence. And it allowed me to visit friends in the area that I had not seen for years.

I once served as president of both the Miami and Gainesville temples. I met people from all walks of life during my terms of office. Back in Florida for a brief while, I not only socialized with the Rich and Famous but also dropped in on the Poor and Obscure.

Doris promised to let me know when she got back to Duke Farms and had everything set up for us. I remember the day she called.

One of my quirks is that at certain times I will not answer the phone. If I'm eating, sleeping, praying, chanting, partying, having sex or in the bathroom, I hate being interrupted. When I go to bed at night, I usually pull the cord from the wall so I won't be disturbed.

I forgot to unplug the telephone. Karina and I were making love. The phone rang and rang. Although pissed off because of my negligence, we continued to have sex. It fell silent after a little while, but the phone started up again after a few minutes. We didn't stop. The ringing ceased. We kept going. The phone rang again.

I gave up and answered it. I was ready to chew out this annoying person. I almost said: "Who the hell is this?" Luckily, Karina made sure I didn't.

Doris was on the other end. For over thirty minutes, she had endeavored to reach me. Like I said, Doris could be most persistent when she needed to get in touch. Tenacious and stubborn.

"Hello?"

"Nischintya, when are you coming?"

"Huh?" Her first words caught me off guard.

"Everything is all set. So, how long before you and Karina come see me?"

"We'll be done in a couple of weeks..."

"A couple of weeks!"

During our get-togethers, Doris would always mention celebrities or people of renown she knew. I took advantage of the opportunity to do some name-dropping of my own.

"Well, I'm visiting my friend Alfred B. Ford."

I could tell Doris was impressed. A little. She knew Christina Ford, the third wife of Henry Ford II, Ambarish's uncle.

Alfred B. Ford, Landlord

Doris was well aware that I had some important clients. In Hawaii, we used to comment about my "business associates." She and I would joke about how these multi-millionaires, who wore three-piece suits and worked in fancy offices, took advice from someone who's as crazy as I am. Any time I would mention a prominent patron, she would have a field day. Doris found it amazing and funny that such respected and influential individuals were actually paying me big money for my consultations. Of course she had made the same offer to me.

"I've got the cottage fixed up." Doris continued telling me all about her preparations for our visit. She was very enthusiastic and doing her best to entice me to cut short our stay in Florida.

I relented. "Alright, Doris, I'll finish up here in about a week or so, and then we'll be on our way. Okay?"

"Great."

CHAPTER 6

Down on the Farm With The Richest Girl in the World

• • • • • • • •

Karina and I wrapped things up and headed to New Jersey. Before leaving Florida, we were plagued by numerous, petty annoyances. Then, really bad things started happening. It wasn't until we left one of our carry-on bags in the Miami terminal that I figured out why.

"O Lord, I've got this frigging, crazy emerald."

That flawed gem had been causing total havoc with our trip. It was a major pain-in-the-ass just to get our luggage back from the airport. To negate the jewel's bad vibes, I did a temporary, cleansing *puja* before our plane set down in New Jersey.

Doris sent a couple of her men to meet us. One of them was the head of security himself; the other was a subordinate. The security chief was not in uniform, but his deputy was. The younger man was holding a sign that said: "Duke Farms." They had identified themselves as opposed to indicating the names of the people they were picking up. The two men took our bags and escorted us to a station wagon, not a limousine.

As we piled in the automobile, I glimpsed a note Doris had taped to the dashboard. "Do not fill this car up with gas. It is being traded in for another." That was Doris for you. She wasn't going to lose money by exchanging a car with a full tank of gas for one that didn't. The lady saved money wherever and whenever she could. Most of the time, it was on such trivial matters. Doris probably got that from her mother, Nanaline.

Unlike the big "locals" in Hawaii, the guards in Somerville were decked out like a great, metropolitan police force. Their badges and patches, as well as the signs on the cars and gatehouses, read: "Duke Farms Fuzz." Doris' idea. Tagging along with the numerous patrol units were dogs. Lots of dogs. Vicious watchdogs.

Security drove Karina and me directly to the main house. Our luggage would be taken to the cottage without us. We had brought presents for Doris and Chandi from Florida. Nothing spectacular, just some herbal soaps, natural cosmetics and organic lotions. What do you buy the richest woman in the world?

Miss Duke allowed her adopted daughter to open her gifts first. Chandi ripped through everything to see what she got.

Not Doris.

She opened her presents very carefully. Doris was so meticulous that there were no tears in the wrapping paper when she was finished. She folded the paper and placed the pieces with the used ribbons and bows.

My mother has been doing that ever since I can remember. Here was one of the world's wealthiest women taking such deliberate care in unwrapping her gifts. I was in stitches.

Doris wondered why I was laughing hysterically. "What's so amusing?"

"Well," I said, wiping the tears from my eyes, "you unwrap things the same way my mother does."

Doris smiled.

I don't know why she was so frugal that day, nor did Doris mention her reason for saving the paper. It was another "Dorisism" that endeared her to me. Like that tank of gas or the costume jewelry brooch.

I had taken photographs of the Deities in the Los Angeles Temple. When we were in Florida, Karina and I picked out frames for the three snapshots. These were among the gifts we gave to Doris.

I mentioned having done the *puja* for Imelda Marcos. Doris wanted to know all the details, so I gave her a complete breakdown on the ritual.

I asked Doris how the trial was going.

"Imelda wouldn't have any problems, if she just got rid of that stupid lawyer. The judge practically told us 'Lose this attorney and I'll let you win the case.'"

Doris wondered when a ruling would be made.

"By her birthday," I predicted.

"That reminds me, Nischintya. I have to be in New York tomorrow. I'll only be gone a day at the most. I'm sorry I have to leave the day after you get here."

I shrugged my shoulders. "No problem, Doris. It'll give us time to recuperate from all our bopping around."

While Doris checked out everything that both she and Chandi received, she explained the arrangements for me and Karina.

"I fixed up a small cottage nearby. The two of you can come and go as you please. Do whatever you like. You can visit the main house any time. You know when we have dinner, so you can eat supper with us."

Doris handed me a set of keys.

"You have access to the whole estate, Nischintya. If you need a ride somewhere, just call up security. If you need something for the bungalow, ask any of the servants or staff. I hope everything is to your liking."

Doris took pride in Duke Farms. She really wanted us to enjoy our visit.

We had arrived around noon at Somerville. Karina and I wanted to freshen up before dinner. Security drove us to our private getaway.

The quaint, little cottage that Doris mentioned turned out to be this huge, two-bedroom house: basement, bathroom, large living room, enormous kitchen and elegant study. The furnishings may not have been as valuable as those in the main house, but I'm sure they must have cost big bucks.

How much, I couldn't be sure. When I look at art or antiques, all I see is a worn-out rug, an old desk or a nice painting. For all I knew, I might have been looking at a 1,000-year-old, Oriental carpet, a Louis XIV writing table or a Gainsborough original.

When Doris tired of something, the *objet d'art* either went into storage or it was shuffled around to various places on the numerous estates. She didn't sell her venerable acquisitions. Anything Doris bought, she kept.

When Doris, Karina and I sat down for dinner that night, it was in the sitting parlor of her personal suite of rooms. I presented Doris with her full-length, astrological research paper. Her eyes lit up. She was impressed with the official-looking binder and the overall, professional appearance.

The servants brought in these little tables for us to eat on. Not regular snack trays but priceless furniture from some maharaja's palace.

Doris read the thirty-page report during our meal. She didn't talk much for the rest of that evening. She was oblivious to us.

While Bernard served, Chandi and James showed up. She was ranting and raving about the fact that security had tied up her dog. The way Chandi told the story, it sounded like the poor German shepherd had been locked up overnight without food or water. In reality, the dog had been a major pest; security had to leash the animal so the gardeners could do their daily jobs.

The incident was another of those "mountain-out-of-a molehill" situations. Typical Chandi. The whole evening, she berated Bernard. During the entire meal, she yelled and screamed at him. And that was only the beginning.

The chef, Tom Rybak, had prepared a dish with eggplant. Chandi exploded. "You know I can't eat that! How many times do I have to tell you? Can't you get it right, for once?"

Karina interceded. Chandi finally calmed down. Tom took my wife aside and told her: "She ate eggplant last week. The lady's a crazy bitch. Chandi doesn't know what she's talking about."

A couple of times, Doris would have a comment or question about what was in the report. After dinner, she thanked me and went into her bedroom. Karina and I never got the chance to say good-night to her personally. Doris was too involved reading the research paper.

That night, before heading back to the cottage, I wandered about the main house. When I reached the bottom of the stairs, I could hear Doris and Chandi arguing.

They had one hell of a fight. Screaming and yelling. Cursing and name-calling. They threw things at one another. I had never heard two people go at it like that. I don't know why they were quarreling, but it had to be about something important. At least, I thought so.

The following day, with Doris away on business, Karina and I decided to take advantage of having the run of the place. To get to the main house from our cottage, we had to walk along a private road, stroll through a Japanese garden, traverse a small wooden bridge, and trek across a huge lawn. That was the way to the back entrance.

The first time Karina and I hiked over that lawn, the guard dogs appeared. Charging toward us were seven of the largest and meanest dogs we had ever seen: German shepherds, Irish wolfhounds and American crossbreeds. Racing at top speed. Fangs bared. Barking up a storm. You could see the look in their eyes: dinner time!

I thought to myself, "Oh shit. This is how it's going to end. Killed at Duke Farms by the guard dogs." With Karina behind me, I tried to recall their names. Chandi and James had mentioned them last night over dinner. I prayed my memory was still intact.

"Kimo! Ike and Tina Turner! Hello! We're friends."

The pack reached us. It was now or never. They sized us up. I put out my hand. They sniffed and licked us. Luckily, the dogs decided that we were "okay." They trotted off.

My heart was still racing. Karina's body trembled, even after we entered the main house.

When Doris returned, I mentioned the incident. She apologized. "It completely slipped my mind. Sorry." Doris had a smirk on her face. "You weren't in any danger."

Yeah, right.

* * * * *

Doris loved animals. So did Chandi.

In Hawaii, Chandi's dogs—really gross old canines—did nothing but pant and plop down wherever and whenever they felt like doing so. Even Imelda Marcos' dog was residing at Shangri-La. In New Jersey, the "attack" dogs were actually Doris' pets. She constantly referred to them as "her children" or "her babies."

The servants and staff working at each of the residences were informed by Doris at the start of their employment: "These animals live here; you only work here. Under no circumstances are you to mistreat them, abuse them, yell or scream at them— no matter what they do!"

Anyone could be terminated for disobeying Miss Duke's prime directive. Many were.

Whenever one of her guests would comment about how mean those guard dogs looked, Doris would laugh. The fact was, these menacing animals were just a bunch of whelps. But only in her presence. If she were gone, they were the most terrifying hell-hounds you had ever seen. I can attest to that.

One night, a major thunderstorm hit the area. Doris and I reveled in nature's awesome display. The attack dogs were scared out of their wits. They barked at the lightning and whimpered when it thundered. As the storm intensified, all of the dogs fled to Doris' private suite.

She calmed their fears. Soothed their anxiety. Hugged them. Doris even gave the dogs *reiki*. "Now, now, now, my children. Everything will be all right." What a scene that was.

Laughing, I retired for the night, leaving Doris with her children. The next morning, she informed me: "The big sissies spent the whole night with me. I had to sleep with them to calm them down."

Despite all Doris' efforts, the dogs ripped up some Louis XIV couch or roll-arm bench. Nuku mentioned to me that when she took in Doris' breakfast, she could see that this valuable antique—worth at least $50,000—had been torn to shreds. Doris only scolded the culprits. "Now, now, now, don't ever do that again."

That was it. The dogs had been chastised by Doris. Just like a mother would do to a spoiled child. Her children could do as they pleased. I bet any servant who spilled something on that piece of furniture or accidentally scratched the wood would have been fired immediately for their carelessness. For the dogs, her precious children, it was a different story.

Later, when the five of us were hanging out, Doris referred to me and Karina as "her children."

Most people would not have gotten this "in-joke." The comment went over the heads of Karina and James. I think Chandi realized Doris' implications.

I thought about her seemingly casual remark. I knew then how deep her affection for me was. You don't get any more accepted than that—unless Miss Duke adopted you.

CHAPTER 7

Hare Krishna Feast

• • • • • • • •

Karina wanted to show her appreciation for our hostess. The next day, she decided to fix this elaborate Indian feast. Though she didn't know that much about what had to be done, Karina volunteered to do all the cooking. She started at nine in the morning and finished at nine that night. She followed various recipes in a vegetarian cookbook. Krishna empowered her that day.

Karina had a great time putting it together. She would call the guardhouse and tell them: "I need about a pound of basmati rice." Cars went out in every direction. A guard came by with a five-pound bag, followed by another person dropping off an even larger package of rice. Minutes later, someone else stopped by with a third bag.

Every time she required an ingredient not found in the kitchen, security would send out personnel to locate what was needed. They always returned with more than what Karina had requested. Much more.

She had their full cooperation. Anything Karina wanted, these men went out and purchased. I checked up on her about mid-afternoon. The whole kitchen was full of stuff for all these Indian dishes. To make dinner for five people, security had bought tons of food. Karina and I laughed at the situation.

When everything was ready, I discreetly informed the servants that Indian food is served all at once. There are no separate courses.

Doris dressed up that evening. Very seldom would she do this while I was hanging out with her. She sported a new coiffure. Jewelry, which she seldom wore. Over her classy, designer outfit, Doris had put on this hand-woven jacket she had purchased in Thailand.

Chandi showed up in an expensive evening gown. James wore a dark suit and tie, looking almost formal in appearance. Karina was decked out in another of her extravagant saris and trappings. I came as myself—casual.

We enjoyed this banquet in the formal dining room. Huge oak table. Candelabra. Paintings worth millions hanging on the walls. Maids scurrying around in uniform. We sat there, ready to be waited upon.

Bernard and one of the female servants come out with the *dal*, which is lentil or split pea soup. I'm not sure which type Karina had made. The two of them started to serve the meal, beginning with this soup, European-style, which is presented in courses.

I didn't say anything, even though I had reminded them about the proper procedure before I had taken my seat. Doris was sharp. Nothing got by her. She knew all sorts of formalities—both grandiose and trivial. She spoke up.

"This is Indian food, Bernard. You serve everything all at once. Now, go back and do it right."

"Yes, Miss Duke. Yes, Miss Duke." Bernard and the maid took the bowls back to the kitchen. Moments later, they came back with the soup and a platter with one of the dishes.

Doris was on his case right away. "Bernard, I said it all comes out at once. I told you that."

"Yes, Miss Duke. Yes, Miss Duke." The pair gathered up the food and disappeared.

Hare Krishna Feast

Doris raised her eyes in frustration and disbelief at their incompetence. Karina and James were trying not to laugh. I couldn't help it. Chandi looked like she would explode at any moment.

Bernard and the maid came out the third time and got it wrong again. Doris lost her patience. Without yelling, she made them aware of her displeasure.

"Bernard, I told you that it all comes out at once. Bring everything out together. Put all of the food on the table and we'll help ourselves. Just do it like that!"

The butler was very apologetic. I felt sorry for him. While he and the female servant cleared the table, he bowed and said: "Yes, Miss Duke. Yes, Miss Duke."

Once they vanished into the kitchen, Doris threw up her arms and exclaimed: "'Yes, Miss Duke. Yes, Miss Duke. Yes, Miss Duke.' But nothing ever gets done around here. No one ever listens."

We looked at one another. I found it very difficult not to start laughing again.

Bernard and several of the maids brought out all the food and placed it on the dining table. Just like they should have done in the first place.

Karina had really outdone herself. The food was good. Very good. Though Doris always ate well, she seldom would eat large portions. That night, she ate a lot. I stuffed my face. In fact, everyone pigged out.

Doris would always have wine with her evening meal. Karina had some. Chandi and James declined. I had some water. After complimenting her on how good the food was, Doris toasted Karina, touching glasses. I went to click her goblet with mine and Doris refused.

"Oh no, that's bad luck." Doris would never touch glasses unless they were filled with an alcoholic beverage.

That night, Karina was in a little pain. Twelve hours in the kitchen had taken its toll on her. She had done something to her neck. She arranged an appointment with a chiropractor in town the next day.

With the extraordinary service she had received the previous day, Karina was spoiled. When she called the guardhouse for a car to take her to Somerville, Doris went into a snit. My wife just told her that: "They're gonna come and get me. I'm going to see the chiropractor."

Doris got huffy, almost vicious. "Call a cab. They're paid to guard this place. They are not chauffeurs."

Complete turn-around for Doris. Maybe it was due to the fact that it was just Karina as opposed to me and Karina. My wife didn't really get along with Doris, especially after that.

Doris and I, on the other hand, got along extremely well. Our friendship deepened—much to the chagrin of Chandi and Karina.

CHAPTER 8

This Is the Life

• • • • • • • •

I *am* offbeat. Doris loved offbeat. She hated people who were proud, stuck-up and snobbish. I wasn't "stuffy," her term for these individuals. Nor was I intimidated by her wealth.

In a past life, as a court jester, I entertained the royal retinue. Being "the fool," I could say things to the monarch that other people—including nobles—would lose their lives over. My reckless commentary brought only laughs. I was protected. Court jesters were usually individuals who weren't "all there" to begin with. They called such persons "touched." No one harmed these "poor unfortunates" who were touched. That would be bad luck. Very bad luck.

I fit that bill even in the present. Especially with Doris. She knew that my wit was as sharp as hers, but Doris was also aware that I was—in most people's minds—crazy as a loon.

I preferred being myself—casual and candid. I would crack a joke, laugh at one of hers or be cynical—whatever struck my fancy or reflected how I felt at the moment.

I can relate to sarcastic humor. Doris possessed a dry wit, what I call a "Mercury-in-Scorpio" sense of humor. She could be very droll in her observations. Whenever Doris came up with a satirical ditty, I would laugh.

I like to laugh. Doris made me laugh. She would have loved to have been a stand-up comedienne. I was a personal and private audience for her jokes.

Doris was pretty funny, for the most part. But if it wasn't humorous, I didn't laugh. She liked that about me. I was real. I wasn't someone who just catered to her whims and fancies. I would not have lasted very long being a "yes"-man.

I was also someone who liked Doris for who she was. I told her point blank if I thought an idea of hers was stupid or brilliant. She respected my opinion.

In my presence, she could be herself. I wasn't "kissing ass" or sucking up to her because I wanted something. I was a person who genuinely enjoyed her company. It didn't matter that Doris was a multi-billionaire, but—believe me—it didn't hurt.

Duke Farms was paradise. It wouldn't have taken much effort on my part to get used to that type of life style. Visiting Doris in New Jersey was like being on a permanent, paid vacation. I could roam over the beautiful, expansive estate at will. Staying at Somerville was infinitely better than any five-star hotel.

A handful of maids cleaned up after me. A personal chef prepared my meals: what I wanted, how I wanted it, and when I wanted it. My laundry was washed every day. Servants were at my beck and call. Drivers were at my disposal whenever I needed a ride.

What's not to like?

Though I was in complete ecstasy, Karina did not like the program. I could see her side of the coin. I wasn't spending that much time with her. I would walk about the grounds alone, meditating and chanting. I hung around with Doris, catching up on things or just shooting the breeze.

There was also the friction between Karina and Doris. Miss Duke did not like to share her friends with other people. Coping with Chandi and James took its toll on her. She and her adopted daughter were fighting more frequently. Many of their arguments concerned the bodyguard/lover. Doris had to contend with my married status as well. I could sense a bit of jealousy on her part.

Dealing with these issues was not easy for Doris. She floundered when faced with these types of situations. I have to give her credit, though. Doris was doing her best. James Burns was "in"—but Chandi was her adoptive daughter. She loved her like a mother would love her own child. She wanted to spend time with the younger woman. Doris just didn't do too well with sharing.

James ate with us in New Jersey when we dined together. Guests and servants understood that he and Chandi were in love. The couple never flaunted it, at least not while I was around. Karina told me, though, that one evening when we were sitting with Doris, the two of them started making eyes at each other. I didn't see it, but that night Karina commented: "Boy, they were really goofing on her, man. What's that all about?"

Doris tolerated their relationship. Although James and Chandi didn't have to sneak around, their affair was not out in the open.

James helped Doris work out. Because of his training, Doris was able to get around. James made sure that she persisted with her therapeutic exercises.

His status was not that of an employee. Employees never ate with Doris—except Johnny Gomez, who was more of a friend. Employees never called Miss Duke by her first name. The distinctions were obvious. The servants and staff wore uniforms. James didn't.

Although I had met James earlier in Hawaii, this was my first opportunity to get to know the man. He was warm and cordial. We got along very well.

James Burns was originally hired as a member of the Shangri-La security force. A muscular, good-looking guy, the role suited him. He always kept in shape: running, lifting weights, healthy foods, and vigorous, military-type drills.

During the time that Chandi was hospitalized for some reason, he was assigned as her bodyguard. James had a military background, so he was a force to be reckoned with. Doris wanted someone trustworthy to watch over Chandi. Miss Duke knew the risks of being rich.

Chandi herself was paranoid. She was worried that because of who she was, there always existed the possibility of being kidnapped and held for ransom. Hers was not an unfounded fear. Doris would have spent her entire fortune to get Chandi back—and Doris Duke was worth several billion.

Wealthy people are always potential targets. Doris and Chandi always drove around in simple, undistinguished cars. The fanciest automobiles they owned were Jaguars and Cadillacs. Not one limousine or Rolls-Royce. Nothing to attract attention or possible trouble. Mother and adopted daughter always maintained a low-key, low-profile lifestyle.

Over time, Chandi and Burns fell in love. Because of this relationship, James was kind of Doris Duke's "son-in-law."

He still took his job very seriously. He was a gung-ho, *kshatriya* kind of guy—a warrior. His unique position in the Duke Organization gave him the opportunity to test his physical and mental skills. The role was meant for him. It was his destiny. For security purposes, he had an unlimited budget.

Everything was at his disposal. Private jets and helicopters. State-of-the-art surveillance equipment. Doris and Chandi even sent James to a private school in Colorado, which taught a course dealing with terrorists and hostage situations. He really got into those training exercises.

In essence, James Burns was the lover of the woman who was going to inherit all of Doris' wealth. Despite this potential power, James was a bewildered individual. He was a friendly person. A good-natured, fun dude. But his situation rattled him. He was always thinking: "Is this really happening?"

It wasn't until Karina and I stayed at Duke Farms that I

was able to do his chart. In New Jersey, Doris had James staying in the Red Room. Red for Mars, the Roman God of War. Very appropriate. The entire room was decorated in various shades of scarlet. A very intense color for living quarters. But James felt right at home.

After the reading was over, we started talking. He told me of the time that Doris had traveled to Africa. James thought it was very far out because all these people were cheering when they arrived. During the trip, Doris hung out with her friend, the King of Morocco.

Doris burst into the room. Accompanying her were the seven guard dogs. "This is an omen," I thought. Something sudden and swift is going to happen in the near future. In Vedic Astrology, dogs represent a problem or denote internal trouble. I anticipated a dramatic confrontation sooner or later, perhaps between Doris and James.

Miss Duke had some errand for James, and he went about his job. As Doris and I wandered back to the main hall, I remained wary of the dogs. I smiled at them, hoping they would always remember I wasn't a threat to their mistress.

I joked with Doris. "So, you're friends with the King of Morocco?"

"Oh yeah," she acknowledged. "But I wouldn't want to be in King Hassan's shoes."

"Why not?"

"It's a very hard job." Doris gave me a brief lowdown on a few of the monarch's royal duties and the immense problems he faced.

On our way through the house, I admired a few artifacts and antiques. If I inquired about anything, Doris was never specific as to when or where she had purchased the piece. Her response was usually: "Oh, it's just something I picked up."

"This is amazing," I said, fascinated by some of her prized possessions. "One of these days, you've got to tell me the stories behind some of these things."

"Maybe. It's not that interesting, really."

Yeah, right.

Doris had traveled all over the world, assembling her massive art collections. Just those particular items that had caught my eye in Hawaii and New Jersey came from Tunisia, India, Persia, China and Thailand. And those were only the ones I could identify or that had been pointed out to me.

Miss Duke stopped and shook her head. Sighing, she reached for a marble ashtray atop one of the cabinets. She moved it to a nearby table, muttering, "The servants never get it right."

That was Doris for you. Nothing escaped her. The woman could go through any of her houses and know if something was out of order, misplaced or missing. She had an amazing mind for detail. Her horoscope indicated such a fastidious nature [Moon in the Sixth House].

"You've got a great chart for treasure hunting. Maybe you and I should discover Atlantis," I suggested.

The idea intrigued her, but we never made plans for an expedition. "Of course," I added, "perhaps it just means that you have hidden treasures yourself."

"Oh? Not me."

"C'mon, Doris, I do this for a living. It might not be real treasure, but just stuff that you've stored in warehouses over the years."

She laughed. Doris knew what she had hidden and what was in storage. She told me one of the stories from her world tour in the sixties.

Doris loved Southeast Asian culture, its art and architecture. She bought an entire village in Thailand. It's not as expensive as it sounds. I've been there myself. The villages are not that large. The people aren't that well off. Labor is cheap. Doris would not have paid them that much to sell their homes. The one or two million that Miss Duke did spend on the village and its artifacts probably allowed these impoverished peasants to build something better than they originally had.

Doris formed a company called The Southeast Asian Cultural Center or Foundation. This venture had been done in conjunction with the Hawaiian spiritual seeker and healer, Nana Veary. Doris was interested in purchasing a few thousand acres in one of the Island's valleys. The government gave her a hard time with the zoning and price of the property. The officials even hassled her about who was going to maintain the acreage and which people were going to be appointed to manage the organization.

Livid with rage against the bureaucracy, Doris' impatient response was: "The hell with them. Put it all in storage." Though she had invested a small fortune in this project, because things didn't go the way she wanted, Doris had everything packed away in a warehouse. She didn't have any problem with changing her plans.

CHAPTER 9

Exploring Duke Farms

· · · · · · · ·

One of the halls in the New Jersey mansion was filled with framed caricatures of famous people. Doris must have had forty or fifty of these commissioned drawings. By the personal inscriptions and private greetings, you could tell she knew these celebrities very well.

This collection was pretty far out. Some of the names I didn't recognize because the individuals were way before my time. All of them were Hollywood people. Not just movie stars, but directors, producers and studio owners.

In the midst of these illustrations was a portrait of Ronald Reagan, from his younger days as an actor in B-movies. I mentioned the fact that the former president and his wife downplayed the role of astrology in their lives.

"Contrary to what they said about just looking it up in the paper like everyone else, Ronald and Nancy consulted their astrologer, Joan Quigley, every time they made a major decision."

Doris was unaware how long the Reagans had been into charts and horoscopes.

"How do you think a mediocre, B-movie actor became the Governor of California—not to mention that later he was elected President of the United States by a huge margin?"

Doris shrugged her shoulders.

"When you've got a good astrologer, anything is possible."

She laughed, knowing I was also plugging myself.

Our conversation reminded Doris about how Ronald and Nancy had turned their backs on Ferdinand and Imelda Marcos. She was appalled by their insensitive behavior: "That's when friends should be there, during the really bad times."

When American foreign policy necessitated a good relationship with the Philippines, the Reagans catered to the Marcoses. But once the exiled couple was in deep shit, Nancy and Ronald spurned these former heads of state.

Doris didn't fault Mr. Reagan that much. She liked Ronald. Doris felt that he was a really cool guy and a great president. Her anger was directed more toward Nancy. Doris felt that she controlled her husband and wore the pants in the family. She did a major Nancy-bashing:

"Nancy Reagan, that two-timing, ungrateful, skinny-assed bitch abandoned my friends, Ferdinand and Imelda. I'll never forgive her for that."

* * * * *

I never saw Doris play the piano, though she practiced on an almost-daily basis. Whenever I would make a personal request, she would politely and modestly decline. Yet Doris constantly informed me that she was working on a particular melody or that she was attempting a new arrangement. Even though she was in her late seventies, the woman still contemplated a possible music career.

I would chant *mantras* over her piano or perform miniature *pujas* so she could play better. In order for the rituals to be more effective, I asked Doris for a picture of herself.

"The more recent the photograph, the more potent the *puja* will be," I added.

"I'll see what I can come up with, Nischintya."

Doris was very particular about her appearance. Her vanity won out. She gave me an old passport portrait—the only picture I have of her.

Chandi had given Doris a Ganesh statuette. The Hindu God with the elephant head helps remove obstacles. I said, pointing to the Deity: "This is very good. He will help you with your dream of being a professional musician."

She showed me a silver medallion with Ganesh's head engraved on it. I instructed her to wear the religious medal whenever she practiced.

In New Jersey, Doris was still reluctant to perform for me. No matter how much I coaxed or cajoled, the answer was always "No."

Atop one of the pianos which Doris would never play for me were the three framed snapshots of the Deities from the Los Angeles Temple that I had given her. In the years ahead, I discovered that Doris took those photographs with her wherever she traveled. They were always placed on top of the particular estate's piano. The servants were instructed to place fresh flowers around them daily.

Doris offered to take me—just me—on a tour of the grounds. She called up one day and said: "Let me take you around and show you my farm. Would you like that?"

"Yeah, sure. I'd like to see it."

I waited at the cottage, chanting on my *japa* beads. I heard a car pull up and someone beeping the horn. I opened the door and looked outside. There was Doris Duke, one of the world's wealthiest women, driving this yellow, beat-up, God-knows-what kind of car.

The auto was rusted through completely. It was trashed and smashed. Dents everywhere. Different colors of paint peeling. The inside was just as bad as the outside. Nothing worked properly. The seat was broken and jerry-rigged so you could lean against it. The dashboard was a mess. The glove compartment had no door. Duct tape seemed to be holding the interior framework together.

I shook my head and started laughing.

Doris turned in her seat, facing me. "What's so funny?" She put her arm around the bald steering wheel. "What's the big joke?"

"Well, Doris, one of the richest persons on this planet just came and picked me up in a car that even the Hare Krishnas wouldn't be caught dead in."

"Hey, it's the only thing they'll let me drive!"

So Doris and I toured her several-thousand-acre estate in this ugly beater. She gave orders to some of the gardeners and inquired about some of the procedures we observed. She showed me where the cows were kept.

While we visited the barns, I launched into one of my many moral and philosophical opinions—this one about dairy cows and beef cattle. Doris merely listened to me; she never admitted her true feelings, because she liked a good steak every now and then.

"You have to protect them. In Hindu culture, there is a correlation between cows and mothers. When you're young, you get milk from your mother. The cow is like your mother because it provides you with its milk. You don't kill your mother just because she stops giving you nourishment. You take care of the woman in her old age. Most cows are sent to slaughter as soon as they stop producing a certain amount of milk.

"In Vedic societies, the bulls are used to plow the fields. The villagers don't have to purchase large tractors to farm the land. The oxen fertilize the soil during their daily rounds. They're also used to turn wheels for power and grind grains for flour and food oil.

"The cows give milk which can be drunk as is or made into other dairy products such as cheese and butter. When both the male and female animals get old, they are put out to pasture. They graze along the countryside, so it doesn't cost anything to feed them. When they die, the farmers use their hides for leather and, if necessary, eat their meat.

"It is a very useful and efficient form of animal utilization. You don't have to kill the beasts to get what you want."

Doris acknowledged the logic in such a system. I reminded her about not having a sense of good fortune. "Such a plan of action will help give you peace of mind, Doris."

Though nothing came of this suggestion with regard to Duke Farms, my little speech would have a subsequent effect on Doris and her eating habits.

On the way to the fruit gardens, Doris and I discussed various farming methods, taking proper care of animals, and the way things had been done in the old days. We talked about the fact that eating meat back then wasn't as unhealthy as it is now.

People didn't eat that much in their diets. Meat was also fresher. The cattle, chickens and pigs ran around freely; they weren't kept penned up all their lives. Nor were the farm animals fed tons of antibiotics or pumped up with hormones and steroids. Even the vegetables and grains they ate weren't tainted with insecticides. Meat was much safer years ago.

We walked up and down the rows in the orchards. Doris pointed out the various varieties they grew. The gardeners were spraying the trees, filling the air with mists. I turned a corner and walked straight into the stuff.

"Oh shit," I cursed. "Son of a bitch." I tried wiping it off my face and clothes.

"What's wrong?"

"I just got sprayed with all that insecticide and chemicals your men use around here."

"What chemicals? That's soap and water! It's all natural and organic. This whole farm is organic. We don't use any pesticides or toxic substances or even chemical fertilizers. Get a grip on yourself, sissy."

Due to her association with Louis Bromfield in the fifties,

Doris was very much into organic farming. She was interested in procedures which were more in harmony with nature. The milk from the cows on Duke Farms was not pasteurized nor was it homogenized. It was fresh and natural.

The farms in New Jersey were a living testament to growing untainted crops and raising healthier livestock. A lasting legacy to her dear friend, mentor, and father-figure, Bromfield.

CHAPTER 10

The Mayor With No Name

· · · · · · · ·

Doris wasn't fond of many people who had money. Aristotle Onassis was an exception. She thought the man had class. Ari, as she referred to him, genuinely liked her company. He didn't need to have her around nor was he trying to get something from her. Doris entertained with his wife, Jackie, due to her prestigious public image. On the other hand, the former President's widow socialized with Doris because of her large donations to charitable causes.

Doris liked people who weren't trying to scam her or finagle money. She was very pleasant to people who didn't ask for things. When someone she liked was in trouble or financial difficulty, Doris would be there for them. I didn't request a fee for my initial services, yet she gave me $3,000.

The woman was pretty perceptive as to what people were after. Many times, she would go along with the con. If Doris was having a good time, she could spend big bucks on the adventure. To make these schemers think they had put one over on her, the money was dangled (figuratively) in front of them. Doris would have them "perform" for her until it was time to say good-bye, then dismiss them without giving the charlatans anything. Doris loved those types of circumstances.

Dollars, Diamonds, Destiny & Death

During our stay at Duke Farms, the Mayor of Newark came by for an official visit. For His Honor, security brought out some new Ford Broncos for traveling around the estate.

The whole episode was hilarious. People really cow-towed to Doris Duke, especially politicians. She could be their bread and butter. She could make or break them if she chose. Most of the time, the woman could care less one way or the other.

Doris showed the mayor all around her farm. Chandi, Karina, James and I tagged along for the ride—and the fun. Everyone put the man through his paces.

The guard dogs were with us in the cars. The mangy mutts were jumping on His Honor's lap and drooling all over him. Karina and I razzed him with Hare Krishna religious spiels. Chandi and James chastised the man about eating meat. You name it, we were on his case about it. Any time Doris made a personal comment or private dig, he swallowed his pride and accepted the abuse.

You could see that the man was being as polite as he could possibly be. Throughout the whole tour, the mayor had to have been thinking: "Why the hell do I have to put up with this crap? Oh, yeah. I need money for my campaign fund." I knew whatever we said didn't matter to him. I have been in similar situations myself. You just can't wait until they're over.

During the whole visit, this guy was very humble and sub-servient. He knew that Doris could write out a check and he would be reelected without any trouble. The man was a true politician. He knew how to "kiss ass" as well as kiss babies.

He must have gotten the impression somehow that Miss Duke had invited him for dinner. I know I did. I thought he was supposed to join us afterward. But Doris didn't invite him to stay. Back at the main house, she said good-bye.

The man was a bit bewildered. Though he had just been brushed off, the mayor was still polite and thanked her for the personal tour. He hopped in his limousine and took off.

Later at supper—we were eating again on those small priceless tables in Doris' sitting room—Karina brought up the subject of our VIP guest. "You know, the Mayor of Newark, he was kinda nice. Do you remember his name?"

Doris shrugged and asked Chandi: "Do you know?"

She shook her head. "Got me." Chandi looked at her boyfriend. "James?"

"Nope."

The four of them glanced my way.

"Don't ask me. I wasn't paying attention."

None of us had any clue as to His Honor's name. Nobody could remember. We started laughing at the situation.

* * * * *

Doris Duke owned one of the finest book collections in the world that I have ever seen. Rare volumes, first editions—you name it. Amazing amounts of stuff. She even had a copy of *Daddy's Duchess*. The mansion at Duke Farms had this huge library. Most of her other estates had similar studies.

Doris had read most of the books she owned, or had, at least, glanced through them. The woman had a difficult time finishing what she started. I had given her a number of books. She was very excited about receiving them, but although Doris started reading them, she rarely made it to the end.

Doris loaned me a hardcover that had been given to her by Mark Spitz, the Olympic gold medalist swimmer: *Quantum Healing*, by Deepak Chopra, M.D. Doris had tried reading this self-help book but only managed to get past the first fifty or sixty pages. She wanted me to plow through the lengthy, cut and dry text, then summarize it for her.

Many times, before in Hawaii and years later, Doris would have me go through some literary work and give her a synopsis. If something seemed fascinating, she would read that particular section rather than weed her way through the uninteresting passages.

What type of publications did Miss Duke like to read? Doris loved the tabloids. Her sitting rooms were littered with the weekly scandal newspapers. She cherished the gossip rags. Doris was also very fond of fashion magazines, beauty and glamour periodicals. Among her favorites were *Vogue*, *The Post* and *Architectural Digest*. This was the stuff that Miss Duke would pore over daily.

Doris was no dummy. When she was in her late teens at boarding school, she had become well-read. She knew about social etiquette and proper protocol. The woman was up on all the major religions, plus a few of the more obscure ones. Her special education—private schools and personal tutors—had given her a well-balanced and thorough historical background. Her own experiences had added to that wealth of knowledge.

As Doris became older, her interests would change as rapidly as her moods. The lady was able to read what she wanted when she wanted. Now in her late seventies, Doris was more into sensational journalism than good literature.

* * * * *

I remember when I first met Doris Duke: the woman did not look that well. Being elderly contributed somewhat, but there was more to it than that. Something was definitely wrong. As I hung out with Doris, I performed *reiki* and provided her with natural remedies and healthful herbs.

A friend of mine suggested beeswax for arthritic pain. Doris experienced major problems and acute pain with her knees.

I asked her about this unusual treatment: "Would you like to try this?"

Her typical response was: "Sure, why not? What have I got to lose?"

That was Doris Duke. The woman always had an open mind. She would try anything, at least once. Two or three times, if necessary, to find out if something worked or not. Should the stuff have no effect or an adverse reaction, Doris would stop using it. If the remedy worked, she was really into it. Doris didn't care how loony it sounded. I made up balls of beeswax in New Jersey, and Doris would ingest these small pellets. Her body would absorb their simple chemicals to help heal itself. This worked, so she constantly ate the stuff.

I also concocted brain tonics for Doris. Elixirs with herbs and natural ingredients to help stimulate cerebral activity. Potions with basic components to keep her cells alive and healthy.

By the time I visited Doris in New Jersey, she began to look and feel much better. Physically and mentally. While James Burns kept her on a strict exercise regimen, it wasn't necessary for him to make sure that Miss Duke ate properly. She already subsisted on a mostly vegetarian diet and had cut down her fat intake. Doris practically eliminated her red meat consumption, replacing the beef with more fish and poultry.

At Duke Farms, she was in pretty good spirits. Doris was able to get around much better and more easily than when I first met her in Hawaii a few months earlier. Between James' physical therapy and my natural medicines, Doris' health had shown a vast improvement.

One evening, I spotted her going up the stairs alone. I called out to Doris: "Look, Ma, no hands." She let go of the railing for a moment and went up another step. Afraid of losing her balance, Doris grasped the banister again for support. She turned around and smiled at me.

* * * * *

I could have spent the rest of the summer—not to mention the rest of my life—at Duke Farms. To me, it was great: I could wander about the estate, chanting and meditating; hang out with Doris; I read new and old books, some from the seventeenth century; and all my needs were taken care of.

77

Unfortunately, all good things must come to an end. Whereas I was contented and felt right at home, Karina needed action: people to see, parties to go to, things to do. My wife needed to get out of there. Duke Farms was not her cup of tea. Nor was hanging out with Doris her idea of fun.

Taking all that into consideration, plus Doris' problem with sharing, and I knew something was bound to end this great vacation.

So, after only a week or two, Karina and I made our apologies to Doris. To Karina's delight and my chagrin, we left paradise. We flew to Los Angeles and stayed there for a bit. Then we headed back to Hawaii.

I had had a taste of idyllic life, and I couldn't wait to get back!

CHAPTER 11

$5 Million
For Services Rendered

• • • • • • • •

The Marcos Trial verdict was reached on or around Imelda's birthday. Doris called me about the judge's decision for acquittal. She was not in New York with the former First Lady, but staying at Duke Farms. I was in Los Angeles.

I performed the *Narasinghadeva Puja* in May, and Imelda's birthday was in June. Pretty fast work, if you ask me.

"When the news broke," Doris said, "I checked it out on the TV. The reporters credited Gerald Spence with winning the case."

"He wasn't the only one who helped," I reminded her. "How much did he get for legal fees?"

"Five million."

"What!" I felt shafted. "Where's my five million?"

"Get it from Imelda," Doris countered.

"Imelda! We both know that she doesn't have any money." Doris and I snickered over that remark. Imelda feigned poverty, yet she could still go out on shopping sprees and spending binges.

Doris wasn't helpful. "Well, what can I say?"

"You're the one who had me do the *puja*," I pointed out. "Imelda didn't ask me. It was you and Chandi."

79

She relented. "Okay, Nischintya, I'll try and get the money."

"Oh yeah," I said in a mocking tone. "And I can add the $5 million to that island I'm getting in the Philippines, right?"

It was an on-going, in-joke that whenever someone performed a special service for Imelda Marcos, she would promise the individual an island in her country. There are several thousand islands in the Philippine homeland.

Doris forgave a great many people the debts they owed her. Imelda was not one of them. Doris stipulated in her Will that Mrs. Marcos was required to reimburse her estate the $5,000,000 that Miss Duke loaned to her for attorney services and court fees.

Perhaps it was Doris' way of showing that she wanted me to be paid for my efforts in Imelda's trial.

* * * * *

In July 1990, I was with friends on Molokai. We experienced a solar eclipse in the Hawaiian Islands. In Mundane Astrology, an eclipse is a good time to predict world events. I had done predictions before, but because very little is written on the subject and you don't always get results, I never felt confident about any of my conclusions.

Perhaps I had been "on line" with the cosmic energies that day. I don't know. Things felt right. I said: "What the hell," and started the ritual. I waded out into the ocean. During the actual eclipse, I started chanting *mantras*. Afterward, I secluded myself in the house and meditated. I drew up a chart and made my predictions.

The world horoscope seemed to be leaning heavily toward war. I thought perhaps I had done the reading wrong. At that time people in the government were talking about a "peace dividend." With the fall of Communism and the end of the Cold War, major military cutbacks had been proposed. These freed-up funds would then be pumped into the eonomy for the benefit of the American people.

I rechecked my calculations. The chart said "war." I recalled what happened when I did George Bush's inaugural chart. His horoscope foretold of a war during his administration. [Mars in the First House connotes powerful military emanations.]

I phoned a few friends. They laughed at my prophecy.

"You're crazy, Nischintya. The Berlin Wall has been torn down. Germany is united again. The Soviet Union is no more. Communism is dead. There's not going to be any war."

"Well, it still looks like trouble to me. Maybe it won't be a major war—perhaps rioting in the streets or nationwide strikes. Something like that. You'll see."

Doris and I regularly communicated since Karina and I had left New Jersey. When we had gotten back to Honolulu, my wife and I moved into a new house—one much closer to Doris' estate. She was very pleased to find out that we would be neighbors. I would be able to walk over to Shangri-La and spend more time with her when she stayed in Hawaii during the winter months.

Doris called every now and then to ask me what I saw as consequences for certain world events. She would want to know my predictions for the months ahead or the good and bad portents of omens. I happened to talk with her the following morning and mentioned my "war chart."

She replied with disbelief and disinterest: "A war?! Whatever."

Nine days after my prediction, Saddam Hussein invaded Kuwait. My phone was ringing off the hook. Doris was one of those callers.

"I'm impressed, Nischintya. I really am. I'll never doubt your abilities again."

* * * * *

Doris returned to Shangri-La in November of 1990, this time without a chef. Tom Rybak had quit earlier because of Chandi. Many servants left because of her.

At the time, my non-profit organization, the Vedic Cultural Association, was expanding. I was into many business ventures. Karina and I were putting together a cultural center. We had brought with us two devotees from the Los Angeles Temple to assist us. One was a salesman; the other was a cook.

Because of the help shortage, Doris and Chandi were going nuts. Many of the domestic employment agencies had blacklisted them because they were both "hard" on servants.

Karina and I had seen first-hand at Duke Farms the true situation. Yes, Doris was difficult. Yes, Chandi was murder on them. But that was their nature. Most of the servants tolerated Doris' behavior. None of them liked Chandi. Based upon the "eggplant" incident, I knew it was only a matter of time with Tom Rybak. No one could take that kind of daily treatment and remain unaffected. You can't even do it for the money. So it didn't surprise either of us when we heard that Tom quit.

The situation was funny. Karina and I, two small-time Hare Krishnas, had their own chef. Doris, a multi-billionaire, couldn't find one that would stay.

Doris moaned and groaned constantly about not being able to hire a replacement. Nuku Makasaile, Doris' personal maid, would cook something one day. Perhaps Bernard would pitch in here and there. Doris even went into the kitchen at one time to fix a meal.

Believe it or not, Doris was a good cook. She learned from one of her former chefs years ago. In her heyday, if something struck her fancy, Doris would do it herself. The lady was not helpless like the majority of rich people. The lady was capable of preparing an elaborate feast. When she was much younger, she liked to cook and took pride in her gastronomical accomplishments. By the time I met her, Doris wasn't into doing stuff herself anymore.

$5 Million For Services Rendered

Doris was the kind of wealthy woman who could hire individuals to paint her toenails, coif her hair and apply her make-up—which she did. But she was capable of doing the little things herself; something her father had taught her: to be self-sufficient. Doris was versatile.

The day I caught her in the kitchen cooking up a storm, I vowed to help her until she found a new chef: "Look, Doris, we've got a cook. I've got access to the Temple. We'll feed you."

Karina and I started bringing meals over for Doris. We had only brought food over a few times before having a run-in with our own cook. The man got a bit cocky. He figured he was some important, hot-shot chef. Someone who was good enough for the rich and famous.

When we first hired the man, he was living in a run-down studio apartment and couldn't pay his rent. We flew him with us to Hawaii, where he now lived in paradise. His room and board were covered, plus we gave him $50 - $100 weekly spending money.

All of a sudden, he now wants $2,500 a month for his services, in addition to living quarters and meals. When we refused his outrageous demands, he made other plans. He figured to cut out the middlemen—me and Karina—and go right to the source: Chandi Duke Heffner. The man was nuts.

Chandi and I discussed the situation.

"Does he have a culinary degree?" she inquired.

"Are you kidding?"

"Has he managed a restaurant kitchen?"

"No."

"This guy's a joke!" Chandi shook her head in disbelief at the man's audacity.

"He knows only the basics—just a few of some Hare Krishna preps. That's it."

Our cook had some great favorites, but his repertoire was very limited. He wasn't familiar with all types of cuisine. Not even in the Indian dishes he prepared was he an expert.

83

Chandi filled me in on the position available. "The chef is responsible for lunch and dinner for Miss Duke, myself and any guests she may have, plus separate meals for the staff, which can be up to ten people or more." Servants and employees did not eat the same thing that Doris did. She had her own particular diet. So did Chandi. The staff was more flexible as to what they ate.

In addition, the chef for the estate would either get a half-day or a whole day off each week. He was not responsible for Miss Duke's breakfast. Doris ate pretty simply in the morning: orange juice, oatmeal, whatever. That was usually one of the maids' jobs. A couple of times, I saw Nuku serve it. Doris always took breakfast by herself in her bedroom.

I have been a cook. As a devotee, I prepared meals for an entire temple. It's a full-time, major occupation. Working for Doris Duke was even more involved. Granted you could earn as much as $500 a week, plus room and board; and you would have access to the lifestyles of the rich and famous. But were all these benefits worth the hassle?

Our cook quit. I don't know if he ever got around to applying for the job at Shangri-La or not. The guy was dreaming. Chandi and I didn't even consider him qualified for the position.

After this guy took off, Karina and I would go to the Honolulu Temple and bring back food for Doris. Every Sunday, Bernard would heat up what we brought and serve it. One time, we stayed and did it ourselves. Doris was very grateful.

She loved the food. Doris would always eat a lot when we showed up with a meal. If the devotees at the temple cook the food in ghee—clarified butter—I would partake of the feast. Though on the heavy side, it's good for you. When the cooks use too much ghee, you can taste it in the food. You want to go to sleep right after eating. Sometimes—to cut costs—the devotees use soybean or peanut oil; that's worse than using too much ghee.

One of those times, we brought over the Temple Feast and it was greasy. The food tasted awful. Karina and I thought it was bad. Doris commented that the meal was one of the worst she had ever had. She added: "Please, don't ever bring me that again."

Doris had to go back to roughing it every Sunday after that incident. She went through a lot of temporary help—when she could even get them. Doris also had some lady who would come by and assist with the meals.

CHAPTER 12

Death Threats and Desert Storm

• • • • • • • •

For her birthday that year, an ever-grateful, but "poverty-stricken" Imelda Marcos sent Doris several hundred dollars worth of flowers. Though she had everything taken from her, the former First Lady could still spend big bucks.

Doris thanked her and ended their phone conversation with one of her witticisms: "Imelda where did you get the money to pay for these flowers?"

The sarcasm and cynicism was lost on Mrs. Marcos. The woman got extremely upset. Imelda went into this long song and dance about how much trouble she went through to get the money for the flowers. She was too sensitive for that kind of humor. Doris shared this joke with me the next time I saw her. I had come over to tell her about a recent dream.

"She's got a hidden stash—just like you!"

"Oh no, not me."

"Yes, Doris, you do." I smiled at her. "You sold some gold, didn't you?"

"Where did you hear that?" she responded. "How did you know?"

I talked to her about my dream. I had envisioned Doris with gold coins, a few of which she sold.

"But you didn't sell all the gold, did you?"

Doris laughed. She didn't say "yes," but then again, she didn't say "no."

Irwin Bloom was the man who transacted the sale of gold bullion from her accounts in Switzerland. He may have converted some of it to cash, but I seriously doubt that he sold all of Doris' precious metal assets.

I tried to figure out why Doris needed to sell any of the gold in the first place. She wasn't strapped for cash. The woman had $80 million in her checking account for spending sprees and "petty cash."

Doris may have been a little cautious, or perhaps a bit paranoid. The Swiss government had cooperated with the United States when they froze the accounts held by Ferdinand and Imelda Marcos. The possibility existed that these same bank officials might do the same to her assets. If you can't trust the Swiss banks, who can you trust?

I could have seen Doris transferring the bullion to another financial institution as opposed to converting it to currency. The lady had money caches all over the world.

Ferdinand and Imelda had probably learned from Doris, who, in turn, was coached by her father and uncle. Even after the former First Lady of the Philippines had her assets frozen, Imelda still had access to other sources of wealth. How else could she have chartered a private plane to take her back to her homeland or have stayed in a $2,000-a-night suite at the Philippine Plaza Hotel.

* * * * *

Doris loved helping people in trouble. Especially when those persons were friends.

I told her about the problems I was having with the Hare Krishnas. My problems became hers. She loved the intrigue. Practically thrived on the stuff.

Death Threats and Desert Storm

Before I met Karina and Doris, I had resigned as the Honolulu Temple president. I was fed up with all the scheming going on within the organization. I had several misunderstandings with the new president and the Governing Board Commissioner (GBC)—both of whom were suspicious and distrustful. Many new administrative personnel saw me as a potential threat, even though I made it very clear I didn't want to have anything to do with their power struggles.

When I returned to Hawaii after my vacation with Doris, I set up my own concession stands at the major tourist spots. I had originally been the person behind the Temple setting up tables to ply their wares for travelers and sightseers. Though my products did not compete with any of theirs, the Temple officials were outraged.

After all I had done for the Hare Krishnas, I couldn't believe their attitude. I used money from my non-profit organization to print books, many of which I donated to the Temple. I fed a good number of the devotees. I made loans to businesses in financial straits. I was the major backer of all of the Honolulu Temple festivals. And I had donated $300,000 in three years to keep the temple afloat.

Still, the new Temple officials saw my tables as competition. They believed I was cutting into their profits and strangling their cash flow. These people were used to having all the business and did not like sharing. I knew there was plenty for both.

They tried to have the Health Department shut me down, but only managed to receive various violations against the Temple due to the negligence of their own incompetent entrepreneurs. Because of that backlash, the man who was the GBC wrote me an ominous letter.

He was extremely critical of what I was doing. The man accused me of setting up a sham non-profit organization. He insulted me, making digs at my third marriage. At the end of this correspondence, he basically said: "So, you had better watch it. You're going to die soon."

To anyone who read this letter, it sounded like a thinly veiled threat. I showed it to other Temple officials. They couldn't believe that a spiritual person would not only say such things, but actually have the audacity to put the words in print. Say what you want, but never put it in writing.

What made the situation even more incredible was the incident took place after the publication of *Monkey on a Stick*. This book revealed murder and mayhem within the Hare Krishna Movement.

Although the message was clear, I wasn't scared. I didn't lose any sleep over it. I knew Doris would get a kick out of it, so I showed her the letter.

Doris got that twinkle in her eye. I knew she was excited about the intrigue. "Want some bodyguards?" she offered.

I shook my head.

She was still gung-ho. "I can have my attorneys start on the case right away."

I laughed. "That's not necessary, Doris. These people can't even answer their phone. They're never going to get around to killing me."

Doris felt I was being a party-pooper. She cautioned me and kept her offers open. At a moment's notice, Doris and her staff could be ready to spring into action. Though I declined her assistance, I promised to keep her informed of any new developments.

During this time, at a Temple board meeting, the administrators took a vote on a special issue—the Vedic Cultural Association, my non-profit organization. They decided upon a hidden agenda to stop me because I, in their words, "was not loyal to the management of the Movement."

I was independent. A troublemaker. A heretic within the organization. Only because I still believed in my Spiritual Master's religious philosophies and principles.

Years ago, I had founded a preaching center in Thailand

where they translated Srila Prabhupada's books. The Temple officials accused me of dealing drugs and laundering money. This center was merely a front for my illegal activities.

I denied all their accusations. I offered to go before the Deities on the sacred altar and speak the truth. One does not tell a lie before The Gods without major repercussions. Misfortune will plague you during your lifetime. You can become ill or physically impaired. Worst of all, you could be struck dead.

In addition to my oath, I stated that I would be willing to undergo twenty-four hour surveillance. With one of their men watching my every movement, they could see for themselves that I was not involved in any criminal activities.

I further declared that I could go before the Deities and name a specific Temple official, the drug dealer he was in cahoots with, and the amount of money changing hands.

When I told Doris about my response to their original charges, she was in stitches. She ate up all this internal intrigue. Doris found it all amusing and exciting. The drama reminded her of the days she served with the OSS in World War II.

The Governing Board Commissioners (also called the GBC) backed off. I possessed the mailing lists of the organization. I knew the names of the individuals and businesses that dealt with the Hare Krishnas. With such knowledge, I could make public my *own* accusations. The Chairman of the GBC wrote me a formal apology, which I gracefully accepted.

Doris was disappointed.

* * * * *

Although Doris and I each kept abreast of the crisis in Kuwait and Saudi Arabia on our own, when she returned to Shangri-La for the winter months of 1990-1991, we saw practically the entire Gulf War together on CNN in Hawaii. Doris usually didn't watch much television.

We talked about Saddam Hussein. She and I discussed the UN proposals. We debated about what would happen in the Middle East.

"Why did Saddam Hussein invade Kuwait, Nischintya?" Doris wondered.

"This war has nothing to do with Iraq's invasion."

"What are you talking about?"

"Saddam's aggression is all bullshit, Doris."

"What do you mean, 'it's all bullshit?'"

"Iraq has always had a traditional claim on Kuwait," I pointed out. "It was part of that country for hundreds of years until the British split the two nations apart for political and economic reasons."

"So, the United States isn't going to do anything about stopping Saddam Hussein?"

"Oh, we'll stop him. He'll be kicked out of Kuwait, at least. But..."

"But what?"

"It's all part of a scam."

"Huh?"

"Any and all armed intervention will be done under United Nation's directives. This is part of the New World Order. President Bush didn't have to petition Congress to authorize troop deployment. The UN formed a coalition and requested men and/or money from the participating members.

"Saddam's invasion plans worked to their advantage. They've turned his aggression into an international cause. The New World Order conspirators want to see, via the media, how much they can manipulate each country and its people into a specific course of action or national fervor.

"The scientists have developed new technological breakthroughs. The Military needs to try out this weaponry, and if it works as good as they think it will, show it off to the world. You know, an impressive demonstration of U.S. power. And an advertisement—free—for our weapons industries."

"You're nuts, Nischintya." Doris didn't just accept what I said like some dummy. She asked very intelligent questions and tried to poke holes in my theories. But she loved hearing about this international intrigue.

"So, you think," continued Doris, "that this is their golden opportunity to forge their single world government?"

"No, it's going to take years before that happens. Not all the constituents of this conspiracy are marching toward the same end. They're fighting amongst themselves, vying for power. They're not united in their cause. When these people finally start working together toward the same goals, that's when they'll make their move."

Events escalated in the Middle East. Doris really got into the hype. The press built up the military capabilities of the Iraqi forces.

Doris became worried. "It's going to be a bloody conflict. Another Vietnam mess."

I was skeptical. "Maybe. Maybe not."

Doris suggested that I do a chart for Saddam Hussein. See what type of outcome I could predict for the war.

The results astounded her.

The UN coalition would rout the Iraqi army. Smash it and all of Saddam Hussein's ambitions. His entire defensive campaign would be a major joke.

Doris' apprehension was appeased. Once the "smart bombs" started falling and the missiles with pin-point accuracy struck, she started believing my prediction that it was going to be a "kick ass" war.

"But they won't take out Saddam Hussein," I emphasized.

"How can they not?" Doris was confused. "They have to remove him from power. President Bush was demonizing him, comparing the dictator to Hitler. What's the point of the whole war if he's still around?"

"I told you it was a scam war." I felt confident. "Personally, I think the man works for the conspirators."

"What makes you so sure?"

"Even if Saddam isn't in on the big picture, he's been very useful so far. The UN will knock him down, take a few things away from him, and impose some restrictions against his country. They'll let him stay in power because he's bound to cause trouble again in the future. The UN will have another excuse to intervene and another chance to impose their will on the nations of the world.

"Nischintya, I think you've finally lost it." Doris was incredulous about the whole concept. "You're crazy—and you're wrong!"

"Just cuz I'm crazy doesn't mean I'm wrong. I was right about war coming. What happened to the 'peace dividend,' huh, Doris?"

"That part, yes, you were correct." She shrugged her shoulders and shook her head. "But everything else you've said is pretty far-fetched."

The Middle East confrontation and its aftermath unfolded almost exactly on the course that I had predicted it would. The ground offensive lasted four days. The invading army was completely routed. Iraqi soldiers deserted by the thousands. General Schwarzkopf maneuvered around Saddam's reserve forces and was ready to march on Baghdad unopposed.

Doris and I watched history as it occurred. The coalition troops were on the verge of annihilating the last remaining aggressor forces. Suddenly, the U.S. advance halted. Hostilities ended. The Republican Guard escaped to Iraq unscathed and intact. Saddam Hussein was permitted to remain as Head of State. The UN imposed a number of sanctions. The Gulf War was over.

Doris couldn't believe what had just transpired. Impressed with my insight, she conceded: "Maybe you're right about some of your theories."

* * * * *

94

The Gulf War brought up a past-life memory. A time when Doris and I were together. Both of us lived as men in the Middle East. Bosom buddies sharing a hookah in an oasis tent out in the desert. Every day, we'd get together, look at life, and talk about stuff. We smoked, contemplated our fortunes over coffee, and enjoyed women and tea.

"That was a good life for us, Doris," I told her. "There wasn't much going on, except that we were really good friends cruising along."

Doris was pleased. She liked hearing about our past lives together. Doris very much identified with the Middle East. She probably had *the* premiere collection, outside of the few royal Arabic houses, of Islamic Art.

"Well, you want me to go and get us a hookah," I suggested, "so we can reminisce?"

"Maybe, but I can't get off on that stuff."

I was taken aback. Stunned by her admission. "What do you mean?"

"Well, I've tried. And I never get off."

I was in stitches at this point. The whole mood and situation struck me funny. I'm with this very wealthy—and elderly—woman, and she's telling me about her experiences with drugs.

"I've smoked pot a number of times," she continued. "It just never gets me high. I wish it would. Believe me." Doris rambled off a half-dozen or more illegal drugs that she had tried in the past.

"I know someone who takes Ecstacy."

"Who?"

"Karina."

"I need some of that," she commented, nodding. Doris picked up on what I was referring to right away. She knew what drug I was talking about.

A look of shock, then doubt, came over my face.

"No, seriously," she insisted.

That night, I debated the issue. I was in another moral dilemma. Should I give Doris something that would get her off? She missed getting high, and I really thought Ecstacy would be good for her.

If I did procure drugs for her, I felt the decision would come back to haunt me. I might not only be implicated in stringing the lady out on dope, but I could also be accused of getting into her confidence by supplying her with narcotics. My credibility as an astrologer and *shaman* would be destroyed.

I decided against any illegal dealings. I regret my choice in the matter. Looking back on what transpired over Doris' final year, I wish I had gotten her loaded, to be totally honest.

Later that week, Chandi told me about Doris partying with the Beach Boys and doing drugs. Doris confirmed it when next we saw each other. She didn't go into details.

"I dropped acid," Doris merely said. "That was fun."

Doris Duke had been out there. A regular on the Sixties Scene. Musicians came over regularly at Shangri-La for jam sessions and pot parties. Although I got the impression from her stories that she experimented with certain drugs, Doris had not been a major abuser.

She confessed to me that the majority of them really didn't work for her. Also, whenever she indulged, rather than getting high, she would merely lose control. Any situation where Doris was not in control of her faculties was frowned upon. The woman was so frightened of such a predicament, that she usually wouldn't take the risk.

Doris told me of the time she was with a musician friend— Joey Castro—who took pot and made it into liquid form. In India, this marijuana preparation is called *bhang*. The drug takes much longer to get you off, but its effect is much more powerful.

Doris said she drank some of the mixture, but all it did was make her feel dizzy. "Oh, Joey, I can't stand up. I've gotta lie down." She disliked the side effects of *bhang*.

If a drug didn't do its job, Doris wouldn't try it again. She wasn't opposed to testing something, at least once. With pot, Doris preferred smoking it.

As Doris reminisced about those care-free days, she recalled that the marijuana in Los Angeles wasn't as good as the stuff she obtained in Hawaii.

The lady was just full of surprises.

CHAPTER 13

Doris At the Movies

• • • • • • • •

One late morning, I stopped over and discovered Doris puttering around on her hands and knees. She had glue and compound all over her fingers. The woman looked a mess. Newspapers were strewn about the room. I had never seen Doris—nor her room—like this.

"What the hell are you doing?"

She paused in her work and looked up, smiling. "I'm restoring some of my antiques." Doris had spent most of the early hours scrubbing off layers of soot and grime on a few of her priceless artifacts.

"Can't someone else do that for you?" When it came to restoration work, Doris usually hired the top people in the field, sometimes museum professionals, to do the time-intensive, back-breaking labor.

"Not if I want it done right."

A stranger walked into the sitting room. Doris introduced him as Roberto. The young man helped her with the Newport Restoration Society. He was going to assist Doris in installing a swimming pool in Rough Point, her Rhode Island estate.

Roberto started to clean up some of the mess that Doris had made while she checked out her handiwork. She was proud of her accomplishments. So was Roberto. I was more impressed with her versatility and skills.

"If you want to do this all day, Doris, I can come over another time."

"No, no, Nishcintya, I'm finished. Besides, I want to do something special today."

"Oh, and what's that?"

"Let's go see a movie."

"You actually go to the movies, Doris? You mean you don't screen them here?"

"No, I don't!"

"Okay, so which one did you want to see?"

"*Goodfellas* with Robert DeNiro."

"Yeah, that sounds good. It's a Mafia movie. I like those."

"So do I. I'll have Johnny pick up our tickets so we won't have to wait in line.

"Great."

That evening, Doris, Johnny Gomez, Roberto and I headed to the theater in the Kahala Mall. Johnny drove. Instead of dropping us off, Johnny parked and we walked together to the cinema.

During our little stroll, I could see how thrilled Doris was. The event was exciting for her. For me and the other two guys, it was nothing out of the ordinary. For Doris, this night was much more. It was a Big Deal. Something she hardly ever did. For many years, the only movies that Doris had seen were either those shown on late night television or were ones she rented on videotape.

There was a long line at the ticket booth, so Doris and I were glad Johnny had gotten ours ahead of time. While we waited for the last show to end, I observed Doris.

The elderly woman was like a little girl with a secret. She was this famous billionaire, but no one knew it. There were no photographers or reporters. It wasn't some gala event or a celebrity soiree. Doris was slumming. She was just one of the crowd. A nobody. And she loved it. Retaining her anonymity the whole time was unusual and fun.

Roberto and I sat on either side of Doris in the theater; Johnny had disappeared once we entered. Doris liked having two handsome male escorts with her. Another thrill on this special occasion.

Goodfellas opens with a violent scene. Doris gasped in shock from the vivid and gratuitous nature of its intensity. Roberto and I were used to such casual depictions of "film realism." A few times during the movie, Doris couldn't follow the plot and asked me what was going on or why something had happened.

On the way home, she commented about how films had become way too violent over the years. "Do they really have to be so gruesome? Filmmakers don't need to show stuff like that. All that's necessary is to suggest it."

Johnny agreed. Roberto and I were pretty much indifferent. Doris elaborated about how the "old movies" didn't contain so much graphic violence or explicit sex to tell their stories.

"They were uplifting and well-crafted," she emphasized. "Works of art. Too many recent films aren't that well made or entertaining."

She did have a point.

Back at Shangri-La, we had a rather lengthy discussion about both the Mafia and criminal activities in general. Doris was really intrigued with the seamy nature of man. She loved "The Dark Side."

For hours, we talked about the workings of the crime syndicate. How the mob underworld was organized. What businesses and fields of operation they controlled.

"How do you know so much about the Mafia, Nischintya?"

I mentioned that I was half-Italian and had been raised in Chicago.

Immediately, Doris responded: "Al Capone."

I nodded. Anytime you mention Chicago to someone out-of-town, they connect the city with gangsters. Doris was no exception, however, she had actually lived during that era.

"Did you know any real life gangsters while you grew up?" she inquired. I could have asked Doris the same question.

"No—but we had a couple of relatives that the family wondered what they did for a living."

"Oh, really. Tell me more." Doris loved to hear tales that involved evil and corruption.

"Maybe tomorrow, Doris." I was forced to cut our conversation short. I had promised Karina—again—that I would come home early. I thought she would freak out if I got back too late, even though I was only five minutes away.

Doris was bummed out. She wanted to have dinner and continue our discussion until dawn. I would have loved to stay, but I was already having marital problems and didn't want to aggravate the matter.

Doris and I were made for each other. I loved to "talk story," as the Hawaiians call it. She loved to listen. We could sit for hours, much to the chagrin of the people around us.

CHAPTER 14

Escape From Shangri-La

• • • • • • • •

My son was born in February of 1991. During that month, Doris flew back and forth from Honolulu and Los Angeles a few times. On one trip in California, she entrusted Johnny Gomez to go out and buy James E. Higgins, IV a gift. The present wasn't anything like a $10 million trust fund or a Tiffany teething ring, but an infant's outfit from one of the best Hollywood clothing stores on Rodeo Drive. Alfred Ford and his wife Svaha sent my son a silver rattle.

Around this time I called Shangri-La asking for Chandi. We were still friends, despite my being good buddies with Doris. Though, at this point, my relationship with Doris was on an upswing while my friendship with Chandi was on the down side.

Chandi had ordered some more books, and I wanted to let her know that they had arrived. Bernard answered the phone.

"Is Chandi there?"

"Oh, Mr. Nischintya. Miss Heffner doesn't live here anymore."

"What?"

Bernard repeated the shocking news.

"What happened?"

"It's a long story, Mr. Nischintya, but we were lucky to escape with our lives."

"What the hell are you talking about? Never mind. Is Doris around?"

"Yes, Miss Duke is here."

"Please tell her I'll be right over."

Doris let me in on the whole story. She milked the turn of events for all it was worth. She sensationalized the incident with melodramatic theatrics.

"Chandi was poisoning me. I was getting sicker and sicker. I was dying.

"The doctor said that Chandi was responsible. He said she was a coke-head, always on cocaine. That's why her nose was all messed up. That's why she was sick all the time.

"Chandi was becoming meaner to the servants. James was walking around like he was the next Mr. Duke. Chandi didn't need me anymore. We were always fighting. It was just getting unbearable."

That was her version of why it happened. Doris told me how she outwitted them. She was in her glory now.

"I made a dentist appointment—I really did. Bernard took me there. I knew Chandi and James were going out that day. So, after my dental work was done, we went straight to the airport. We flew out to California and escaped with our lives."

Doris called Shangri-La and made the necessary arrangements for Chandi's expulsion. From Falcon Lair she sent out faxes to every estate, notifying them that her adopted daughter and lover were *persona non grata* at all residences. Their belongings were to be packed and shipped to her ranch on the Big Island.

When Chandi and James returned to Shangri-La later that day, they found the gates closed to them. Security informed the couple that "You're not allowed on the property anymore."

Doris ranted and raved about how the two of them were trying to kill her. That they were plotting her murder. But she thwarted their plans and turned the tables on them.

At the end of her stories, it was always: "That's it. She's out."

The whole situation took me by surprise. After thinking it over, I could see how the whole predicament had developed. Chandi and Doris fought; I had heard them arguing in New Jersey. Chandi was a total bitch according to the servants. Doris could also be a pain in the ass, but you had to do something major to get her pissed. Chandi seemed to be always looking for a fight, something to complain about. Doris may have just given up trying to share Chandi with James.

I thought back to that day at Duke Farms when Doris burst in on us while I did James' chart. The omen had proven true.

Days later, when things had calmed down and the daily routine was back to normal, Doris asked me to perform a cleansing *puja*. This was to get rid of any lingering "bad vibes" from Chandi. She insisted on witnessing the entire ritual.

I cautioned Doris: "You might get a little bored while I'm doing all these repititious *mantras*."

Doris watched the whole ceremony from start to finish, both inside the main house and outside on the grounds. She stayed with me for each particular ritual. First, I did an *aratika*. Then, I sat down and recited the *Narasinghadeva Kavaca*. Walking around the estate, I burned incense, rang a bell, and blew a conchshell. Finally, I went into every room, every closet, every bathroom—except the servants' quarters. Doris followed me as I chanted. She instructed me where to go. I repeated the proper procedure each time.

Later that year, she had me do a cleansing *puja* both at Rough Point in Newport and Duke Farms in Somerville. For some reason, we never got around to performing the ceremony at Falcon Lair in Los Angeles.

I enjoyed helping Doris. Doing *pujas* for her was always fun. She felt relieved after I worked my *shaman* services. She calmed down. Started to put her life back together.

Another ritual she had me perform was the pouring of Ganges water into her salt-water swimming pool. Whenever you mix water from the Ganges River in India with another body of water, it becomes, in effect, the Ganges. Devotees who make the pilgrimage to India will bathe in the Ganges River for spiritual cleansing.

One of the servants, Tija, took me out past the beach house, where I poured Ganges water from a couple of vials I had brought into Doris' pool. I chanted *mantras* and burned incense as needed. I knew the man must have thought I was nuts. Being part of the Duke household in Hawaii, however, I'm sure he had seen a lot of stranger things.

Doris didn't actually swim in this pool, but she exercised, just like James had taught her. I never saw Doris in the water, though I knew she continued her daily, rigorous regimen. In her younger days, Doris not only swam but surfed a great deal. I could tell she missed those days.

During the first year that I knew Doris, her health issue was a mystery. The situation was really weird. I would pre-scribe herbs and natural tonics, in addition to performing *reiki* over her. Whenever I finished one of my treatments, which might take a few days, Doris would be in good spirits and feeling much better. A week or two later, the woman would be in bad shape and dragging. Both her mental and physical condi-tions could go from one extreme to the other in the course of a couple of weeks. I couldn't figure it out.

After Chandi's expulsion, Doris started asking me to per-form more *pujas*, ones where I would just pray for her and her health. The break-up with her adopted daughter sent Doris into a depression. The doctors put her on major medications. The lady had a whole table full of bottles for all the drugs that the doctors wanted her to take.

I told her: "Doris, you don't need all these friggin' pills. Let's just get you some proper herbal remedies."

"What do you mean?"

Doris wasn't as sharp as she used to be. She was sluggish. All those drugs had messed her up, mentally and physically.

"You need to clean out," I told her. "You're clogged up. We have to flush all this garbage from your system."

Doris was impressed because I knew what was going on in her body. She was also touched by my concern.

I went to one of the natural health centers and bought this really disgusting mixture that would do the trick. After a short prayer ceremony, I brought the whole kit over on my afternoon visit.

"Did you do it? Did you do the *puja*?" Doris always had me perform an offertory prayer with any remedy or medication I gave her.

"Yes, Doris. I offered up all the ingredients to Dhanvantari. That specific Deity was the incarnation of Krishna connected with Ayurvedic medicine. This particular branch of treatment was made popular in the United States by Deepak Chopra, M. D.

Doris checked everything out. She read the list of ingredients carefully. She was very interested in anything I found that would help her.

"Psyllium seed husks?" Doris asked.

"They're a natural laxative. It acts like a broom going through your colon and intestines."

Wary, she watched me measure out the precise dosage.

"Don't worry, Doris. I've used it before. The stuff may be gross, but it works. I usually do a clean-out at least once a year," I added.

"Make a batch for yourself, Nischintya."

"Sure."

After administering the herbal medicine, I left and went back home. Natural or not, the remedy still took time to take effect. I figured I would see Doris the following evening and check on the results.

For me, that concoction works wonders. Doris was another story. Before noon she called, almost cursing me: "I'm dying,

I'm dying." The stuff had gone all through her system, but it hadn't come out.

I rushed over. Sitting next to her bed, I rubbed her stomach and performed *reiki* to make her feel better. In a short while, Doris fell asleep. According to *reiki* handbooks, that was a good sign. It meant that I had connected with Doris' body energy.

Doris was out of it for about fifteen or twenty minutes. Her breathing became heavy and noisy. Here was a lady who was very particular about her appearance—both in public and privately—passed out on the bed, snoring with her mouth open, and with my hands on her belly.

I tripped out on the whole incident. As I sat in Shangri-La, I could hear the roaring surf crashing against the lava rocks. Seagulls screeched as they searched along the breakwaters. The servants were milling about, concentrating on their duties. I glanced around her bedroom, admiring its "maharaja motif."

When Doris came to, she was a little embarrassed.

The *reiki* worked. She went to the bathroom. Doris emerged feeling much better. That little sparkle was back in her eyes. She was happy.

"Now, remember, you're supposed to do the clean-out a few times to make sure every—"

"No way, Nischintya. I'm not having anything to do with that shit again."

"But—"

Doris was adamant. She never took that remedy again. The first time had been too traumatic.

* * * * *

Over the next couple of months, Doris started getting better. She ate the herbs I brought her. The *reiki* sessions eased the chronic pain in her knees. She saw her acupuncturist two or three times a week. Her health definitely improved.

Though Doris was no longer depressed, she was still lonely.

She definitely needed company. Despite the fact that I was having numerous and more frequent spats with Karina, I couldn't abandon Doris. She required my personal attention and constant support.

Many times when I would walk over to the estate, Bernard would greet me with open arms. "Oh, it's so good when you come, Mr. Nischintya. Miss Duke is so happy. She has such a good time. It's very beneficial for her."

Doris' mental and physical state improved, but the woman was still carrying a torch for Chandi. She would alternate between telling me about how Chandi had tried to kill her and asking me if I had heard anything about her and James.

During her frequent discourses concerning the alleged murder conspiracy, Doris would regularly make references to "Harry" or her "doctor." I thought she was talking about the same man, Harry Demopoulos, her main physician. Doris never mentioned another doctor that she was seeing.

Dr. Roland Atiga, a second consultant, helped convince Doris that she was being poisoned by Chandi. He would make a diagnosis and prescribe crazy treatments to counter the adverse condition. Atiga would always tell her: "This is why you're in such bad shape, Miss Duke."

Doris told me of her discussions with Atiga. "He said that Chandi was slipping me something. I asked Bernard who had access to the food I ate. He told me that except for Chandi, the chef and himself, none of the staff even knows what I eat. So it had to be some of the medication that Chandi gave me or the pills she recommended for some of my problems.

"Even Bernard was worried about my health. He kept telling me that I was 'getting sicker and sicker, and nothing seemed to help.' Many a morning, when he would bring me my breakfast, he'd say to me: 'Chandi's doing something to you, Miss Duke. Be careful.' "

Doris paused and shook her head. "Did you know that it was Bernard who recommended I see his doctor friend? I'll never forget how concerned he was about my health."

Something sinister had been going on. Anyone who had contact with Doris could have been up to no good. There were too many suspects. Every one of them had the same possible motive—money.

It could have been Chandi. Or possibly James and Chandi. On the other hand, one of the doctors might have been the guilty party. With all those prescriptions, Doris might have been experiencing unusual side effects. She could have been taking the wrong drugs based upon a misdiagnosed condition. Bernard and the chef were suspects themselves. Anything was possible. With what little information I had, I couldn't make a judgment call.

"Atiga also told me that Chandi was a coke addict," Doris continued. "That's why she was always up late at night and couldn't get out of bed until noon. It explains all her so-called health problems, Nischintya."

I've *been* around people who were coke addicts and individuals who are substance abusers. Chandi didn't act like either. The actions and temperament of an addict are very obvious, if you know what to look for. They're very hyper and completely paranoid. Chandi was much too calm, despite her many outbursts with the servants. There was no way I could believe Chandi was strung out on cocaine. From my talks with James Burns in New Jersey, I learned that Chandi had a congenital defect. Chandi had to constantly see a doctor for her condition. She was required to take specific medications daily for the rest of her life.

Both Atiga and Bernard had convinced Doris that Chandi was out to get her. Any time she would reiterate the "rumors" these two men told her—which was frequently—I thought it was just a way for Doris to justify her actions in getting rid of her adopted daughter.

No matter what Doris believed, I could still see that she was in love with Chandi. Despite what had happened, Doris wanted to know what was going on in Chandi's life. Any gossip about her was welcomed. If I didn't have any, Doris volunteered new information she had come across.

A couple of times, I suggested that she *call* Chandi. "Maybe she wasn't really trying to kill you. Perhaps you should call her. It's obvious that you miss her."

I found out that I wasn't the only one in this frame of mind. Dr. Harry Demopoulos had told Doris: "You're just pining away for Chandi. Why don't the two of you get back together?"

Doris was adamant and stubborn. Once she cut someone from her life, they were out. No turning back. This was something she learned from her father, Buck Duke. When a person lets you down or betrays you, you cut them out of your life—for good and forever.

Doris had done that; only her heart strings were still holding on. The situation was very difficult for her. Chandi had exaggerated a number of the stories she had told Doris. It was part of her nature. Doris now took them as boldface lies—deliberate falsehoods to gain her confidence. Doris' frustration and aggravation with Chandi had been manipulated and altered into a festering vehemence and a seething hatred.

I was not convinced that she had made the right decision. I talked with Doris. "If you can't work things out with Chandi, at least part on good terms," I suggested.

It was a futile request. Doris had the will and determination to stick by her guns. She had made her decision and would live with its consequences.

* * * * *

What was the story between Doris and Chandi?

After her expulsion, Chandi retreated to her horse ranch on the Big Island. The newspapers had a field day with the situation: "Doris Duke disowns adopted Hare Krishna daughter." The tabloids hinted about a possible lesbian dalliance between Doris and Chandi. Even the servants and staff had their own suspicions about what had gone on between them.

The question about that relationship was something I could never ask Doris. To be honest, I think there may have been some physical connection, but the levels of intimacy were too many to comprehend.

To me, it was as if they had been a mother and daughter or sisters in some past life. Doris and Chandi were two peas in a pod. Soul mates. Twin flames. The two of them possessed an extremely strong, emotional bond.

I felt that Chandi wasn't there just for the money. Doris' wealth was only a part of the picture. Chandi had not been looking for a "mark," happening to pick Doris. They took a liking to each other from the start. Just like both women had taken a liking to me when I met each of them.

Doris and Chandi shared genuine love and affection. Doris might have been the mother that Chandi never had. Chandi may have been the daughter that Doris never had. Their temperaments meshed. They also clashed. Every relationship has its ups and downs. Theirs was no exception.

Many articles and biographies state that Doris believed Chandi was the reincarnation of her long-dead daughter, Arden. Doris never said anything to me to confirm this supposition, nor did Chandi claim that "Doris thinks I'm Arden" or postulate "I am Arden."

Chandi Duke Heffner was to have been Doris Duke Junior. Doris trained her during those years they spent together. She groomed Chandi to follow in her footsteps. Doris expected the young woman to carry on her legacy after she was gone. The same way that Doris took over her family's fortune when Buck Duke passed away.

She had a good time during those years. Chandi knew who she was and used that fact to her advantage every chance she got. Nobody can blame her for that. The situation went sour.

All those involved had a part in the break-up: Doris, Chandi, James, Atiga and Bernard. Even me. Circumstances had escalated out of control until there was no turning back.

Maybe their split was inevitable. What a waste. It was a damned shame. Knowing Chandi's ability to get things done, I can't help but wonder about how much Doris and Chandi could have accomplished together.

CHAPTER 15

Doris The Healer

· · · · · · · ·

In May of 1991, I attended a Temple President/GBC meeting in Los Angeles. When I got back to Hawaii, things on the home front were coming to a boil. Karina had been up to no good in my absence. Our marriage was falling apart. Another divorce seemed more likely as each day passed.

Though concerned about my welfare, Doris was in ecstasy over the bad news. My third wife moved out by the end of the month. I was down in the dumps. Because of our mutual partner problems, Doris and I became almost inseparable.

We were like two people spurned by their lovers. We needed each other's company more at this point in our lives than ever before. Though we continued to "talk story," she and I commiserated a great deal of the time.

I was really "in" at this stage. Doris had my full, undivided attention. We would relate back and forth about all we had done for certain individuals and how badly they had treated us in return.

Even before Karina left me, I had been experiencing stomach problems. After she was gone, the condition became much worse. My ability to digest food properly failed completely. I hardly ate.

I grew very thin. I don't weigh that much to begin with, so the weight loss took even more of a physical toll on me. I was down to about 105 pounds, which made me look emaciated. Because I was all knotted up inside, my appetite was almost non-existent.

A friend of mine had received his first *reiki* attunement around this time. He stopped by and performed the full ritual over me. He washed his hands, rubbed his palms together, inscribed the *yantras* on his flesh, chanted *mantras*, and meditated. Finally he gave me the actual treatment. After an hour or so, he finished, washing his hands a second time.

Nothing happened. No effect. No change. I sighed in frustration and decided to accept the persistent pain.

One night after dinner in Shangri-La, Doris noticed that I hadn't eaten much.

"What's wrong, Nischintya?"

I mentioned what was ailing me. She was very concerned about my failing health.

"Oh, you poor thing," Doris consoled me. She placed her hand on my stomach while we talked. It wasn't a true *reiki* session, like my friend had done for me. No proper preliminaries. No formal ritual. She just put her hand on me.

We continued our conversation for another half-hour or so. All during our lengthy discussion, Doris kept her hand in place.

On my way home, my stomach started rumbling. I realized then and there that I was starving. Later, I ate one of the first big meals I had eaten in months. After one casual treatment, my appetite had returned. I remember thinking: "God, this lady is really potent." I was truly impressed with Doris' healing abilities.

I augmented her *reiki* with some Ayurvedic medicine called *dracsha*, which is almost like a wine and aids the digestive process. Within weeks, to Doris' delight, I was back to my old self.

Doris The Healer

* * * * *

A few months before Karina and I went our separate ways, I met the renowned Hawaiian healer and spiritual seeker, Nana Veary. Karina met Nana's granddaughter, Kathleen, who later introduced me to this remarkable woman.

After a shopping trip to the Kahala Mall, Karina couldn't get the car started. Kathleen approached Karina in the parking lot and offered to give her a ride home.

She and I got to talking while Karina called for a tow truck. I happened to mention Doris. Kathleen's eyes lit up.

"Oh, Auntie Doris? I know her." As a little kid, Kathleen hung out at Shangri-La when Nana visited her friend. Doris knew Kathleen by her Hawaiian name, Noelani.

Kathleen told me all about Nana Veary. The woman recently had a stroke. She wasn't doing that well. I asked if I could meet her grandmother. Though Kathleen said yes, she warned me about what to expect. That I shouldn't get my hopes up.

Nana acknowledged my presence, but she couldn't speak. To communicate, she usually wrote things down. Her handwriting had suffered, and the woman limited her scribbling to phrases or simple words.

It is difficult to be friends with someone who has had a stroke—a person who basically just sits there. But I did feel connected to Nana. I would chant for her or perform *reiki* like Doris had taught me.

She was very happy to see me. My visits lifted her spirits. Nana would nod or sway to the rhythms as I meditated and chanted. Her family was also grateful for the time I spent with their invalid relative. I really liked the woman. Just being in her presence made me feel good. Hanging out with Nana Veary gave me the same pleasure and satisfaction I received when I hung out with Doris.

The next time I saw Doris, I mentioned to her about meeting Nana Veary. When I told her about the stroke, Doris was a little concerned. She fondly recalled those times with Nana.

Doris had become instant friends with the lady. She respected Nana not only as a healer but a fellow seeker of "The Truth." The two women traveled all over the world together. Although they were best of buddies, Doris almost revered her friend as a saint.

Nana Veary later wrote a book about her quest in a spiritually-enlivening work called *Change We Must*. She referred to Doris as her rich, philanthropic friend named Ruth, which was a goof on "truth." A chapter in the book told about an incident that happened during the time Doris and Nana were making a pilgrimage to several holy places.

When Doris related the experience to me, she used all her dramatic skills to embellish the tale:

"We were staying at this inn. It had been a long day. Nana and I were extremely tired. We had just unpacked and started to rest when, suddenly, Nana received a warning from her spiritual guide, Grandfather Thundercloud. He told her to leave immediately. Though exhausted, we left right away.

"Later, when we arrived at another town, Nana and I heard that the building we were in earlier that day had collapsed. Everyone who was inside was killed."

Doris and Nana had not seen each other for many years. There had been a falling out with some members of her family. Doris lent Nana's daughter's husband money for a business venture. The loan was never paid back.

I suggested to Doris that she visit Nana, before something worse happened to the wonderful lady.

"Yeah, I really should go over and see her," Doris agreed.

Though Doris said she would make it a point to arrange a visit, she never did. I harassed her every chance I got, especially after each time Kathleen took me to see her grandmother.

One day, I just forced the issue. I knew where Nana lived. Originally, Kathleen was going to take us, but something came up and she couldn't make it that particular day. Since I figured it was going to be now or never, I got directions. Johnny Gomez volunteered to take us. He also knew Nana and wished to see her again.

The day we left, construction workers were rebuilding the highway near the town where Nana lived. We encountered one major traffic jam. Johnny wasn't familiar with the area, and since I don't drive, I couldn't be any help at all. For twenty or thirty minutes, we didn't move. The road was wall-to-wall cars.

I was thinking to myself: "Oh, God, no! This isn't a good sign." I glanced at Doris. I could see that scared look in her eyes. She was starting to freak out. Doris was not the type of person who was used to waiting, especially when she traveled. I imagined her backing out, telling Johnny to get on the car phone: "Call a helicopter—and get us out of here!"

Doris surprised me and held out until we finally reached Nana's place. I have witnessed many reunions in my day, but none was ever as poignant as this one.

When Doris and Nana saw each other, tears flowed like rivers. They embraced and kissed. It was a very touching moment in both their lives. Johnny and Nana exchanged hugs. Even his eyes were watery.

Johnny and I sat off to the side. For a long time, Doris and Nana were oblivious to us. As Doris talked, Nana would nod or shake her head; sometimes she would write something down. Doris started giving Nana *reiki*.

Suddenly, Nana spoke for the first time in years, which was a special thrill in itself. She said: "*Kahuna haha.*"

Both Doris and Nana pointed to me. I came closer. They touched my chest and said almost in unison: "*Kahuna haha, kahuna haha.*" I laughed because I thought they were making a joke. But, the two women merely smiled at one another and then, together, they gave me their own version of a *reiki* attunement.

Dollars, Diamonds, Destiny & Death

During the rest of our visit, Nana and Doris held hands and looked at one another. Doris would remember an experience they shared and Nana would nod. A few times they communicated by sign language. To my astonishment, Doris stayed quite a while. I could see that being in each other's presence was some sort of spiritual connection.

I believe I received some mercy on my karma for bringing the two of them together after so many years apart. I had been touched by their lives in a way I can never describe adequately.

On the ride home, I asked Doris about what she and Nana had called me. *Kahuna haha* is Hawaiian for a *kahuna* (someone with specialized knowledge) who diagnoses and heals by touch. This designation includes individuals who give massage, perform *reiki*, or just take a person's pulse and temperature.

As far as I know, that was the last time Doris saw Nana Veary. The elderly Hawaiian healer and spiritual seeker died in May of 1993. No doubt, she was escorted to Heaven by Grandfather Thundercloud.

* * * * *

Doris and I hung out together a great deal until it was time for her to return to Duke Farms. Before she left for New Jersey, we shared a special evening of dinner and stargazing.

In the newspapers, we read about a unique astronomical event that was going to take place. This important alignment of celestial bodies happened only once every 175 to 200 years.

Doris invited me to see it with her, pointing out that she had her own telescope. From her ocean-front patio, we had an excellent view of the night sky. Candles illuminated the terrace. The water crashed against the breakwater as the waves crept up the shore. It was a spectacular setting and evening.

The only drawback was the fact that Doris didn't own a decent telescope. You could see the particular configuration with the naked eye, but the event was more impressive through the optics. Her spyglass looked like it had been purchased from a cheap department store. My own, expensive telescope was much more powerful. I regretted not bringing it along as I had originally intended.

In the midst of our heavenly observations, I commented to Doris: "You know, we were probably together the last time this occurred. We were somewhere in Europe, I think." I didn't have a psychic flash or a past-life remembrance; it was more of just an off-hand remark.

Doris left for the East Coast a few days after that, stopping off in Los Angeles for about a week. We kept in touch. No matter who called whom, Doris would always ask: "When are you going to come and visit me?"

I had to keep postponing a reunion because of urgent business matters. Things started to slow down, but I wanted to be able to spend as much time with Doris as I could. My schedule looked totally free in the Fall. I told her that I'd be able to visit in October.

That wasn't convenient for Doris. "No, no. I won't be here.

I'm going to Europe then. Better come now. I'm staying at Newport. You can see my cottage in Rhode Island."

So I did.

I wrapped up all my loose ends in Hawaii and flew to California. I spent some time in Los Angeles seeing friends and taking care of Temple business. Then I headed for Newport.

I was looking forward to this vacation. I was traveling alone so no one would spoil my second stay in paradise.

CHAPTER 16

Rendezvous At Rough Point

• • • • • • •

Although I traveled First Class during the years I knew Doris, I never touched airline food, except the water. I did not have a direct flight to Rhode Island and had to switch planes in Georgia. A friend of mine from the Atlanta Temple was supposed to meet me in the airport with a cooked meal. Something went wrong, and we missed each other.

Doris had asked Ben Reed, the director of the Newport Restoration Foundation, if he could send someone to pick me up at the airport. Ben sent one of the freelance workers, Tim, who did carpentry for the Foundation, as well as some odd jobs for Doris. He brought along his girlfriend, Kim.

When Ben told him my name was Nischintya, Tim figured I was some Oriental guy. He had printed a sign but forgot to hold it up while they were waiting in the terminal. Numerous people were at the airport, with and without signs, looking for others. As I exited the gate, I went right up to Tim. Somehow, I just knew he was the one taking me to Rough Point.

Both Tim and his girlfriend were impressed with the fact that I picked them out of all these other people searching for friends and relatives. I think Tim was disappointed and bewildered because I wasn't some Eastern religious dude. They were fascinated, though, that I was Doris Duke's astrologer. Tim and Kim couldn't believe she had her own personal soothsayer.

On the trip to the mansion, I received a few psychic flashes about this couple. Like I said before, the less I know about someone, the more I can access "past-life" information.

I looked at Kim, pointing out: "In one of your previous lives, you were a Southern Belle. Tim was a Northern Yankee."

Both Tim and Kim got what we call "chicken skin" in Hawaii. Your hair stands on end and your flesh breaks out in goosebumps when you hear something eerie.

One of the first things I asked Tim, and I knew nothing about him since we just met, was: "Are you a politician? Or are you contemplating a career as a legislator or a diplomat? I see you as the mayor of some town."

They looked at each other. "Oh my God," Kim exclaimed.

"This is so weird," Tim explained, "because all my friends call me the 'Mayor of Newport.' That's because I know everybody in town and have lots of connections."

"Oh. You should try to become the real mayor. I could probably convince Doris to kick in some money for your election campaign."

Tim smiled. Kim laughed.

As I went on for a bit, we kind of became friends. They both sensed what I was revealing about them was true, that this had really happened to them. It just felt right.

Kim gave me their number so I could keep in touch with them while I was in Rhode Island. We planned to get together later on during my visit.

When we arrived at Rough Point, a ten-acre spread right on the Atlantic Ocean, Bernard met us. He showed me inside. Tim and Kim weren't invited to stay, which surprised me, because I thought Doris would have wanted to thank them personally. Instead, Bernard expressed Doris' appreciation to Tim. The couple then got back in their car and drove off.

Doris was thrilled to see me. We kissed and hugged. Ever

thoughtful, Doris had supper waiting for me, which was great, because, by then, I was starving. While we ate this huge dinner, she and I talked story and caught up on things. Too bad Tim and Kim couldn't have joined us.

After this evening meal, I was shown to my quarters. It turned out to be this one little room. Pretty small compared to what I was used to as Doris' guest. This room was definitely tiny by Duke standards. But it was comfortable.

While a couple of the maids helped me unpack, they told me how grateful all the servants were to have me visit. "Miss Duke is always easier to deal with when you're around," one of them confided in me. "Life is not as complicated or as stressful."

"She's always in great spirits when you visit," the other one added.

No wonder the staff like me so much and were always happy to see me.

The next day I awoke early and, after breakfast, went outside the mansion to chant. The main house had this circular driveway, which was ideal for me because I prefer to pace about while I meditate.

So I strolled around in a circle, fingering my *japa* beads and chanting. Out of the corner of my eye, I saw one of the groundskeepers with a pair of dogs. From a distance, they looked like Dobermans. It looked like any minute this guy was going to let them loose, and the dogs would come charging.

Déjà vu. Duke Farms all over again. I'm going to die because Doris forgot to tell security I was visiting. It must be my destiny.

The dogs were straining at their leashes. I could now see they were only Greyhounds, but the pair was vicious-looking. Snarling, sizing me up for breakfast. Their master seemed to be debating on whether or not to call for reinforcements to handle an apparent intruder alert.

I threw my arms up in the air and screamed: "Whoa! Hold

on! I'm Miss Duke's guest."

The man approached me cautiously. "Who the hell are you? What are you doing here?" he demanded to know.

"I'm Nischintya Dasa, Miss Duke's astrologer. If you don't believe me, just call and ask."

Luckily, I convinced him my story was legitimate. The man was extremely apologetic. "Security didn't notify me that Miss Duke had a guest. I'm sorry. I should know about these things. Nobody informs me of nothing around here. I have no idea about what's going on.

"Why doesn't Miss Duke ever tell us about her friends?" The groundskeeper muttered to himself as he and the dogs went on their way, "I see some nut out here in the yard, and I don't know who it is." The man was probably worried that he was going to lose his job.

I made it a point to remind Doris about notifying security each and every time I came to visit her after that. Once was bad enough, but two close calls! I wasn't about to let the third time be my last.

Though still shook up by the incident, I went back to my spiritual contemplation. At lunch, Doris commented about seeing me practice my daily prayer rituals.

"I have to get back to my meditation," she concluded.

Being a religious seeker, Doris had probably seen and done anything and everything over the years. From Catholicism, which she almost converted to when she heard Spanish monks performing Gregorian Chant, to Black Gospel, when she sang with the Angelic Gospel Choir in Harlem two decades earlier. Doris had been exposed to the Self-Realization Fellowship, as well as meeting such celebrities as L. Ron Hubbard. Whatever spiritual form it took, she had checked it out.

"What's the problem then?" I asked.

Her excuse: "It's so hard."

"That's because," I pointed out, "the meditation you do is 'Contemplating the Void.' You're trying to make your mind blank, right?"

"Yeah. So?"

"Think about how difficult that is. Just the thought of making your mind a blank is a thought. And another thing. Where can you go in this day and age and not be disturbed? It's just not possible. You've even got mountain climbers bothering you in the Himalayas.

"The meditation that you've seen me do," I continued, "works the opposite way. I'm chanting on beads, so my sense of touch is engaged. I'm reciting the *mantras* out loud, so I am both speaking and hearing the words. I usually burn incense, so my sense of smell comes into play. And I either look at the Deities or gaze at natural surroundings. All five of my human senses are being used. It's very easy for me to meditate."

"I like that," Doris agreed. "Smart thinking. Sounds like it might work for me. Trying to block out everything is much more difficult to do versus being able to focus on what's around you."

Doris may have liked my approach, but she never did chant as much as I did. She did get out her *japa* beads, a set I had given her in Hawaii, and began saying a few *mantras* on a daily basis. She preferred watching me offer incense to Krishna or listening to me chant.

Doris Duke was someone who would do something for a while, even to the point of obsession, and then become bored with it because there were always many more distractions to interest her.

After lunch, she and I discussed the Hare Krishna cult. Doris was well-versed in that religion. She owned most of my late Spiritual Master's books and was interested in his philosophy of life. Doris was always very respectful when she talked about him.

"I regret not having met Srila Prabhupada," she reflected. "He must have been a great man, like Ghandi." Doris now wanted to know how important Chandi had been in the organization. "Was she very close to His Divine Grace? Chandi told me she was an important figure in the Hare Krishna organization hierarchy. Was that true, Nischintya? Because lately I've had my doubts."

Chandi had been initiated by Srila Prabhupada, but she never really hung out with her Spiritual Master. Her husband was one of his first disciples and a member of the Inner Circle. But not Chandi. I knew the woman. She didn't really lie, but merely stretched the truth. That was just how she was.

Doris took the news in stride. "Yeah, I thought so. She wasn't that spiritual. Chandi would say things a true devotee shouldn't have."

Chandi had gotten Doris interested in Krishna Consciousness when they first met. For Doris, it was all part of her search for "The Truth." With me, Doris found an individual who was more into the philosophical aspects of the cult—what was behind the Movement. I could explain the religion to her without ramming it down her throat, like many devotees did to the "unenlightened."

Doris also liked getting her information from me because I was a black sheep in the organization. I was a troublemaker and a heretic. Because I was dedicated to my late Spiritual Master's vision, I became *persona non grata* in the scheme of things.

I also possessed a wealth of knowledge of other religious principles. I could hold my own with someone like Doris Duke. Due to my own experiences and education, I was able to tie together many far-out, in-depth, physical and metaphysical aspects of the world's religions for Doris.

I used the example of six blind men and an elephant. Each of the men described the animal only by the particular part of its anatomy they were touching. The man holding the tail said it was a rope. The guy with the trunk believed the pachyderm to be a snake. The third one caressed the long tusk and fancied the creature to be like a polished rock. The man with his arms around one of the legs claimed the animal to be similar to a tree. The fifth one, feeling the enormous ears, cried out that it was like a huge fan. The last blind man, touching the side of the animal, thought the beast was an odd-shaped wall.

Each of them was right, yet none was correct. All had failed to describe the entire elephant. It was the same way with man's numerous theologies.

I told Doris: "Every important spiritual personality has seen The Truth. They all have a valid claim. But because their followers are not self-realized, they maintain that their particular religion is the "One and Only True Path." Man is limited in his capacity to understand the cosmos. Only one being knows everything and that is God.

"If all the religious leaders would accept the fact that there can be many paths to the Absolute Truth, the situation in the world would be a lot better."

Doris liked my perspective. I made her feel that all her soul-searching had not been in vain. For the next hour or so, she and I trashed a number of religious organizations and philosophical institutions because the people who ran them were "blind" to the opinions of their contemporaries.

Usually when we discussed spiritual matters, I would tell her a joke or two. That day we sat down and talked about the problems that the Hare Krishnas had after His Divine Grace A. C. Bhaktivedanta Swami Prabhupada passed away. I told Doris a joke about God and Satan.

`God and the Devil were walking together one day. During their stroll, they talked about how they did things. Suddenly, God stopped. He bent down and scooped up something in His hands. Satan wanted to know what He found. "What is it? Whatcha got, Lord? Let me see it." God showed it to the Devil, calling it "Truth." Ever ready to exploit things, Satan replied: "Let me organize that for you."

"The Krishnas are like any other religion," I said. "A great teacher comes and expounds so many truths. Once he's gone, someone else steps in and wants to organize that doctrine in his own fashion."

Doris liked my mode of thinking. I wasn't set in my ways like so many people she had met in her lifetime. When it came to religion and philosophy, I was more open-minded—like Doris herself was.

When Doris was ten years old her father, James B. Duke, the
ninth richest man in America, began to train her to manage
and increase this fortune. Here she is at age ten wearing a
Japanese kimono. (Introduction)

A glamour photo of Doris taken in Europe, where she worked as a journalist and an agent for the OSS, the forerunner of the CIA. (Introduction)

When I told Doris that Scorpios like her have a fierce look, she laughed. Later on I had an intuition that she had been on the higher planets in a previous life but had fallen, much the same way that the crocodile who attacked Gajendra the elephant had also been on a higher planet previously, but had fallen. (Chapter 3)

Top: Chandi and I aboard Doris' $25 million 737 jet. Chandi always carried her own portable oxygen supply to help deal with jet lag. (Chapters 1 and 25) **Bottom:** $20 for 20 years. Alfred B. Ford, a Hare Krishna devotee, leased his estate to the Honolulu temple for only $1 a year. I paid the temple's past-due rent with a twenty from my own pocket. (Chapter 5)

Above: My third wife, Karina, modeling on the ocean side of Shangri-la. (Chapter 4)

Inset: Karina styling in her silk sari and silver bangles.

The Honolulu Temple. Alfred Ford bought the Coelho estate now worth over $2 million and rented it to the devotees for only a $1 a year. (Chapter 5)

Fire *yagna* (sacrifice) for
Imelda Marcos. I predicted that the court
would rule in favor of Imelda; the verdict
of "not guilty" was rendered on her
birthday.

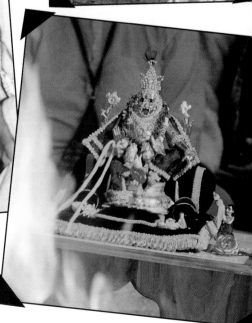

Bathing Lord *Narasinghadeva*. Despite
what it looks like, I am pouring straw-
berry juice over the Deity, not blood.
(Chapters 4 and 11)

Lord *Narasinghadeva*, a powerful Deity, gives protection to those in need. I asked for His intercession on behalf of Doris' friend, Imelda Marcos, the former First Lady of the Philippines. (Chapters 4 and 11)

To visit Doris in the nearby Manor House at Duke Farms, Karina and I daily crossed this tiny trestle from our guest cottage on the vast estate.

Clock Tower and stables on Duke Farms. Doris housed her two camels here.

In the "back yard" of the main house at Duke Farms, Karina and I encountered vicious guard dogs roaming about the property. (Chapters 6 through 10)

A man-made lake on Duke Farms. In the 1920s, Buck Duke spent more than $10 million to landscape 750 of the 3,000 acres he owned in New Jersey. Duke Farms contains more than twenty-five miles of paved roads, lagoons, fountains, sculptures, woodlands, gardens, pastures, heated stables, cottages, and a huge chateau-like Manor House. (Chapters 6 through 11)

Buddha statue and fountain. This piece is one of the numerous art treasures collected by Doris during her long lifetime. The artifacts alone at Duke Farms have been appraised at over $1 billion. (Chapters 6 through 11)

Saying good-bye to Bernard at Duke Farms. This shot was taken during the good times the two of us shared. Later, I and others would accuse the butler of murdering Doris. (Chapters 6 through 10, 17, and 29 through 31)

Top: The formal dining room at Rough Point where I enjoyed a late-night Indian dinner cooked by Doris' personal maid, Nuku. (Chapter 17)

Bottom: The after-dinner sitting room at Rough Point where Doris and I would "talk story," discussing religion and philanthropy, trading UFO tales, or telling one another jokes and personal anecdotes. (Chapters 16 through 24)

The grand staircase at Rough Point in Newport, Rhode Island. **Top:** On the second floor, to the right of the stairs, were Doris' personal apartments. **Middle:** A handful of the numerous, priceless paintings found at Rough Point adorn the walls of the main stairwell. **Bottom:** This is only a glimpse of the ornate, detailed woodwork showcased throughout the building. (Chapters 16 through 24)

Gaura (right) and *Nitai* (left). I gave Doris three snapshots of the Deities in the Los Angeles temple. Because these Deities could help Doris with her music and dance, she always traveled with those photographs. Setting them atop her piano, Doris instructed the servants to place fresh flowers next to them daily. (Chapters 6 and 9)

Rukmini (right) and *Dwarkadisa* (left). Doris was enthralled by the Vedic understanding of God, the Divine Couple, engaged in amorous pastimes. The habitual arrangement of those framed photographs on her grand piano was the closest that Doris ever came to having a personal altar in any of her estates. (Chapters 6 and 9)

Jagannatha (right), *Baladeva* (left), and *Subhadra* (middle). These three Deities are each given Their own limousine and 40-foot-high float in the lively Festival of the Chariots parade held annually at Venice Beach. (Chapters 6 and 9)

Top: Sitting room. Down the hall from Doris, in a separate wing of the mansion, was my three-room guest suite at the "Doris Duke Hilton."

Bottom: My "office." Despite the luxuriousness of my temporary professional accomodations, I worked as little as possible. (Chapters 16 through 24)

Bedroom views. To the right I could see the angry surf of the Atlantic Ocean. To the left was Senator Pell's estate, hidden behind a thicket of trees.

Above: My bedroom. The gourmet meals, service, and lodgings were far better than any five-star hotel in the world.
Right: Mural in the hallway (Chapters 16 through 24)

Reading room and library. Though Doris owned vast amounts of handbound first editions of the world's greatest authors, she preferred to read the tabloids and scandal sheets. (Chapters 16 through 24)

Collection of my spiritual master's books. Doris bought fifty-volume sets for four of her five estates. (Chapter 1)

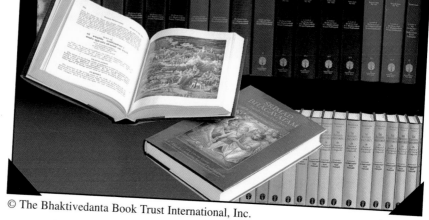

For the first time in my life, I wore a tuxedo. My brother and co-author, Joseph P. Higgins, assists me by fastening my bow tie. Doris never believed that I had ever been "dressed up." (Chapter 21)

Here (posing with my grandmother) is the proof that I did wear a tux. But Doris never saw these; the photographer took two years to deliver them! By the time he finished them, Doris had died. (Chapter 21)

My newborn son, James E. Higgins IV, and I resting peacefully. Doris purchased swaddling clothes from Rodeo Drive; Alfred Ford sent a silver rattle. (Chapter 14)

Production crew from Outpost Films. This company was commissioned by British ITN and American A & E to produce a biography on Doris Duke. **Above:** Associate producer, Helen Twigge-Molecey, sitting in the foreground, oversaw the set-up of equipment at the Honolulu temple. **Below:** During a break in filming at Shangra-la, I posed with the crew members. Next to me is the producer, Philip Dampier. (Chapter 29)

Posing with Colin
Shanley, Doris
Duke's personal
chef, at a party
hosted by *People
Magazine's*
Denelle Morton
after Doris passed
away.
(Chapter 30)

Left: I almost missed
a ride on Doris' jet
after an all-nighter
with my new girl-
friend, Susie.
(Chapter 24)

The Beach House at Shangri-la. Although it appears quite palatial, this building merely houses the cabanas for the swimming pool.
(Chapter 2)

"Cleaning the vibes" at Shangri-la. Doris requested this ritual to purge her Hawaiian estate of any negative energy lingering from her now-exiled, adopted daughter, Chandi.
(Chapter 14)

I did the *puja;* I finished the book; I'm out of here. Aloha!

CHAPTER 17

A Motley Crew

· · · · · · · ·

The main people connected with Doris' intimate entourage seemed to have been hired not for their skills or competence, but because they appeared to be non-threatening personalities. Not overtly ambitious, career-wise.

Friends have told me that wealthy persons seek out individuals who are down and out, alcohol or other substance abusers, clean them up, help them get their act together, and give them a new purpose in life. They will remain loyal to their masters and mistresses for the rest of their lives. These people remember how bad things were before they were given a second chance.

Many of Doris' employees were either from Third World countries with a caste system or emigrated to America from European nations which still retained an aristocracy and/or royalty. Bernard was an illiterate Irishman. Nuku hailed from Fiji. Jenny, a servant at Rough Point, had been born in the Philippines. Tija came from the South Pacific. Many of the maids in New Jersey, as well as the housekeeper in Newport, were Irish. Kupee, stationed at Duke Farms, was Indian. One of the maids at Shangri-La had left Brazil and ended up working for Doris.

If I called and Doris was not home, I always left a message with whomever answered the phone. Doris would rarely know that I had tried to contact her. Whenever it was necessary to get in touch with her, I dialed the Duke Farms Gate House. These people were very efficient. They would always know where Doris was and see to it that she received my message.

I'm not saying that any of the regular staff were inefficient. They just didn't seem like the types of individuals that someone like Doris would hire. Someone with her wealth could afford top-of-the-line domestic help. You know, hire the very best that money can buy.

These people were just operating in a manner that reflected their different cultural backgrounds. Each of them knew his/her place in the Duke household hierarchy. All of them were very much at home deferring sole authority to Doris.

Whenever Miss Duke was "in residence," the official designation, everyone at that particular estate was hyper. The staff seemed to be on pins and needles the whole time. A couple of exceptions were Johnny Gomez and Nuku Makasaile. Johnny hadn't lasted as long as he did by being bent out of shape because of Doris; her outbursts and eccentricities didn't bother him at this point. Nuku was mellow, much more easygoing. The majority of them were on edge; a good portion of them feared their employer. Doris' reputation always preceded her.

I grew extremely fond of Doris' personal retinue. Many I considered dear and close friends. An outsider would, to a certain degree, probably consider them a little "spacey." Perhaps because I was a bit like them, we got along so well. I felt like I fit in their unique little world.

Although I had a great rapport with the staff and hung out with them, they all knew I was Miss Duke's guest. They were never disrespectful; none of them ever gave me a hard time. Unless Doris was away or the setting was extremely casual, they would still call me Mr. Nischintya. Bernard was always formal, no matter where we were or what the circumstances.

A Motley Crew

Johnny was different. He called me Kimo, which was Hawaiian for James.

* * * * *

Johnny Gomez was the first of Doris' entourage that I met. On the way to meet Miss Duke for her first astrology reading, we talked and got to know one another.

Johnny was a unique and unusual character. A short, portly man, he stood about five feet. He was probably in his late sixties or early seventies. But he got around extremely well. Balding, with a large nose and his big belly, the guy reminded me of The Penguin from the Batman show. He would always wear inexpensive—almost cheap—polyester clothes. Most of these were fifteen or twenty years out-of-date. Hawaiians refer to this type of wardrobe as "Filipino clothing."

In his heyday, Johnny had been a beach bum. He was now the *majordomo* at Shangri-La. For the past quarter-century, he worked for Doris. Of all the domestic help, he had been with her the longest.

I always got the impression that Johnny knew on which side his bread was buttered. The man put up with whatever Doris dished out. He was also the closest of the staff to her. Whenever he visited her at any of the other estates, Doris would come out and greet him. She was always pleased to see him, embracing the man like a long-lost relative. She never showed that type of affection with any of the other servants—not even Nuku, her personal maid.

I wondered if he did certain "services" for Doris. At Newport or Duke Farms, I couldn't figure out the situation. I would constantly ask myself "What's he doing here?" Days would go by before he did anything remotely considered work. At Rough Point, while the new pool was under construction, Johnny was put "in charge of things." Though he really didn't have anything to do with the project, the man walked around looking official and important.

In one sense, Johnny Gomez was a special friend of Doris Duke. He ate at the dinner table with her. He was allowed to watch television. No one else possessed these privileges. When Doris stayed in Shangri-La, though, Johnny was just one of the servants. At any of the other residences, he was treated more like a "working guest." He performed some tasks and chores, but he spent time hanging out with Doris.

Johnny was proud of a ruby ring he wore, a gift he received from Doris. It wasn't a very valuable piece of jewelry; the star ruby was cloudy and its color was banded or speckled. It may not have been worth that much, but the gem certainly was huge.

Johnny was always polite to me, almost fatherly in his manner. We spent some time together, either just the two of us or with Doris. He explained how things got done on the various estates. He would tell me stories about Doris when she was younger or reminisce about the "good old days" in Hawaii. In Shangri-La, the only time Doris ate dinner with Johnny was the night that he accompanied me, Doris and Roberto to the movies.

In the evenings at Newport, he usually wanted to watch television. Doris disliked his choice of programs, so we ended up renting videos. Most of the stuff Johnny brought back was junk. Either Doris or I would be telling him: "Turn it off! Turn it off!"

"Okay, Dorschka." Johnny always called her that. I think it's Russian for Doris. Don't ask me how someone with a Portuguese surname could come up with personal Russian references. Since Johnny could never please Doris with his video selections, I was put in charge of renting the tapes. We had planned to do a gangster marathon one day—all three *Godfather* films—but Doris and I never got around to it.

One night, she noticed that a Ginger Rogers/Fred Astaire movie was on television. Doris was really excited. I was trying to figure out some way to get out of watching the old picture, but it would have been awkward and impolite to excuse myself. The three of us watched the vintage flick. To my astonishment, I enjoyed the movie. Doris was pleased that I had had a good time.

* * * * *

Bernard Lafferty was the one who escorted me to Doris whenever I visited her in Shangri-La. Because of his constant devotion to Doris, I assumed that he had been with the woman after a long tenure of service. Like Johnny Gomez. I later found out that he had only been in her employ for a few years.

Chandi's sister had originally hired him. But they got rid of Bernard because he drank too much. Chandi dried him out, cleaned him up, and gave him his prestigious job—butler to a billionaire. The young woman practically saved his life, yet, every time I stopped by, Chandi would be yelling at him. And he couldn't stand her. Go figure.

I liked the guy. He was an eccentric loon in his own right. Reminded me of myself. Bernard talked with an Irish brogue and was as gay as they come. He wore his hair in a pony tail and sported a small diamond earring. Contrary to rumors or what has been written, he did not go about his duties barefoot.

He was very affable. The man wasn't too competent or all that together. Bernard bungled his chores on a regular basis. He was your typical devoted—yet inept—butler. Doris would regularly chastise or make fun of him.

Bernard's hands shook when he served during a meal. I think it was because of nervousness. With Doris and Chandi around, I could see why. No matter what he did, though Bernard performed his best, he got screamed at for being incompetent. He took every insult with a silent stoicism. Or so it seemed.

The man was always nice to me—at least to my face. I sympathized with him. Doris wasn't noted for her patience. She wouldn't go overboard like Chandi, but she could achieve the same results with a raised eyebrow or sharp comment.

He appeared very concerned for Doris' welfare. He was always there to assist. Bernard cared for her. He wanted to make sure Doris was happy. After remarking when I arrived about how beneficial for Doris my visits were, he would always inquire about my next visit as I left: "Are you coming by tomorrow?" He made me feel like I was the best thing to happen in Doris' life.

Bernard never wanted me to do his chart. He never accepted any gift from me. When I wished him a happy birthday, the man burst into tears because I was the only one who remembered. I was touched by his sincerity every time he broke down emotionally.

A couple of days after I arrived in Newport, Doris had to go away on business. I decided to catch up on things with the staff. We gathered in the kitchen, where the servants seemed to be acting like "Thank God! She's gone. Let's have a party." It reminded me of that commercial on television: the one where the lady of the house leaves on vacation and all the domestic help rejoice and celebrate her absence. All the maids, footmen and the butler cut loose with a major pool party.

As I sat down, I started to say something to Bernard about Chandi. "Oh, Mr. Nischintya," he interrupted me, "we all made a solemn vow to ourselves that we would never mention her name again."

"It was just a nightmare that really happened," one of the maids added. "We don't ever want to talk about it again."

Then, for the next two hours, Bernard, Nuku, Johnny and Colin proceeded to bash Chandi. Every so often, a few of the servants milling about would also add their vicious comments.

"She hated you, Mr. Nischintya."

"Yeah, Chandi really didn't like you. She would be in the

worst moods whenever you were around."

"When you would leave after a visit," Bernard pointed out, "she would always ask me 'What was he doing here?' or 'Why was he here?'"

"After Miss Heffner was adopted, the woman became more and more obnoxious. For petty, little things, she'd go ballistic and start screaming and bitching at everyone."

"Yeah, she would go nuts over the most insignificant details. What a bitch!"

"Her lover strutted around the place like he owned it. James Burns thought he was going to be the next Mr. Duke. He became such an asshole."

"Serves 'em both right for what they put us through."

After listening to their tales of woe and resentment about Chandi, I could imagine some of the complaints they might have concerning Doris. The group could have gone on for the rest of the day speaking ill of Chandi. Despite their vow not to mention her name ever again, she seemed to be a favorite topic for discussion.

Colin Shanley, the chef, knowing I was vegetarian, warned me about what was going to happen: "You may want to leave now, Mr. Nischintya. It's going to be a slaughterhouse here in a few minutes. I'm going to be cooking up a lot of meat, and I wouldn't want to offend you." I appreciated Colin's concern for me.

* * * * *

One of the pleasures I got from my visits and vacations with Doris was seeing Nuku. She was a rotund woman with a heart of gold. A real sweetheart.

Nuku, like Bernard, was always with Doris wherever she went, except if it was a brief business trip with Doris expected back the next day. On some occasions, Doris might go on ahead of her entourage, but the staff was expected to follow in a day or two. Even in those situations, both Nuku and Bernard would be "on call." Those times away from Doris, Nuku could relax with the rest of the staff. I would hang out with her.

Polynesian "aunts" traditionally take care of their wards. Nuku fit her role ideally. She doted on Doris—and me. Nuku reminded me of Aunt Bea from *The Andy Griffith Show* and Nell Harper of *Gimme a Break*.

She could be funny. She was always sweet and compassionate. Nuku was extremely sympathetic when my third marriage broke up. Losing Karina had hurt. Not being able to always see my son was even more difficult. Nuku was a warm shoulder to cry on when things got rough. The woman had been through some personal crises of her own, so she could relate to many of the people around her.

Nuku had many talents. Not only was she Doris' personal attendant, but she was a good cook in her own right. Many times she fixed my morning meal. We shared a special ritual every day when I was a resident guest.

"Mr. Nischintya, where would you like to eat your breakfast today?"

I did not eat breakfast with Doris. She would do her own stuff in the mornings. I wouldn't usually see her until lunch, though occasionally I might run into her around ten-thirty or eleven o'clock.

Some days I ate with the staff in the kitchen, which they got a kick out of. Other times I would say to Nuku: "I'd like my breakfast in the Morning Room, please."

Being served in the Morning Room was a blast. This room overlooked the Atlantic Ocean. Seated at this private retreat, while Nuku or one of the other maids brought me hot oatmeal, honey, cream and fresh strawberries, made me feel like a king. It was fun having a taste of royalty. I could get used to such service on a daily basis, believe me.

The night that Doris was gone, I went out to the movies with Tim and Kim. We caught the eight o'clock showing of

Terminator 2. I got back late. Most of the household were asleep or had retired for the evening.

Not Nuku. Not only had she waited up for me but she fixed me a special dinner: "I made you something Indian, Mr. Nischintya."

"You know how to cook Indian food, Nuku?"

"Oh, yes. Half the people in the Fijian Islands are of Indian descent." She smiled at me. "Where would you like to eat your supper?"

I smiled back at her. On a whim, I said with an upper crust British accent: "I'll take my meal in the formal Dining Room tonight, Nuku."

She and I laughed. We could share moments like that. Have fun. I asked her to join me, but Nuku declined, saying that she had eaten already. She may have, I'm not sure, or it's possible none of the help was allowed to eat in that room with any of Doris' guests.

So there I was. Alone in this huge room. Seated at one end of a long, antique oak table. Candelabra. Gold plates and flatware. Fancy linen napkin. Expensive paintings on the walls. The ocean right outside. And I'm eating dinner. I couldn't have passed up that opportunity.

*   *   *   *   *

Doris regularly made sure that I had transportation to and from Shangri-La. When we were neighbors, I usually just walked. It didn't matter to Doris who picked me up or took me home, just as long as it was taken care of. Could be Jin, one of the servants, or security. Whoever was available.

Doris would usually tell Bernard: "Nischintya needs a ride. Get someone to drive him."

He would always respond: "Yes, Miss Duke. Yes, Miss Duke." Since Bernard had no license, he was never my chauffeur.

One time, Bernard was taking care of something else for

Doris. He wasn't around, and it was time for me to leave. Doris picked up the phone and called each of the rooms in the great house. She punched all of the buttons, trying to locate someone, anyone.

Nobody responded to her calls. Either no one was around, or no one wanted to answer the phone. Doris cursed the communications system and kept trying.

I have to admit, I laughed at her predicament. Here was the wealthiest woman in the world, and she couldn't even get the service of a single servant.

Fifteen minutes later, Doris finally located someone to take me home: good, old, reliable Johnny Gomez.

CHAPTER 18

Colin the Cook

· · · · · · · ·

When I stayed at Rough Point, I met Doris' new chef. Colin Shanley wasn't really new, though. He had worked for Doris earlier but quit because of Chandi. Colin could not stand the woman, and rather than take the abuse, he left. With Chandi now out of the picture and Doris desperate for a personal chef, he was invited back into the fold with wide open arms.

Colin was a high-strung individual. Nervous and hyper. Probably even more so now that he was back cooking for Doris. From my former chats with Chandi, I knew what kind of high-pressure position he was in. Talk about frantic.

The man was a terrific cook. I don't think Doris appreciated his talents. Doris would give him hell. Half an hour before a meal, she could change her mind and decide upon eating something totally different.

Colin stood his ground. He would always make Doris aware of the problems she caused: "I'm sorry, Miss Duke, I can't do that. It's just not possible." He knew his limitations and his abilities. Colin would never agree to fix something he couldn't prepare. He was always up front and honest about his capabilities.

He felt great satisfaction when someone complimented him on his culinary expertise. I would tell him: "Man, these meals are great!" Colin would be thrilled and excited. He never got that from Doris.

He would ask her daily: "Is everything to your satisfaction, Miss Duke?"

She would either mutter: "It's all right," or give him a silent "no comment" response.

Colin was sensitive about his cooking. I couldn't figure out why he wanted to work for someone who didn't care one way or another about how he prepared a dish. Don't get me wrong. Doris loved his cooking. She just didn't tell him that to his face.

One day, he came to me and said: "Oh, Mr. Nischintya, what am I going to do?"

Puzzled, I responded: "Do what? You're in a pretty good situation here. You've got a great job. What's wrong?"

Colin proceeded to tell me about the problems he had with his employer. Cooking for the entire staff for a whole week was a piece of cake compared to preparing one simple meal for Doris. He would give her a sample menu for the day and ask Miss Duke if she had any questions about what was on it. Big mistake. Doris never failed to make revisions. Then, later, she would change her mind again. He couldn't win.

I could see how adversely his job affected him. Colin was stressed out most of the time. So I told him: "Decide on what the menu is going to be. Tell her this is what you are fixing on a particular day. Don't give the woman any choices. Discussing anything with Miss Duke means headaches and more trouble, right?"

He nodded.

"Colin," I continued, "avoid asking Doris any questions, at all costs."

"You're right. That's what I was thinking, too. Thanks, Mr. Nischintya."

Colin the Cook

For me, he was extremely accommodating, especially considering my unique needs and complicated, vegetarian diet. Some days, I fast; on others, I abstain from certain foods. Not only was he a fantastic cook, but Colin was always on top of things. Very meticulous. He would always check with me in the morning: "Is today the day that you don't eat beans and grains?"

Several times he would warn me: "Keep away from that chocolate mousse dessert. I made a separate one for you without eggs." Or it might be: "I prepared a special hollandaise sauce for you. Everything in it, you can eat."

He was always friendly and courteous. A fun guy. Colin was a flamboyant, Irish New Yorker. His parents hail from Long Island and were fairly well off.

We became buddies in a short while. Shared some good times. Whenever we would get the chance, he and I talked. I even went shopping with him for groceries and other necessities on a couple of occasions. Colin loved to be able to go to the store and pick out whatever he felt like buying. The estate had an account—and unlimited credit.

When I accompanied him, he would always tell me: "Anything you want, anything you need, just let me know."

I would look around and make suggestions. He would reassure me if I thought I was choosing too many items: "Get whatever you want. And as much as you think we'll need." As they totaled up our purchases at the check-out lane, Colin merely reminded them: "Please put it on Doris Duke's account."

We walked out of the health food store loaded up with vitamins, herbal teas, natural dietary supplements, and organically-grown vegetables. More than we could possibly use in a year or two. Must be nice not to worry about food bills.

Colin was interested in astrology and horoscopes. He constantly asked: "What do the stars say? What's going to happen to me?"

I did his chart, however, we never actually got to sit down and discuss it. We never had sufficient time to do a proper reading. Colin was busy most of the time in the kitchen or out shopping for the estate. He worked most of the days I spent at Newport.

Every now and then, he had a break, relaxing with the staff. Colin was good-natured with his fellow employees. They were a close-knit group and enjoyed a good laugh together.

During my stay at Rough Point, some nights I was told by the servants that "Miss Duke is busy tonight" or that "Miss Duke will not be joining you for dinner this evening." Colin would ask me what I wanted for supper. I would eat alone or with the staff.

I recalled that a few nights when I had stayed the previous year at Duke Farms, the same thing happened. I didn't think much of it then, because Doris had business matters to attend to in New Jersey. Her estate there was a working farm.

Here in Newport, the situation was different. Her mansion was like a private retreat. If Doris had any business, she would have to travel to either New York or New Jersey. Something was up.

I thought about it for a while. I knew Doris wasn't a vegetarian. She was conscientious about what she ate, though. Mostly healthful foods, including meat a few times a week. Doris was well aware of my strict herbivorous habits and dietetic regimen. As I pondered the situation, I couldn't remember the last time a dinner was served that included beef, poultry, or seafood.

Then it dawned on me what was happening. Doris was basically holed up in her room, eating meat. I recalled my big speech about cows and cattle when I toured Duke Farms with Doris. I don't know if she was worried about offending me or concerned that I might not like her anymore. I thought her behavior very odd, but that was Doris for you.

I confronted Colin with my suspicions: "Doris is hiding in

her room and eating meat, isn't she? Those nights she doesn't dine with me, you cook steak, pork, fish or chicken for her, right?"

"Yes, Mr. Nischintya, it's true."

"Well, God, please tell Doris that I'm a guest in her house. It's not the other way around. I have plenty of friends and relatives who eat meat. It doesn't bother me. I don't curse or hate them. They're still my friends and relatives. Please tell her that I think it's a bit ridiculous, considering the circumstances. Doris doesn't need to sneak into her room to eat what she likes."

Colin appreciated my comments. He spoke to her. The next day, Doris and I silently acknowledged what had been going on. I didn't want to get into any debate. Knowing Doris, she probably felt a little embarrassed about the whole matter.

From that day on, if Doris requested a meat entree, Colin would inform me: "This is what Miss Duke is having for tonight's menu. What would you like instead?"

Every time, he offered to cook something else for me, so I wouldn't have to just eat the vegetable and fruit portion of the meal. I think both he and Doris wanted to make sure that I didn't starve and always had enough to eat.

CHAPTER 19

Camels, Cliff Walks and Chairman Mao

• • • • • • • •

While Doris was away in New York, I decided to shoot some pictures in Newport. I was unaware that no one else was allowed to take photographs at any of the estates.

The previous year at Duke Farms with Karina, I recalled Doris seeing the two of us armed with Instamatics. We used up a whole roll of film with shots of the grounds and some of the staff. Doris never said anything to me about "no photos."

Neither staff nor guests were permitted this privilege, however, I was one person she let slide on that particular rule. But Doris was adamant about herself being photographed. She would never let me take a picture of her. Nor would she consent to being in one with me.

In her twilight years, she was extremely concerned about her looks. Doris did not like to see a photo of herself which she thought unattractive and preferred pictures that had been taken years ago. Doris felt that she was much prettier then.

I have snapshots of me with my other celebrity clients, such as Timothy Leary and Alfred Ford. None with Doris, though. I should have badgered her until she had conceded. All I have of her is that old passport photo she gave me when I performed a protection ceremony before her trip to Europe.

That day at Rough Point, I took some shots of the view from my cramped accommodations. The few I have are of the bedroom, including the priceless paintings hanging on the walls. Outside my room at the bottom of the staircase stood this impressive piece of statuary. Knowing Doris, this sculpture was probably some damned, long-lost, important, archeological artifact, but it was just a fancy statue to me.

I always removed my shoes when I roamed around Shangri-La and the manor house at Duke Farms. Out of habit, I did the same at Rough Point. In Hawaii, similar to the Japanese custom, you take off your "outside" shoes and put on slippers that are worn only on the inside of the house.

I had brought this ragged pair of Nikes for my "outside" shoes at Newport. For contrast, I placed them at the base of this statue and took a snapshot. Unfortunately, the picture did not quite capture the effect I wanted.

Doris returned the following day. She invited me on a tour of the grounds. I accepted, wondering what sort of car they let her drive here in Rhode Island. Security pulled up in an almost-new Jaguar. We hopped in and took off. Despite the automobile being a fancy luxury car and an earlier gift from Chandi, Doris loved it.

Our "tour" was very brief. Compared to Duke Farms, the estate wasn't that large. Doris merely wanted to check to see if part of the chain-link fence around her property had been fixed properly and to inspect some landscaping that had been finished recently.

With Doris back home, I sort of settled into the routine at Rough Point. Some citizens of Newport were still cleaning up after the devastation caused by Hurricane Bob the previous month in August. All of the debris and downed trees had been cleared away from Doris' estate.

Rough Point is located on "The Strip," where other mansions of the wealthy are situated. Among these great houses was The Breakers, summer home of the Vanderbilts. Though the numerous visitor guides stipulated that Doris' place was more impressive than her rival's, I didn't think so. The Breakers was not only more interesting architecturally, but the Vanderbilt residence seemed more stately. Rough Point was rather a majestic cottage than an imposing mansion. But it still reflected the life styles of the Rich and Famous, believe me.

Because of their historical significance, these American palaces attracted thousands of travelers from all over the world every year. Tour buses made daily rounds to The Strip. Whenever a motor coach would stop in front of Rough Point, you could see the passenger's faces pressed against its windows. Several times when I was walking around the estate chanting, I would interrupt my meditation to wave at the tourists.

Also along The Strip, on the ocean side, is the Cliff Walk. Citizens and visitors alike love to stroll along this pathway. They gaze out across the water or take in the sights of the famous Newport summer homes. Seeing the area from the Cliff Walk gives the onlooker an even more dramatic view.

By following this route, passersby could get within a stone's throw of the various mansions. A person could even wander around through the numerous well-kept lawns. When you came to Doris' estate, things were much different. A high chain-link fence prevented you from setting foot on the property.

When this barrier had been erected, the tabloids spread the rumor that Doris was frightened of people. They alleged she was terrified that someone, having access to her estate, could harm or kidnap her. Her decision to fence in her grounds only fueled reports about Doris being a scared and paranoid recluse.

The truth of the matter was Doris would at times be eating lunch while tourists and gapers roamed loose over the estate. They would walk up to her cottage and gawk at her while she was inside. "I wasn't afraid," Doris told me. "I just got tired of people watching me while I ate."

Doris had nothing to be frightened about. She was surrounded by vigilant security guards and vicious sentry dogs. The woman had plenty of servants and staff to protect her.

* * * * *

There was another important resident at Newport: Chairman Mao—another of Doris' dogs, not the Chinese dictator. He looked mostly like a bulldog. This canine—though I never mentioned it to Doris—reminded me of her father, Buck Duke. He looked like Doris' dad; and there was a peculiar energy about the animal.

Each day, I would walk and chant. On those mornings when the weather prevented me from going outside, I would do my daily meditation inside. Rough Point had this long hall which was decked out in flags, coats of arms, and suits of armor. It was there that I would pace back and forth, fingering my *japa* beads as I recited the prayers.

In the center of the hall was a huge table resting on this enormous Oriental rug. Now, it was much more comfortable to walk on this carpet than the parquet floor. As I strolled up and down the rug, Chairman Mao would watch me. I, in turn, would keep an eye on him.

Every time I chanted my *mantras* in that room, we kept each other company. I observed his mannerisms and demeanor. He was puzzled by my behavior. One day, he gave me a weird look, pissed on that antique rug, and strutted off.

Later, on our way to lunch in the Morning Room, Doris and I detoured through that particular hall. I was on her right, away from the walls and close to the table. Doris was walking on the floor, while I had to step on the rug.

I had gone only a few feet when Doris stopped and admonished me: "If you walk on that rug, there's a $50 fine."

"What?"

She repeated her warning. That was enough for me. I wasn't

going to pay any fine. I switched around to the other side, where there was more room to maneuver. As we sat down to eat, I thought about what would have happened if Doris had caught me earlier in the week. Or worse, in the morning when I had paced up and down that rug for over an hour.

It must have been a very valuable rug if Doris didn't want anyone walking on it. Colin informed me that the carpet was from the First Century B.C. and probably worth several million dollars. Any of the servants could lose their job for even stepping on it.

I commented to the servants later about what Chairman Mao had done on the rug. "Think about it," I said, "this mangy dog enjoys the unique pleasures of this estate. All of you know how much more important he is than any of you are."

I further pointed out: "None of you are allowed to even go near that rug, but Chairman Mao can piss on it. If Doris found out, the worst that mutt would ever get is a little scolding. You'd be out of here in nothing flat.

"He has complete run of the house. Goes wherever he wants. Does whatever he wants. His *karma* is to enjoy this place. But it's not strong enough for him to experience it as a human. He's trapped in a dog's body. He's probably some old rich guy who still had the *karma* left to enjoy some of his money, but not enough to be reincarnated as another human being."

That's when it dawned on me. Everything I had observed about the dog reminded me of what I read about Doris' father. "He must be the reincarnation of Buck Duke!" I exclaimed.

The staff looked at me. From their expressions, I knew they thought I was crazy. Yet, after that incident, the servants saw Chairman Mao in a new light. "Maybe you're right, Mr. Nischintya. He does look like some old codger."

That bulldog swaggered about the mansion like he owned the place. It was so weird. And Doris never caught him pissing on that rug.

Chairman Mao was not the only unique animal at Rough

Point. That year in Newport I got to meet Doris' exotic pets, the two Bactrian camels. Princess and Baby had been previously owned by the Kuwaiti prince who sold his 737 jet to Doris. I think she bought that plane just because these two, extraordinary creatures were part of the deal.

Doris loved those camels. Usually they were housed in the stables at Duke Farms. Since Doris was going to spend a substantial amount of time in Newport, the two camels had been transported to Rhode Island. For the most part, wherever Doris was on the East Coast, that's where the camels were.

Set up on the grounds was this enormous tent—something out of the Arabian Nights. The animals would use the tent as a refuge from the cold to keep warm. When Hurricane Bob hit the Atlantic seaboard, Princess and Baby were kept in the Morning Room until the storm passed. Contrary to what the tabloids printed, they did not have complete run of the house.

From the amount of dung covering the lawn, I pitied whoever had to clean up after their brief stay in the mansion. While I wandered the grounds, a team of workers was constantly shoveling up the stuff.

Princess and Baby loved graham crackers, especially the ones made with honey. On my morning meditation rounds, I fed them these special treats. I remember one day after giving the camels some crackers, they wandered off just before a bus pulled up outside the property.

I went back to my chanting, pacing back and forth along the chain-link fence. Minutes later, I was interrupted by a group of tourists.

"Excuse us, is this Doris Duke's estate?" A couple of them were checking out a local map which indicated the homes of the Rich and Famous.

"Yes, this is her place," I replied. I could tell what their next question was going to be.

"Who are you?" All the sightseers on the cliff walk were hoping that I was someone rich and famous.

"I'm her astrologer." That tweaked their interest. I really made their day. "And yes, the camels are here." I could hear the "oohs" and "aahs."

Because the cliff walk is much lower than the fence, I had to disappoint them. "Unfortunately, from where you are, you won't even be able to get a glimpse of them. You have to be even higher than I am to see the camels. But you never know, you might get lucky. They're wandering around right now. Perhaps they'll come close enough to the fence for you to see them."

"Really?" The group moved off, filled with hope.

I spoke to Doris about the incident while we ate lunch. She told me about the problems her "children" posed when she tried to ship them to Shangri-La in Hawaii.

The Pacific climate would have been ideal for her Bactrian beasts. But she discovered that Princess and Baby would be required to spend several months in quarantine before they would be allowed access to Shangri-La. Doris knew that such a lengthy detention would have been fatal for the exotic animals. She couldn't even transfer them there permanently.

The isolation and confinement—plus the fact that Princess and Baby could not receive the proper care required or be housed in adequate facilities—would have surely killed them. Doris was mad as hell that the government wouldn't lift the quarantine for her. Not even promises of substantial amounts of money worked. Rather than risk the lives of her special children, Doris resigned herself to keeping them on the East Coast.

The photograph Karina took of the two camels did not come out; it was all fuzzy and out of focus. Too bad. It would have made a great addition to the collection in this book.

CHAPTER 20

What a Vacation!

· · · · · · · ·

My vacation with Doris on the East Coast in 1991 was one of the most pleasurable times in my life. Without Chandi to antagonize Doris and no Karina wanting to leave, life was blissful and uncomplicated. We could do what we wanted, when we wanted, without any repercussions. I had seen Paradise. This was Heaven.

When I was a little boy, during summer vacation, I used to spend a week with my maternal grandparents. With Grandma Fiela, I could do no wrong. She loved me dearly. She would fix whatever I wanted to eat. Let me play with whatever I wanted. My grandmother would listen whenever I wanted to talk. Coming from a family of eight, staying at Grandma's and Grandpa's was like being an only child. I was totally spoiled.

Staying at Rough Point was more luxurious than any all-expense paid trip anywhere. Better than the Hyatt Regency or Kahala Hilton. Now that Doris had me all to herself, she took very good care of me. Totally spoiled me, just like my grandmother had done. It was like being a kid again. Reliving all those wonderful memories.

On vacation with Doris, I had only one duty—enjoy myself. I could chant and meditate at my leisure. I burned incense, rang bells, blew on a conchshell, and made daily offerings to the Deities. It didn't matter to Doris. As long as I had a good time. How many people do you know would have tolerated such strange behavior? Rich or otherwise?

Once I left my room in the morning, a maid entered and tidied up after me. My clothes were washed each day. Whatever clothes I had worn the previous night would be cleaned and pressed by afternoon. My room was stocked with dozens of toiletries, in case I had forgotten anything or could use something new. Whatever I needed, I merely had to ask and it would be taken care of right away. Where in the world can you get service like that? For free, no less!

Despite the many times I asked Doris to show me her priceless antiques, art treasures or painting collections, she would never give me a personal tour. She knew how uneducated I was when it came to valuable works of art. Doris got a real kick about my *naiveté*. Whenever I referred to something as "old stuff," she would start laughing. The concept of antiquated value was a little beyond my comprehension.

I knew people paid big bucks for these things, but I couldn't figure out why. Later, when I heard about how some collector paid several thousands of dollars for a comic book, a copy of which I had bought when I was a kid, my business interest in "collectibles" grew. I owned items of antiquity, but they had more of an historical or religious significance than a monetary value for me.

When matters are put into perspective, I can grasp the notion. Or if someone takes the time to explain the history behind an important relic. Doris never had the time nor the patience. Her chef and my new friend, Colin, did.

Though he never actually took me around the entire mansion, he would point out several of the art pieces Doris displayed at Rough Point. "That tapestry hanging there, Mr. Nischintya, is one of a pair. Only two of them exist in the entire world."

"Where's the other one?" I inquired.

"It's on exhibit at the Louvre in Paris."

Boy, was I impressed.

He indicated one of the more grandiose paintings. "That one's a Raphael. Miss Duke purchased it at an auction for several million dollars."

Doris entered the room when I turned to Colin, pointing at another painting. "I saw that one with the dogs in a magazine once."

"You mean *Riding the Hounds*?"

"Is that what it's called?"

Doris broke out in laughter. Colin merely smiled. Hey, I never claimed to be an art connoisseur.

Friends, who are artists, would regularly razz me: "We'd die to be able to see Doris Duke's collections. We'd give up our first-born just to get a brief tour of one of her estates." Whenever I told them about my latest visit to a Duke residence, they always wanted a low-down on what I saw while I was there. Like I could remember everything. Doris' estates were filled with more treasures than most national museums.

I usually had them bring me an art book, and I would look through it. If I came across anything owed by Doris, I would tell them: "Oh, yeah, I saw this sculpture in Newport." Or it might be: "She's got that painting in a room at Duke Farms."

* * * * *

Doris, single-handedly, revived the town of Newport. At one time, the prosperous site was an important resort area for wealthy East Coast families. Once the Gilded Age of America had ended, people who owned those magnificent mansions moved to other summer homes. The town suffered financially. Property and buildings were neglected. Soon, everything was in ruins.

Doris Duke stepped in. To restore the landscapes and structures to their original splendor and grandeur, she created the Newport Restoration Foundation. Millions of dollars poured into her pet project. Newport was resurrected.

One day, Doris took me, Colin and Bernard for a tour of one of the neighborhood museums she had established in town. A few of the reconstructed houses actually had people living in them. Others had been refurbished more for their historical significance. We strolled through an old sea captain's cottage. After that, we wandered about a farmhouse powered by a windmill.

Though Doris knew a great deal about Newport, she had someone else give the actual tour—Ben Reed, the Foundation's president. Between the man in charge and the woman who made it all possible, Colin, Bernard and I were treated to a deluxe excursion.

Doris and Ben alternated in telling interesting anecdotes about Newport's history. They joked about some of the problems they had in finding and verifying a few of the original articles.

Doris had really been into authenticity. Her major concern was to recreate the mood and lifestyle of that by-gone era. I thought she had done a marvelous job. We had a fun outing that day. For Doris, it might have been merely a way to pass the time. For me, that tour was not only an interesting trip but was a meaningful insight into the woman who had made it all possible.

I might not have been the ideal candidate to appreciate the determined dedication and total commitment the Foundation members demonstrated in their restoration of this venerable settlement, but I could comprehend and acknowledge the museum's timeless beauty and consequential influence in the state's—and country's—history.

* * * * *

What a Vacation

One night, after a couple of short videos, we finished earlier than usual. While Johnny Gomez cleared away our snacks and munchies, I rewound the tapes. The television was still on. A commercial played, advertising some of the soul hits from the Sixties and Seventies. One of the tunes was James Brown's "I Feel Good."

All of a sudden, Doris jumped up. She did this little dance while singing the words to the entire song. When she was done, I clapped. Doris bowed and sat down, smiling to herself. She was definitely feeling good. Almost frisky. The woman looked like she was ready to Rock and Roll.

I razzed Doris again about her long-denied ambition. "Poor Doris, all your life you've wanted to be a dancer, perhaps even a ballerina. But, instead, you became a billionaire. Life is so cruel."

With a straight face, she answered: "Yes, isn't it."

Doris still had problems with her knees. My herbal and *reiki* treatments helped, as did her acupuncture sessions. But she was able to get around much better than I had ever seen her before.

Her dry sense of humor and that sharp, sarcastic wit were back. I knew how important jokes were to Doris. It's true what they say about "laughter being the best medicine." Doris was in a good mood, too, so I knew she was fully recovered, mentally as well as physically.

Doris Duke was very concerned about her health and appearance. If Doris had been alive when Ponce De Leon searched for the legendary Fountain of Youth, she would have been right behind him. The woman would not only have funded his expedition, she would have joined it as well.

Doris was not some nut case obsessed with beauty, though she might have appeared that way to many people. She kept up-to-date with the latest medical breakthroughs and scientific advancements. If any procedure or miracle drug sounded like it might help her, Doris would at least give it a try.

Both she and Chandi had gone to Romania for GH-3 treatments. Rich and famous people go to this spa in Eastern Europe to receive therapeutic injections. At present, these physicians are trying to mass market their discovery. Once the drug became available in pill form—I'm not into shooting stuff into my body—I tried it myself. I was not impressed with the results.

Doris may not have been a vegetarian, but she ate healthful foods. Mostly organic vegetables and grains. I supplied her with Chinese herbs. She no longer smoked. In addition to her beneficial diet, Doris exercised. Despite her age, she still practiced *yoga*.

The woman was a firm believer in plastic surgery. Even in her seventies, Doris underwent a couple of cosmetic skin operations. She also invested a great deal of money in makeup and aloe-based dermal creams. To supplement these physical restorations, I prepared numerous potions and lotions. I knew I wasn't going to turn Doris into any raving beauty with my elixirs, but they did make her feel more attractive, inside and out.

After one particularly successful batch, Doris commented: "You know, Nischintya, you and my acupuncturist are responsible for saving my life."

I mentioned to her about a new technological breakthrough in the scientific medical market that produced similar results. "All these healing devices are based upon the body's own natural bio-electrical field."

"Oh, I've got something along those lines," Doris responded. "It's called a Dynatron."

"Well, where is it?"

"I think it's in one of my closets. Why don't you go get it." She told me what the Dynatron looked like and where I might find the electronic machine.

I searched her closet. Way in the back was this metal case. I pulled it out and dusted it off. Doris hadn't used the device for a long time.

What a Vacation

The machine would scan your body and let you know the precise location of your acupuncture points. By firing a low intensity laser beam at the skin, the Dynatron worked the same way as the actual Oriental needles. The device was actually a high-tech version of the ancient practice. Like having your own acupuncturist at home.

When Doris and I first operated the machine together, we used diagrams from a book on acupressure as a guide. Once I had familiarized myself with the procedures, it was easy to give Doris regular tune-ups. She was extremely happy I learned how to operate the controls in such a short time. I even used it on myself. The Dynatron was a pretty, far-out, futuristic gizmo. The machine helped prevent colds, relieved aching muscles, and invigorated you. Doris paid $10,000 for that thing.

For those of us who don't have that kind of money to spend, there are a couple of other gadgets that do just as well. One device is called a Lightshaker and the other is called Electro Acupuncture. They give advanced pain relief without needles. Both are small, portable, and battery-operated.

Various versions of both non-invasive inventions range in price from $80 to $150. I have tried them, and they worked for me.

Doris loved the effects of the Dynatron so much that, while living on the East Coast, the device was transported with her luggage as she bopped back and forth from Rough Point (Newport) and Duke Farms (New Jersey).

CHAPTER 21

We've Corrupted You

• • • • • • • •

Doris read all the fashion magazines. She kept current with the latest trends and fads. The woman was always invited to the most important fashion shows. She was on a first-name basis with many designers, both here and abroad. A number of her outfits were made-to-order, but I think Doris got discounts on them.

If Doris was "in residence," she dressed casual, but expensive casual. When the woman got dolled up, she did it to the max. Between salon visits, her hair was coifed daily, either by Nuku or Bernard. She always wore make-up. If Doris felt that she didn't look particularly good, she would not entertain guests that day. Miss Duke hated to have anyone see her when she wasn't at her best.

One evening, Doris dressed up for dinner. She wore this stunning, full-length gown. I wore my maharaja costume, which was the fanciest thing I owned. We were sitting down to a formal supper, though for some reason the meal was served in the Morning Room and not the official Dining Room.

Doris and I ate from gold plates and drank from gold goblets. The flatware was also gold. I recall that I had four forks, three spoons and two knives. I was trying to figure out which one I was supposed to use with which course. I was just like Julia Roberts in *Pretty Woman*. For years, I was used to either eating with my fingers or using a simple spoon at the Krishna temples. I watched Doris and followed her lead. At least this time, I remembered to place the cloth napkin on my lap.

Servants were scurrying back and forth from the kitchen. Bernard wheeled in the serving cart. He brought Doris a bottle of wine and poured her a sample. She nodded approval, and Bernard filled her goblet. To both the butler's surprise and Doris' astonishment, I offered my glass for some.

Aghast, Doris commented: "Oh no, we've corrupted you."

I allayed her fears.

The entire first year that I had known Doris Duke, I never drank liquor with her. Wine was always served with dinner, but I would only have water. After my third marriage failed, I started drinking wine to ease my stomach problems and aid my digestion.

I read an article in one of the temple magazines where my Spiritual Master spoke to some devotees who owned and worked a farm and vineyard in France. He commented: "You grow grapes. Very good. What you do is squeeze the grapes, take the juice, and let it ferment. The resulting beverage is very good for your digestion."

The devotees retorted: "But, Prabhupada, that's wine." He merely restated the procedure and its beneficial results. No matter how hard his followers tried to point out that the finished product was wine, Srila Prabhupada avoided acknowledging it.

So, I figured if my late Spiritual Master believed fermented grape juice was okay to drink, who was I to argue with him? From then on, I started taking wine with my evening meals.

Doris was happy that I joined her. She had someone to touch glasses with for toasts and good luck.

A couple of biographies stated that Doris drank too much. She was not an alcoholic. The woman did not strike me as a person who overindulged in liquor. In all the time I was with her, she only had wine with her evening meal. If she drank privately in her room after everyone retired for the night, I wasn't aware of it.

Doris talked to me about the printed rumors. "Chandi said that I drank too much. You've seen me, Nischintya. I only have a glass or two. I don't abuse alcohol, do I?"

"No, Doris, you don't," I reassured her.

As the weeks went on, Doris observed that soon I drank more than she did. Which was true. Bernard would always come in and try to give us more wine. I'd be: "Yeah, okay." But Doris usually said: "No, that's enough." Most of the time, she barely finished her first glass.

Sharing this formal dining experience with one of the wealthiest women in the world was fantastic. We were eating our dessert and talking, enjoying ourselves like we always did. Suddenly, we heard this crash of metal, china and crystal hitting the kitchen floor.

"There go the profits," Doris said straight-faced. I lost it right there. I laughed so hard it hurt. She got a real kick out of my reaction to her witty comment. The woman had a knack for timing. Too bad she was born rich. Doris would have made an excellent comedienne.

The whole setting that evening was classic.

Later that night, Doris received a phone call. I was ready to excuse myself, so she could have some privacy, but she signaled me to stay. It was one of the women who took care of the stables in New Jersey.

Toward the end of her conversation, Doris looked at me while she gave this lady advice: "Oh no, honey. Definitely not. Don't get married. Just shack up. Believe me, getting hitched won't work. Whatever you do, don't make it legal."

Doris hung up, and we had a good laugh about the situation. Doris had two bad marriages, and my third one went down the tubes just that year. Both of us had resigned to the fact that both Chandi and Karina were gone for good.

* * * * *

When Johnny Gomez had flown in from Hawaii, the pool project in Newport was well underway. Doris, Johnny, Bernard and I inspected the progress the workers had made so far.

The swimming pool was being installed in one of the basements. You had to go down a couple of levels, past a series of boilers, and through a maze of cavern-size corridors. Despite this lengthy and tiresome journey, Doris would be down there every day supervising the construction. She was always on top of things.

Something was wrong that day. Bernard had screwed up big time. I don't recall what he had done, but Doris was pissed. Bernard thought of himself as foreman. Doris constantly made fun of it with disparaging remarks. This time his incompetence cost her time and money. Doris lost it.

"Bernard, you're fired! You have nothing to do with this anymore. I don't want you down here at all until the lap pool is finished." She turned to Johnny. "Call Roberto. Tell him he's in charge of the installation project now."

Doris relied upon Roberto's skills both as a historical restoration expert and an interior designer to maintain the grounds and buildings of Newport and Shangri-La. He showed up at Rough Point the next day.

During the time he was there, Roberto was a "working guest." I didn't see him that much, probably because getting the pool project reorganized and back on schedule took up most of his time.

Bernard warned Roberto when Doris was not around. "You'll regret this. I'll get even with you." He later made good on his threat.

* * * * *

We've Corrupted You

That week we flew from Doris' Newport estate to Duke Farms in New Jersey. Via helicopter, no less. After packing a light suitcase, I sat in the kitchen with the staff waiting for the chopper. I looked around at all these characters with me. They were all unique individuals in their own rights. Put them together, and it was even more out of the ordinary.

"This is like a television sitcom," I commented. "I mean, really, think about it." I got up and went around the room to each of the staff.

"We've got crazy New Yorker, Colin the cook. Johnny's our elderly beach bum and surfer dude. Nuku can be the lovable, Fijian 'aunt.' The Old World butler with an Irish brogue wears a diamond earring and his hair in a pony tail. I'm the Hare Krishna astrologer. And don't forget Doris Duke as herself, the eccentric billionaire."

Everyone started laughing. We really had a strange and eclectic mix of personalities, looks and styles. The perfect cast for a situation comedy.

When Doris Duke's personal helicopter landed on the estate, the pilot and co-pilot disembarked to greet us. The two men were in uniform, all prim, proper and formal. Totally business-like as they prepared to transport Doris Duke's entourage. Meeting this pair of professionals across the lawn was our motley crew.

Nuku had slipped on slacks for the occasion. Johnny was in his typical, Seventies, polyester attire. I wore a combination of Hare Krishna colors and Hawaiian florals. Bernard sported his penguin suit. Colin was dressed casually, though a bit flashy. Doris wore one of her charming lounging outfits.

We hung out at Duke Farms for a couple of days. Doris had some things going on in New York City, so she needed to stay at New Jersey for an easy commute.

Doris had me do a general "good vibes" *puja* at Duke Farms. Same routine I did at Shangri-La, though this time, Doris didn't stick around for the entire ceremony. I performed an abbreviated ritual at Rough Point the day before we left.

She had a formal soiree to go to that evening and invited me to go along with her to the Big Apple. Because the event required a strict dress code, I knew I would have a problem with the black-tie requirement.

"I've got nothing to wear," I pointed out.

To this day, I don't know whether or not Doris was too cheap or if she just didn't want to deal with the hassle that my situation presented. Doris simply said: "Okay, stay here." I had thought she might have suggested we go out and buy me some decent clothes.

When I visited Chicago to stand up for my youngest sister's wedding, I rented a tuxedo. Doris never believed that I wore one. She would always say: "Sure you did, Nischintya. Where's your proof? Got any pictures?" Unfortunately, the official photographer took two years to assemble my sister's wedding album. Doris passed away during that time, never having seen me wearing that tuxedo.

A Cadillac pulled up to the Manor House that afternoon, and Doris was driven to New York City. Party time at Duke Farms.

Though there weren't many servants around, none of them wore their uniforms; most wore jeans or casual wear. Doris was supposed to be gone for only a short time.

Doris phoned the following day. Bernard left to join her. We were to visit later. After a small breakfast, Nuku, Johnny, Colin and I drove to the Big Apple in a Ford Bronco. Colin was our tour guide. During the trip, Nuku, Johnny, and I made some vicious remarks about why anyone would want to live in New York City. Colin took them in stride. After bopping around the world with Doris Duke, I bet he felt the same way we did.

We were to meet Doris at her penthouse on Park Avenue— 475 Park Place. What struck me was that in this supposedly posh neighborhood, where some of the world's wealthiest families can be found, homeless people were sprawled out on the sidewalks. Even on the block that Doris lived, I saw some pretty scary characters. A few grimy, scruffy people were passed out on the pavement only yards away from her entrance.

Doris met us out front. Bernard was with her. She was wearing a new outfit, something I had never seen her in before. It was an elegant—and very expensive—designer ensemble. The woman looked radiant. A Princess among the Paupers.

Doris lived in this old building, which wasn't that high. Her penthouse apartment was on the fifteenth floor. The elevator operator took us up. The whole time, I was thinking that Doris could have gotten something a lot nicer.

Her suite was dark, furnished in a very strange black decor. A weird combination of disco and imitation leopard skin. I went out on the veranda, strolling across the roof of the building. I looked out over the city. That was cool. At least she had a good view. Compared to her other residences, this place was not up to snuff. Almost a dump.

Doris showed me her crystal collection. I have seen many in my travels, but this was one of the best I had come across. Doris was proud of that collection. She had a huge assortment from all over the world. It occupied an entire wall in a specially-designed cabinet. Exquisite glass craftsmanship, but the crystals were filthy. All of them looked like they had not been used, let alone washed, in years and years.

I warned Doris: "You need to scrub all these crystals. Make 'em sparkle. It's bad luck to leave them dirty. You also have to use them once in a while."

"Maybe you're right," she agreed with me. Doris never got around to having that collection cleaned.

We didn't stay long at Doris' penthouse. After lunch, a driver took us to this landing field not too far from where Doris lived. A helicopter landed, and we got in. We flew back, not to New Jersey, but to Newport. Our luggage had been sent on ahead.

Dollars, Diamonds, Destiny & Death

The rental chopper was very noisy. To have a conversation, we had to speak quite loudly—almost shout—otherwise no one could hear you. After ten minutes or so, we gave up trying to talk. We just sat there, reading newspapers or magazines.

The six of us, three to a side, sat in the passenger compartment: Doris, me, Johnny, Bernard, Nuku and Colin. Doris made do with the inconvenience of substitute transportation. She commented: "One of my Newport neighbors, Senator Pell, is too cheap to fly around via helicopter."

"Why is that?" I asked.

"Because it costs $4,000 a flight."

I could see why.

That was a fantastic day. Three estates in less than twenty-four hours. I ate breakfast in New Jersey at Duke Farms. Took lunch in her New York penthouse. Dinner was being served in Rough Point on the famous Atlantic Cliff Walk.

Not bad, wouldn't you say?

* * * * *

That night at Newport I did a little, personal fortune-telling with my set of Viking runes. They're sort of an Icelandic version of tarot cards. "Disruption in daily life" was the main prediction. I interpreted the message as meaning that I was going to be moving or leaving.

I first thought maybe I was going to say something wrong; Doris would be offended and she would throw me out. But after some wishful pondering, I figured that maybe we would be leaving for one of the other estates again.

The very next day, I got up early. While I was still in my room, one of the servants knocked on the door.

"You have to get out," she informed me.

I thought, shit, it's happened. "I have to get out?" I asked with trepidation.

"Oh, no. I'm sorry, Mr. Nischintya. You have to vacate this room because we're going to move you to another one. This room and the spaces above and below it are going to house an elevator shaft."

The planners and builders for the swimming pool, after looking over Rough Point's floor plans, decided that this section of the house was the ideal place for an elevator, its shaft, and mechanisms. To eliminate the exhausting hike through that subterranean jungle, Doris decided to put in her own personal lift. This elevator would take her from the upper floor to the sub-basement.

I was brought a few doors down the hall. My previous, humble accommodations offered only a glimpse of the grounds and surrounding area. My new quarters were much larger and boasted a spectacular view of the estate and ocean. The bedroom connected to a parlor and a study. I now occupied a three-room suite at the "Doris Duke Hilton."

Not only that, but these chambers led to another wing of the house. I investigated this whole new series of rooms. Wandering about that section of the mansion, I marveled at all the neat things I found.

My grandparents had this enormous house with almost two dozen rooms. As a kid, I would go exploring, which was great. I was reliving that wonderful time all over again in Rough Point. The whole without-a-care attitude and mood swept over me. I remembered those special summers with Grandma Fiela while I checked everything out.

Visiting the Grand Ballroom with its crystal chandeliers, renaissance paintings and oak paneling, I thought to myself that the room would have made a great Krishna temple.

Atop the grand piano were the three portraits of the Deities that I had given to Doris. Next to them, as always, were fresh flowers. The Ganesh statue was nowhere to be seen. Then I remembered that it had been a present from Chandi.

I came across the second of Doris' huge libraries. I checked

171

out the wall-to-wall bookcases. More rare first editions. One of the initial printings of Shakespeare's complete works. A whole series of the classics bound in expensive leather with gold edges.

I discovered a rather worn copy of Patton's *War as I Knew It*. The book reminded me of Doris' affair with the general. I was surprised that this memoir was not signed.

Doris poked her head into the room. I held up the book and asked: "How come it's not autographed?"

"Georgie died in 1945 from injuries received in a car accident. That edition was printed posthumously." Doris sighed. "Every now and then, I used to read sections of it. Helps bring back the memories. Georgie was such a dashing and debonair soldier." She winked at me. "A great lover, too."

"I've got to write that book about you, Doris. Nothing like what's been printed. The real you." A thought came to me. "We could make it into a mini-series. Maybe George C. Scott can do a cameo as General Patton?"

"That'd be great."

"Who would we hire to play you?"

"I don't know. I'll have to think about that."

"What about someone for Chandi?"

"The Wicked Witch from *The Wizard of Oz*."

"You mean Margaret Hamilton?"

"Yeah."

"But she's dead!"

"Even better."

"I wanna be myself."

"You'd have to, Nischintya. No one else would fit the part."

"Well, maybe Robin Williams."

I thought Danny DeVito should play Johnny Gomez, and that Bill Murray would make a perfect Bernard. We figured Rene Russo or Uma Thurman as Doris. Though Doris and I talked about the possible book and television show, we never got around to setting either project in motion.

CHAPTER 22

The Trouble-Making Philantrophist

• • • • • • • •

After leaving Hawaii, Doris got fired up enough to meet with representatives of the Anti-Vivisection Movement. This was part of her agenda when she made the trip to New York during my vacation on the East Coast.

Every now and then, Doris would be inspired enough to follow up on her desires and take action. Through her attorneys, she arranged a meeting with these people. When Doris Duke talked, people walked.

The various organizations sent her tons of material. A good twenty or more associations mailed the woman business proposals. Doris had me read through all these suggestions and give her my recommendations. After the initial meeting with the lobbyists, she asked me: "What's your opinion?"

I had spent a great deal of time weeding out the good from the bad. I showed her one pile: "These people obviously just want your money. These other groups," I indicated another batch "would like your financial backing, but they're still debating on what to do with the funds once they get some."

Doris listened to what I said; she even took notes.

I got a kick out of the situation. Important and influential people had drawn up these humane proposals. Many had given much thought to which direction they wanted to take their organizations. Here I was, some crazy, Hare Krishna astrologer and *shaman* telling their potential, major financial supporter whether their plans were good ideas or not. I had wondered why Doris didn't take me with her when she met these officials. Maybe, if I had been there, she figured they might have tried to influence my decisions.

I told Doris: "I have a friend in Hawaii who's really into this particular cause. She would probably know more about each group's history and background." Debbie Cravatta sent me a breakdown of each organization's managerial staff and how much they made. I also received a "reputation summary" of all the associations involved in the protest movement.

Doris and I weighed this new information during our subsequent discussions. We discovered that the people I thought were clowns were in reality bozos. Those individuals I dismissed as phonies happened to be the ones who didn't have that great a reputation or were drawing huge salaries compared to their organization's overall income.

"You were right," she concluded.

After all this, Doris asked me what I personally thought should be done about the situation. I deliberated a whole day before telling her: "You could definitely spend money, helping a few of these groups. But you don't have to give them a lot. Just dangle the funds in front of them; they'll jump through hoops for you."

Doris preferred my type of advice.

She had done that many times before. The woman knew when people were just after her financial support. Doris would make them dance for her, make sure they performed a few good deeds before she would throw a little money their way.

My overall opinion to her was: "I would concentrate on requiring the various groups in the League to spend the money in specific ways. First, educate people in general through exhibits in shopping malls. Second, reach the students in the elementary and high schools. Get in touch with the young minds who haven't been corrupted yet. They're still impressionable. Kids will relate to what you show them. And when they grow up, they can change things for the better. Third, you get a bunch of lawyers together and sic them on the animal-killing companies you want to stop."

Doris liked my last suggestion best. "Attorneys are just hired guns," she pointed out. "You can use them for good, or you can use them for evil."

"Right. Just let them go to work. Find a few hot shots right out of law school who want to make a name and reputation for themselves. You won't have to pay them that much."

Doris smiled.

"I probably know a few guys who would be interested," I added as an afterthought. Jokingly, I commented: "You could always funnel some money to a guerrilla group. One that goes in and busts the animals out of the labs."

As my advice became more extreme and outlandish, I could see the twinkle in her eyes. Doris perked up, rubbing her hands in anticipation. "Yeah, their exploits would be all over the front pages. The tabloids would have a field day."

"Just be certain," I warned her, "that there are a lot of buffers between you and the people who get the money. You don't want to get in serious trouble for it."

"That's for sure." A thought came to Doris. "Hey, even if these militant guys get taken to court, I can hire a whole team of defense attorneys."

"We could launch a publicity campaign on their behalf. Any other major issues you'd like to tackle, Doris?"

"Such as?"

"Pollution. The environment. Destruction of the rain forest."

"Why?"

"You could sponsor a task force of lawyers and lobbyists who would attack opponents of environmental reform."

"Have them file lawsuits against the companies that produce toxic wastes or the ones who destroyed ecosystems?"

"Right. Tie them up with years of litigation."

Despite our major discussion, Doris merely left some not insubstantial funds for a few of the more deserving groups in her Will. She should have gone much further with the Anti-Vivisectionists. The woman could have made a tremendous impact on their protest movement.

But like I said, Doris would get fired up about something, then her interest would fade. Before you knew it, she would be involved in something else. Her attention span could be very short.

She never had a set program or true agenda when it came to donating money. Certain charities or organizations she hated right out. Of those that she liked, Doris would listen to their proposals. Sometimes, the more outrageous a plan sounded, the more she would be willing to discuss it.

I could never tell with Doris if she ever intended on following through with a particular idea or stratagem. Whatever had merit interested her. Anything that sounded like it might be fun to pursue captured her attention. No matter what the outcome, Doris liked to talk—and talk—about what she could do with her enormous wealth.

One idea that Doris contemplated was supporting the movement to legalize marijuana and hemp. We both knew its effects—both adverse and medicinal.

"Look," I told her, "your father was famous for tobacco. But the health risks of that product tainted his generous philanthropic ventures. You could be remembered for something that's good for people.

"Doris, with your money and your connections, you could change history. Let's kick some ass. Save the planet."

She considered the matter extensively. Doris was fascinated with Prohibition and Pot. The former Act of Congress had failed. She wanted to know why the latter issue was still illegal. I even brought her a book called *The Emperor Wears No Clothes*, which was all about hemp. The book details how the petroleum conglomerates, the timber companies, and the Hearst newspaper syndicate ran this industry into the ground.

During our talks, Doris and I got off on a tangent. We contemplated about where to get the best "stuff." The woman was very knowledgeable about the subject.

I could see the glint in her eye. Doris felt that legalizing marijuana was more controversial than beneficial. That alone appealed to her more than anything else. She could leave her mark on society and raise a few eyebrows at the same time. Doris loved to raise eyebrows.

We even argued over AIDS research.

"That's a lot of bullshit," I said. "Look at how many studies they've done on cancer. $30 billion in twenty-five years. And have they come up with a cure? No. They're going to be researching cancer until the end of time. None of the scientists really want to come up with a cure."

"Why is that?"

"Because these people are making too much money on their investigations—what to speak of all the worse-than-the-disease treatments they've come up with."

"So, it's just a scam," she conceded. "What do you suggest then? Forget about donating any money to research?"

"Yes. Not a nickel for research! What I think would be even better is if you gave the funds directly to the people who have AIDS."

"I see what you mean. It will help them."

"Right. The quality of their lives will be improved before they pass away. Spend the money on facilities where these people can live what little time they have left in comfort—and with dignity. See to it that they have hot, nutritious meals. Round the clock care."

"My donations can help support the families involved, too," Doris pointed out. "Allow friends and relatives to visit.

Relieve them of the financial burden."

"You could even see to it that those unfortunates receive herbal remedies, natural medicines, oxygen treatments, acupuncture therapy—you know, the same stuff you're into." I could see that this idea was interesting to Doris. It was both beneficial and controversial.

I fed the fire. "Think of the headlines and their consequences: 'Doris Duke Gives $1 Million to AIDS Victims.' The drug companies will be shaking in their boots. The doctors will be freaking out. Researchers will be going nuts."

Doris was an intelligent woman. She understood what technology was available. The woman knew how expensive medical assistance was and how that help was used. Doris saw the advantage of giving some of her money directly to the suffering individuals. She also knew that with special care and comfort, some of them might possibly be cured.

Though it was more of an on-going joke between us, Doris and I contemplated creating a Chair of Astrology at Duke University. Or, at least, a Department of Metaphysical Studies.

That scholastic institution had so many numerous and varied fields of study, we figured ours would fit right in with the rest of them.

The university people, despite hundreds of millions in endowments, were so anxious for funds, they would have accepted her proposal. For Miss Duke's money, they would tolerate anything. Doris knew that. The thought in itself brought a smile to her face.

She and I always had a good laugh knowing that whatever hare-brained scheme she wanted to finance, there would be more than enough willing people to take the matter seriously to get the money.

I brought up the topic about rebuilding the old Hawaiian temples. Doris thought such a restoration was a worthwhile cause. She knew how the United States government had stolen the country from its inhabitants, just like Congress had done with the American Indians.

I told Doris: "Yeah, we'll get the Hawaiian Gods to come back and kick their *haole* asses." *Haole* is an Island term for foreigners or white people.

We talked about reviving The Southeast Asian Cultural Foundation, the organization she had coordinated with Nana Veary. In conjunction with my museum at the Vedic Cultural Association, Doris and I would have an amazing and tremendous collection of ivory statues, brass and bronze weaponry, religious carvings and scrolls, andßΣ archaic paintings.

"You could finally get that village out of storage," I pointed out.

Doris snickered at my comment.

I suggested that we could mix all the cultures together. Indian civilization, Hawaiian heritage, Hare Krishna rituals, a dash of Catholic ethics and a dollop of Buddhist philosophies. "Hey, Doris, we could organize our own cult. Do our own version of The Truth."

Doris smiled. "L. Ron Hubbard always said that if you wanted to make money or a name for yourself, you should start your own religion."

Unfortunately, at that point in her life, Doris didn't have the energy or total enthusiasm to become involved in any major undertaking. A "typical day" was like: read the tabloids, play a little music, do a few exercises, chant or meditate a bit, donate some money here and there, talk story, eat well, and call it a day.

CHAPTER 23

Spirits and Spaceships

· · · · · · · ·

"Whatcha reading, Nischintya?"

"The UFO report."

"Really? You finished it?"

"No. These are just some of my conclusions."

"Tell me about them."

Somewhere around 1990, I started working on a research project concerning the existence of UFOs. I engaged the services of a collaborator who was going to actually write the book about our discoveries.

Dr. Richard Thompsen, another Hare Krishna devotee, had published a text about *Vedic Astronomy and Cosmography*. His first book included documentation on alien encounters, religious events and near-death experiences.

I met with him and suggested that he write about the historical and theological "truth" on UFOs. Show how the ancient Vedas constantly make reference to interplanetary travel. Illustrate that throughout man's history, "mystical ships" and "magical beings" have come into play numerous times. I offered financial assistance; my non-profit organization, the Vedic Cultural Association, funded his initial research.

On my own, I started looking at various documents and case studies. I read numerous old books and dozens of non-official reports. I wrote down my findings.

Though Doris was not interested in reading drafts of this rather lengthy manuscript, she wanted to be kept abreast of any information I uncovered. We constantly compared UFO theories.

With Doris, I had my best audience in which to present my arguments and suppositions. She really drank it up. How much of it Doris actually believed, I couldn't say. But the woman listened. She asked intelligent questions. She loved to hear about my speculations and, a few times, offer her own.

"Did you know that UFOs are both man-made and extra-terrestrial in nature?"

Doris shook her head. "Really? You mean they're not just from outer space?"

"Some of them are. Not only from other planets, but different dimensions as well." I brought up the fact that space is so vast and interstellar flight takes a considerable time. "A more believable concept," I pointed out, "is that these visitors to Earth hail from another dimension occupying the same space as our planet but in a different or parallel universe."

"Yeah, I kind of thought it was something like that," Doris admitted. She was familiar with many of the numerous scientific theories at the time.

We debated over the Roswell incident.

"I remember when that happened. The official report said that it was just a weather balloon. But why did they have to have their top military intelligence personnel investigate such a trivial matter? I wasn't taken in by their lies," Doris boasted.

Doris was a firm believer in UFOs. She told me that the day I met her in Hawaii.

"I saw one myself," she now confessed. "It was here in Newport. A few years back. I saw this bright light. First, it just hovered there. Then the object started moving around. I know what planes and helicopters look like, and how they operate. This was something different. You couldn't explain how it maneuvered, because nothing we have moves like this thing did."

She asked me if I had ever seen a UFO. I did have a "Close Encounter of the Third Kind." Mine was more recent, though.

I told Doris about the time I was visited by non-terrestrial entities. "One night I was in my house in Hawaii Kai. This was shortly after Karina had left me. I was still living in that house we had shared.

"A UFO appeared in the darkened sky and landed outside. It was a small ship."

"What did it look like, Nischintya? What about the aliens? What did they look like?"

"Doris, I don't really remember. It's like something was taken out of my memory."

She signaled me to continue my story.

"So, they got out of the ship. I didn't know if they were there just to talk to me or take me away. All I recall was that I was pretty scared."

"Why were you frightened?" Doris interrupted. "You're usually not terrified of anything—except the guard dogs."

"I don't know." I've been through earthquakes, panicking mobs, encounters with vicious hoodlums. For the most part, I'm pretty mellow in such circumstances. Very calm in the face of adversity. This particular incident terrified me.

"I started praying to my Lord Narasinghadeva Deity for protection. All of a sudden, these aliens just packed up and left."

"Do you think you dreamed it?" Doris inquired.

I shook my head. "It wasn't like any nightmare I ever had before. And I've had some pretty spine-chilling visions." I continued with my narrative.

"I've done lucid dreaming, Doris. You know, where you perform reality checks. But this apparition was totally unlike what you'd experience in a dream state. It was more along the line of an actual occurrence. That it really happened. I was in bed, but I was sitting up. I don't recall falling asleep that night."

"Can you remember anything else?"

"No. It's so weird. I knew that it had taken place, but I can't recall any details. Nothing about the ship. No images of the aliens."

"Be truthful now, Nischintya. What do you honestly think it was? A dream or a real alien abduction attempt?"

"Is there much of a difference?"

Doris was puzzled for a moment. Then the realization came to her. "Dreaming is a form of traveling on the other planes of existence."

"Exactly. There are different realms, some occupying the same space but in another dimension. These beings visited me on the earthly plane. Not wishing me any harm, they left because I was terrified of them."

"Interesting."

"When you dream, things are going on. But they are happening to your subtle body, not your gross body."

"Yes, I know," Doris elaborated, "in Vedic culture, you're gross body is composed of earth, water, fire, air and ether. But your subtle body is made up of mind, intelligence and false ego. Both are real, only you can't measure your subtle body in the physical sense."

"How do you measure an emotion?" I asked her.

Doris shrugged.

"You know what you're feeling, right?"

She nodded.

"Your emotion can be one of love, hate, jealousy, or whatever. You might be able to measure brainwave activity, but how do you gauge the actual sensation?"

"You can't," Doris pointed out. "It's not something tangible to the five senses. But it's very real. Just like your mind is very real. Your brain processes information, but your mind conceives of concepts and ideas."

We went on for hours discussing the scientific reasoning versus metaphysical aspects. Doris may not have believed my theories about many issues, but she loved to talk and listen. She and I did agree that something was happening, but the people who knew the truth weren't coming forward with any of the answers.

* * * * *

During my more-than-a-month stay at Newport, I would usually awaken completely rested and energized. Solid in mind, body and soul. Only one night I didn't sleep well.

I could feel this whole aura or energy about the place. I remembered what Ben Reed had said during the tour of the museum. Slave trading had been prominent along the East Coast. Many of the murdered blacks haunted this particular coastal area.

That night, a ghost or spirit was active and disturbed my rest. I got a few psychic images of the tragic incident that had taken place inside the gates of Rough Point. Some of those restless phantoms were responsible for the death of Eduardo Tirella. Eddie hovered around the mansion, now a ghost himself.

At lunch the following day, I mentioned my vision. "I know what happened when the car went out of control, and your friend was run over."

"What?" Doris was caught off-guard.

"It was a ghost. The troubled spirit of one of those innocent slaves caused that accident."

Doris raised her eyebrows. She thought about it. Didn't say a word for a few minutes. Then she merely acknowledged my explanation. We moved on to another topic.

We did not discuss the matter—ever. Eddie's death was not a subject that Doris wanted to remember. Too painful.

185

A dear friend of hers had lost his life under very mysterious circumstances.

I do not believe that Doris murdered him. No way. Not at all. Considering how much the woman had partied around that time, she and Eddie could have been intoxicated or doped up. With Doris incapacitated, the ghost could have taken over her body without any difficulty.

If a person sleeps with his/her mouth open or passes out because of alcohol and drugs, a malevolent spirit can possess the unconscious individual. Harmful ghosts search for victims who are not in control of their faculties.

Later that day, I went to the library and pulled out Doris' second copy of *Daddy's Duchess*. I looked up the date when that incident had occurred. Yesterday—the night before—had been the twenty-fifth anniversary of Eddie Tirella's death.

I got "chicken skin" from that bit of news.

CHAPTER 24

When Are You Leaving?

· · · · · · · ·

For just over a month, Doris and I were constant companions. During my extended stay, I had begun to neglect my own businesses and affairs. I did call a few people, checking up on things via telephone. I just was not in any hurry to do "real work." Can you blame me? I was having too much fun.

I should have visited a number of places where I had deals in progress. I was supposed to see my son back in California. I was to have arranged travel plans for a trip to India. Yet I kept putting off things.

At the beginning of my fifth week on the East Coast, reality set in. Bernard came into the room and asked: "Mr. Nischintya, Miss Duke would like to know when you're leaving?"

That took me by surprise.

"Miss Duke has some people coming who will be working guests," he further explained. "She just wants to know."

I didn't think much of it that morning. Later, I thought the request a bit odd. Rough Point had many, many rooms. (This "cottage" boasted more than seventy.) Doris had working guests in and out of the mansion all the while I was there. She could deal with these new people and not worry about me. She had done it before. Doris knew that I didn't need to be entertained. Maybe she wants me to go, I pondered. Perhaps I had overstayed my welcome. Since I had a whole list of things to do, I figured I should be getting to them.

At dinner, I mentioned to Doris that I would be packing in a few days. She looked hurt.

"You're leaving?"

"Well, I do have to run my organization, the VCA, remember? And I should take time to visit my son," I added.

Doris recovered from the initial shock. "Yes, you should see him. I know how important family is to you."

* * * * *

The day I arrived back in California, I hadn't been in the door more than five minutes when the phone rang. It was Doris.

"Oh, I miss you. It's too bad you had to go. God, I really got used to having you around."

Her whole attitude confused me. First she wanted to know when I was leaving. Then she calls to say she missed me. Since I knew how easily she changed moods, I dismissed the notion and didn't give it another thought.

For two weeks in a row, Doris called every day. Since she had all my numbers, Doris would try to track me down. If I wasn't home, she would leave a message. Each time I talked with her, it was the same routine:

"I miss you. What are you doing? What's going on? When are you coming back, or are you going to meet me in Hawaii at The Beach House?" Doris always referred to Shangri-La as "The Beach House."

Doris finally flew to Europe. Only it wasn't the vacation trip she had planned. She went to Switzerland on business. A royal jewel collection was on auction. Doris had me perform a *puja* so she wouldn't get taken if she bought anything.

When Are You Leaving?

Her visit didn't last long. She called, thanking me for my mystical help. "Thank you for everything. That *puja* helped a lot. I knew immediately that the gems were overpriced. I didn't buy anything, but I had a great time. Thanks again."

I was still in Los Angeles when Doris stopped off at Falcon Lair on her way to Shangri-La. I put in a brief appearance and mentioned that I would see her in Hawaii around February 1992.

"I'll probably be staying at the Kahala Hilton," I informed her. I no longer rented that luxury house near her estate.

Doris was disappointed. "You won't be staying with me?"

"Well, no. I'll be working. I don't want to inconvenience you. "

"You're never a bother, Nischintya."

"Doris, I'll be seeing a number of clients. I've got a hundred or more calls that I'll have to make. A hotel suite is ideal for business purposes. The clerks take messages. They let you know when your clients arrive. The people there make all the arrangements for company functions."

"All right. But you promise to visit?"

"I'll just be down the block from you."

I kept my promise, however, I didn't stay long.

In March or April of 1992, I flew to Chicago to see my family. I also helped Karina with a personal problem. Doris was impressed that I was still considerate toward my ex-wife.

"You must be a good guy after all," she commented.

From October 1991 through November 1992, Doris and I had been long-distance friends. We saw each other occasionally, but it wasn't like before. I didn't get a chance to visit her on the East Coast that year. But we kept in constant touch.

Since I was now based in Los Angeles, hanging out with Doris posed a problem. She did not spend that much time at her California residence, Falcon Lair. Doris extended her stayovers in Beverly Hills whenever I planned to see her, though.

It was there that I met Ann Bostich, the housekeeper. Ann was one of the select handful of Doris' staff who was extremely efficient. She was friendly toward me, but maintained a professional distance because I was Miss Duke's guest. She would join in conversations when I hung out with Colin in the kitchen. Whenever I stopped by, Ann seemed happy to see me. I also noticed that she was happy whenever Doris left for either Hawaii or the East Coast.

Ann was petrified of Doris. Scared to death of the elderly woman. She was very conscientious. Ann knew what had to be done and how to take care of things. The less time she spent dealing with Doris, the better operations at Falcon Lair went.

Doris employed about two hundred servants and staff members total. They were divided up among the five estates. I did not know all of them. I was friends with those who were part of her daily or intimate entourage. In the past, I might have been considered "over-friendly" with the hired help.

Though Ann was a nice person, she didn't reveal much about herself. Whereas Colin and I were almost buddies, Ann always treated me like a guest. She always called me "Mr. Nischintya." Colin would switch off and on, depending upon the setting.

When Doris had been into the Hollywood scene in the Fifties and Sixties, she spent a great deal of time at Falcon Lair. She mingled frequently and partied even more. When I met her, Doris only used the Los Angeles residence as a layover point between flights to Hawaii and the East Coast. If Doris went on a shopping spree along Rodeo Drive, she had a place to stay close by. Falcon Lair was like her penthouse in New York; it wasn't a residence *per se*, but a temporary lodging. The house formerly belonged to Rudolph Valentino.

* * * * *

In my extensive, personal travels, I had come across many

people who knew Doris Duke. Yet, when I stayed with her, I was never introduced to more than a few of her close friends. That select group was more along the lines of business acquaintances such as Roberto and Ben Reed.

I think Doris rearranged her social calendar when I was around. Except for Nana Veary, the only other person that I met who was close to Doris was Ellie Dawson. The woman was a dance instructor who lived in Culver City. The three of us shared dinner at Falcon Lair. Miss Dawson was a charming lady, very cordial; I could see that she and Doris were very fond of one another. Miss Dawson, I think, regarded me as one of Doris' eccentric friends.

I remember that meeting because Doris wore these "hippy beads" at supper. I complimented her on them before we sat down to eat.

Modest as ever when it came to her personal effects, she replied: "Thanks. They're just some trinkets I have."

During the meal, my attention constantly focused on her necklace. I kept staring at those "beads." Then it dawned on me. Doris' little necklace was actually comprised of precious gems—emeralds, rubies and sapphires. Lots of them. Odd shapes. Uncut. But flawless. Worth several million dollars easily.

* * * * *

One week, when I was scheduled to drop in, Doris wanted me to come earlier so I would be in time for Aretha Franklin's birthday. Unfortunately, I couldn't make it to the celebration.

Another time, we made plans to party at a B.B. King Blues Night. Doris loved jazz and Black rhythms. Despite her age, the woman still got around.

During the years I knew Doris, I don't recall any of her relatives ever visiting her. A few times when we were hanging out, she did not speak too highly of them. They considered her a "black sheep." Because I was in the same situation, Doris and I once discussed the matter.

"I get so frustrated dealing with them sometimes," she confessed. "Most of them think I'm spoiled and selfish. How do you handle people like that?"

"Doris, because of karma and destiny, you're related to certain individuals. Those persons with blood ties are important in your life. Somehow, you've been put together for a purpose."

"You mean I shouldn't be so hard on them?"

"Right. Be a little more open and tolerant."

"I'm fond of my half-nephew, Walker Inman, Jr.," Doris admitted. "He's always welcome to stay at any of my estates."

"And does he?"

"Yes, but he usually chooses one of the residences I'm not living in at the time. To tell the truth, I don't really like hanging out with him, but he and I share a special bond."

Of all her relations, Walker was the one family member that Doris empathized with the most. If anyone knew the problems and pitfalls of being a "spoiled Duke," Walker Inman, Jr. knew them. Despite the fact that she considered him a popped-out klutz, Doris really loved him.

"In my family, despite our differences, we're still close. I don't see us fighting over things that might well happen in a very wealthy environment. When all else fails, I could probably trust my relatives more than you could trust anybody you've met."

"That's interesting," she noted. My statement must have had a profound effect on Doris. Toward the end of her life, she tried to reconcile both family and friends. No matter how much her feelings may or may not have changed, Doris still preferred talking about my own family relationships rather than discussing hers.

* * * * *

One day, after taking care of business at the Los Angeles

When Are You Leaving?

Temple, I spotted James Burns. Since Chandi's expulsion, he had begun to spread vicious rumors around town about me. That I was the person who split up Chandi and Doris. I found out about it because the two of us have friends in common. I confronted James about the lies he had been telling.

"Hey," I said, pulling him aside, "we've got to talk. Look, I wasn't responsible for breaking up Doris and Chandi. It's just not true. I'll go in front of the Deities, if you don't believe me."

James interrupted me at that point and explained: "This is the story that Chandi got from another devotee. He said that you told Doris the two of you were lovers in a past life, and that Doris should get rid of Chandi and give you all the money."

I pointed out how ludicrous the story was. "I never said anything of the kind. First, you know Doris. It may have been possible to fool her, but do you really think she would have been suckered in by a line like that? Gimme a break. Doris may be a bit eccentric, but she isn't stupid."

James pondered over what I said.

"Second," I continued, "supposing what you heard was true, how come I haven't moved in with Doris? Believe me, if I was inheriting all her money, I wouldn't be hanging around here trying to make ends meet, would I?"

"No, I guess not."

"James, Doris and I are good friends. I still visit her, but I have my own independent life."

He admitted his mistake. "You're right. What the hell was I thinking? I'm sorry." I accepted his apology, and we shook hands.

"You know, after Doris kicked out Chandi, she was still pining away for her. I wish they'd forgive and forget what happened."

"Do some *ho pono pono*?"

"That would be nice, but I don't think either of them would agree to the ritual. Perhaps, if Chandi gave Doris a call... "

James shook his head. "I wouldn't be able to convince her. Chandi and I are having problems ourselves."

"I hope you work things out."

We parted friends that day and kept in touch.

In April of 1993, Chandi Duke Heffner filed a "Galimony" lawsuit against Doris. That legal action destroyed any chance of a reconciliation between them.

* * * * *

Once I had settled in Los Angeles, I started "dating" again. In the Fall, I began going out with a new girlfriend, Susie. I don't think Doris was too thrilled that I was seeing someone.

Doris called in early November informing me that she would be returning to Hawaii. "Do you want a ride?" From her tone of voice, I knew the invitation only applied to me. "We should be going in a few days."

"If you leave now, I'll catch up with you later."

She called me back at the end of the week. "We won't be leaving for a week or two, now."

"If you head out around the end of the month, Doris, I'll hitch a ride. Just give me a call before you leave."

"Fine."

Doris would regularly change her mind when it came to traveling. Departure times fluctuated. Days could become weeks. Weeks sometimes turned to months. Doris would make specific plans for a particular destination, then decide on a completely different itinerary. Because she flew in her own jet, Doris could do that without any problems—at least for her.

The day before Thanksgiving, she called and informed me of her new travel plans. "We're gonna go tomorrow and leave at three o'clock."

"Great. I'll be there."

Doris was pleased that I was coming along.

After an all-nighter with Susie, I wandered back to my apartment between ten-thirty and eleven the next morning. I figured that I had time to eat lunch, pack the rest of my things, and straighten out a few business deals. Deep inside me, though, a little voice said: "Check your messages."

Sure enough: "Nischintya, this is Doris. We'll be departing at noon tomorrow." Which meant today.

I went: "Noon! Oh, shit!" Scrambling around the flat, I cursed Doris for always changing her mind. I threw all of my stuff into a suitcase. I had most of what I was taking set out on the bed, however, I hadn't really packed anything. I called up a friend who could give me a ride. I got to the Duke estate a couple of minutes before twelve.

I found out there had been no need to rush.

Everybody was still getting things together at Falcon Lair. Ann Bostich, the housekeeper, and her husband the handyman were still making final preparations. Colin and Bernard were busy loading the luggage in two cars—a couple of station wagons, not limousines. My stuff was put with the others.

About one o'clock, we drove to the Burbank Airport. Our entourage pulled up to a gate. After it was opened, we continued out onto the runway. We parked right along side of Doris' personal jet.

God, this was service. Right up to the plane. No hassles. No problems. No waiting. Better than First Class. Men came running out of the 737 to assist us. They grabbed everything. We didn't have to take anything with us to the plane. Not even our "carry-ons."

I thought to myself, I could get used to this. No lines. No waiting for seat assignments. No baggage checks. What a way to travel. Book me with Doris Duke Airlines from now on.

The crew greeted Doris. They were extremely courteous to me. I was the only guest. Bernard, Colin and Nuku came on board. A single mechanic joined the pilot and co-pilot in the cockpit.

Off we flew to Hawaii.

Whenever you took off in Doris' plane, it was like lifting off in a spaceship. Years before, when Pushkar and I had flown with Chandi from Honolulu to the Big Island, I was allowed to visit the cockpit. "God, it's like a rocket," I exclaimed. "Did Doris have some special engines put on this jet?"

The pilot explained the reason for the powerful sensation. "No weight, Mr. Nischintya. A 737 is made for transporting a full load of passengers and their luggage. With only a handful of people, the plane is extremely light. So the jet takes to the air very easily and very rapidly."

He wasn't kidding.

CHAPTER 25

The Fateful Warning

· · · · · · · ·

Contrary to expectations or rumors, Doris Duke's personal plane was not luxurious. It wasn't a gilded residence in the sky. Totally unlike Hugh Hefner's extravagant Bunny Jet. Her 737 was more Bedouin on the inside—simple, yet functional—which seems more appropriate since it was purchased from an Arabian prince.

At the front end of the plane was a small galley. The appliances were not for cooking, just reheating food. Near the entrance and cockpit were couches on either side. Nothing fancy, but similar to what you might find on a jumbo 747 jet. These small sofas could accommodate three or four people across comfortably. Further down was open space, carpeted, but without seating. You could look out the windows without having to lean over any obstacles or furniture. Following that area was a section with chairs—about eighteen or twenty seats, half on each side. Though they were all standard airline issue, the ones in the front row must have been First Class types because they were much larger than those behind them.

In the middle of the plane, curtains divided the front half from the rear. The aft section was filled with large, double mattress futons. No beds or elegant sleeping facilities. These futons, even though they had no framework or supports, were extremely comfortable; the mattresses were filled with fluffy cotton instead of the usual foam rubber. Behind this area was the lavatory. The bathroom was spacious and included a shower stall. All of the fixtures were gold-plated. The toilet was the same type that you have on all airlines, only you weren't cramped and boxed in like on a regular aircraft.

The interior of the jet was very Spartan. The decor reflected the simple and austere lifestyle of the previous owner. Except for a few minor changes, Doris had left the plane as it was.

We sat on the port side. Doris always took an aisle seat. I was next to her by the window. For the beginning part of the trip, I worked on another chart for Doris. She wanted to know what could be happening in the near future.

When Doris excused herself to go to the restroom, Colin approached me. He seemed very upset. "Look, I didn't know you were coming. I'm really sorry, but I didn't make anything special for you."

"Don't worry about it," I assured him. "I won't starve." The fact that Colin was unaware of my coming along was interesting. He always knew when I would be a guest. He would always make sure that if I stayed for lunch or dinner, I could eat some of the food that he had prepared. I never had to worry about what I was going to have when I ate with Doris.

I didn't think much of it at the time. Since Falcon Lair had been in chaos when I arrived earlier that day, I figured Doris had not got around to telling the staff I would be joining them on the plane. Because of Doris' usual forgetfulness, I dismissed the whole incident.

Mid-flight, at 30,000 feet, we shared our Thanksgiving dinner. Because Colin had prepared a standard holiday meal, there were plenty of things I could eat and munch on. He had cooked this spinach and mushroom dish; everything had been finely ground, and it melted in your mouth when you took a bite. Between that, the vegetables, fruits and nuts, I filled my stomach with no problems whatsoever.

After dinner had been cleared away, Doris inquired about her horoscope. "So, Nischintya, what do the stars say?"

"The portents don't look so good."

"Oh?"

"Soon you'll be entering a 'very bad time.'"

"When?"

"This dangerous period lasts from February 1993 through the following February in 1994."

"How 'bad' is it going to be?"

"Worse than the time when I first met you. And you remember how sick you were then—how poor your health was."

"Yeah, I know," Doris reflected. "I thought I was ready to turn in my suit." The woman firmly believed that she could have died during that time.

I gave Doris hope. "Nothing is certain. We can always take precautions. Remember what you did back then? You exercised. Kept up with your acupuncture therapy. I performed *pujas* for your health and gave you *reiki* sessions. You took your herbal medicine. You had treatments with the Dynatron machine. You're still here today, right?"

She nodded.

"If we stick with the same type of program, you can make it through the bad time. We can beat it again."

Doris inquired further about what I "had seen." She wanted all the details. I was not to pull any punches.

When you do someone's chart, the horoscope is not specific. The reading only gives you a general prediction. You have to look at what the overall picture might be. At the time, I never took any foreboding omen as fatalistic; pre-warned of disaster, you can take protective measures to prevent the potential calamity.

"There's evidence of a conspiracy, a possible plot against your life. It entails poisoning or bad food, drugs . . . could be surgery."

"Another plot? Who's involved this time?"

I had a mental flash of the players in Parker Brothers' *Clue* game. I merely replied, "Doctors, lawyers... you know, the usual suspects."

Doris laughed. She told me about some of the attorneys and law firms she was trying to get rid of who were mishandling her business affairs. The woman, as usual, was one step ahead of the game. She was in the process of weeding out those employees or financial staff she didn't feel comfortable with. She had even consulted her cousin, the ambassador, about trustworthy legal counsel.

"Look, you're going into a phase where adverse conditions and life-threatening circumstances may prevail. It's a time when you can get really sick—be in the hospital. You might even die. But I don't think you have to."

I elaborated: "Why don't you start taking herbs as a precaution. They fall into the same category. Better watch out for sharp instruments or cutting yourself. Don't schedule any cosmetic surgery either." Doris saw how serious I was. "Beneficial safeguards can't hurt."

"So, if I heed this warning, I can live another ten or fifteen years, huh?"

I shook my head. "If we use forethought and intelligent planning, I can keep you alive until 1998—maybe 1999. But between 1999 and 2001, I envision you going through a series of even nastier experiences."

I put all my cards on the table, so to speak. I'll be honest with you, Doris, I can't see how I'll be able to keep you alive through all that."

"Because of my age?"

"You turned eighty four days ago. You've lived a pretty good, long life."

Doris smiled and winked at me. "I have, haven't I?"

We debated on a particular agenda during the upcoming "bad time." I offered suggestions. Doris made the final decisions.

In February, she and I were going to fly back to Shangri-La for a brief stopover before heading on to the South Pacific. We agreed that the winters in Hawaii had gotten a little too cold for our mutual comfort. Temperatures got down to almost sixty degrees at night. (I know, both of us were really spoiled.)

With Doris' international connections, we would be able to stay at various places until it came time for her to head back to the East Coast around mid-Spring or early Summer. She and I would spend the entire "dangerous year" together, with me taking only a few, brief time-outs to take care of my business affairs and visit family. Doris wanted me to be her companion as much as possible during that time. I was to "be on for the duration" as Doris put it.

I would perform any necessary benevolent *pujas*, gather all the required herbs and natural medicines, administer regular *reiki* and Dynatron treatments, and do whatever I could to maintain her health. It was basically the same as I had been doing, but on a daily basis and a more rigorous schedule.

Doris was very serious about the prevention program. I was pretty sure that I could see her through the forthcoming perilous period. I just hoped that she would stick with the agenda and not lose interest because it was such a lengthy and involved undertaking.

After our animated discussion, Doris went to the back of the plane. Resting on a futon, she reflected upon what I had revealed to her.

I, in turn, went forward to the cockpit. I was allowed permission to enter. The pilot and co-pilot did not look like they were watching the lights and gauges. Seemed like they were playing video games on the instrumentation. I joked about it.

Both of them kind of agreed with my observation. "Oh, yeah, we don't fly the plane. All we do is take off and land. Everything else is done by computer." The pilot further instructed me: "See this triangle, that's the tip of the plane. A radio signal from there bounces back and forth off a satellite to keep us on course."

"Sort of like, 'Look, Ma, no hands!'" I commented. The mechanic laughed. The two others smiled, noting that my remark was not only funny but accurate. The four of us talked about the plane and its capabilities.

"I mentioned to some of my friends that I was getting a ride on a private jet from Los Angeles to Hawaii. One of them said: 'Oh, you're going on a Lear jet?' I laughed at him, pointing out: 'Oh, no. She owns a 737.'"

The pilot smirked. "A Lear jet would be roughing it, wouldn't it?" We all laughed.

I had a good time hanging out with the crew. Contrary to my usual "blah" feeling when I fly the normal, conventional way, whenever I took a trip on Doris' private jet, I never felt tired. Must have been due to the fact that the plane had more oxygen to go around because there was only a handful of people on board. I never suffered jet-lag on Doris Duke Airlines.

I remembered flying with Chandi. She instructed me on how to prevent jet-lag. "For every hour you fly, you breathe five minutes of pure oxygen." That was why Chandi always carried her own personal air supply when she flew.

I was in pretty good spirits. Restless, I walked around. Chanted up and down the long, wide aisle. Checked out the various views from the windows. Eventually, I wound down. I went to the back to relax. By this time, Doris was asleep. I plopped down on the mattress opposite from hers and took a nap. About a half-hour later, I made a pit stop. When I came out of the restroom, Doris awoke. After she freshened up, we talked story for the rest of the flight.

Once we landed in Honolulu, cars were waiting for us. An airline crew and some of Doris' staff had anticipated our arrival. Some of them held leis, others had signs reading: "Welcome back to Hawaii, Miss Duke." Without any delays, we were whisked away to Shangri-La. Literally and figuratively.

On that particular trip, I was only hitching a ride. I had business to take care of, plus family and friends to visit on other islands. Doris was only staying at "the Beach House" for about a month.

I stopped in to see Doris when I returned to Honolulu. We caught up on things over dinner. Doris wasn't sure of her immediate plans. She mentioned taking a trip to Vietnam. She had even invited Roberto to come along as her guest. I had work to do in California and wanted to spend more time with Susie. I told her I would keep in touch, that maybe we would see each other during the holidays.

I flew back to Los Angeles by myself. Economy coach on Continental. What a disappointment that was. I suspected that I was so spoiled, even flying First Class would never be as pleasurable.

Around the holidays, I tried calling Doris. If we were out of contact with each other for more than a week, the woman would be upset. Doris would phone me to find out what was going on or inquire about what I was doing. I couldn't get a hold of her, so I left messages at all the estates. But I didn't hear from Doris for a while. I started to worry.

One day, I came home and found a message on my machine. It was from Doris. Only the woman sounded like she was dying. "Nischintya, you've been neglecting me. You haven't called. I'm in the hospital. I'm at Cedars Sinai. Here's the private number. Call. Please. Don't abandon me."

I was aghast.

"Jesus Christ," I thought, "it's happening a little early."

CHAPTER 26

Superbowl Sunday

• • • • • • •

I dialed the hospital right away.

"Nischintya, why haven't you called?"

"I've been trying to get in touch with you for the past two weeks, Doris. I left messages at all five estates."

"I never got any of them. It's so good to hear your voice."

"What's wrong, Doris? Why are you at Cedars Sinai?"

"Please don't be angry with me, but I decided to have the knee surgery. I know you were against it."

Even though Doris could move quite well by herself at the time, she had constant pain in her knees. Daily exercise therapy, weekly acupuncture treatments, and periodic *reiki* sessions helped, but they weren't a cure-all. All these temporary reliefs took too much time.

Doris was convinced that surgery was the easy way out. One quick operation, and she'd be her old self again. A few weeks of recovery and no more pain. Doris didn't care about how much it cost. Nor was she scared of the procedure.

Her doctors had told her the medical procedure wasn't that big of deal. "All we have to do, Miss Duke," they told her, "is pop those bad knees of yours right out. We put in artificial ones and stitch you back up. You'll be walking like new in no time." Doris believed that it was something she had to do.

I thought it was unethical and unnecessary. An eighty-year-old woman. Double knee surgery. Even if Doris was adamant about getting the prosthetic replacements, I figured the doctors should have done only one knee at a time. I felt that all these unscrupulous characters were concerned more about the money than her health. I don't know what they charged Doris for their services, but I'll bet it was an ungodly amount.

"You want me to come visit you, Doris?"

"No, no, no. I should be home in a couple of weeks. You can see me then."

Until she was released from the hospital, Doris called me or I phoned her every day.

Since Doris would not let me visit her, I decided to cheer her up with a floral arrangement. I got a hold of the hospital gift shop. "I'd like to send my friend, Doris Duke, some flowers."

The person on the other end went: "Doris Duke?"

"Yes, Doris Duke," I reiterated.

"*The* Doris Duke?"

"Yes, *the* Doris Duke."

"She's in *this* hospital?"

"Yes." I gave the woman the information. Afterward, I got to thinking, "Uh-oh, maybe I shouldn't have done that." Doris had checked in under an assumed name. I called Bernard about my *faux pas*. He really got on my case.

"I can't believe you did that, Mr. Nischintya. Miss Duke will be most upset."

When Doris received the flowers, she called me up right away: "That was so thoughtful of you." She never got on my case about revealing her identity to the hospital staff.

I had sent flowers to Doris on other occasions in the past. I didn't do it all the time, just once in a while. Usually on her birthday.

A few days after thanking me, Doris found out when she would be coming home. She had me wait until late January before I was allowed to visit. The healing process took longer than she thought it would.

The last day of the month, Doris called and said: "Why don't you come on over." It was on Superbowl Sunday, January 31, 1993, that I stopped by.

Doris and I had not seen each other for months. Because I had been doing more personal readings for important clients, my girlfriend, Susie, had given me a whole new image. I sported a different hairstyle. I was wearing better clothes than I was used to.

When I came over, Doris checked me out. As a fashion authority, she could be very critical of a person's attire. She looked at my clothes. Had me turn around a couple of times. The woman took in my changed appearance. She didn't miss a thing. All the while, Doris hinted and hawed.

"You're a Hollywood Pooh Boy now, Nischintya."

"Huh?"

"A Hollywood Pooh Boy."

"What's that?"

Doris didn't answer, but laughed and laughed. She never told me what she meant. She really enjoyed her secret joke. It was nice to see her in good spirits.

Physically, Doris was weak. She could not walk. She stayed in bed the entire time I was with her that day. Doris needed assistance to even get out of bed. To move around the house required a wheelchair.

We talked about her surgery. Even though I was upset, I didn't get on her case about it. I had never seen Doris so frail. She pulled up her pant legs and showed me the scars. Her knees looked gnarly. Those doctors must have done a vicious butcher job.

"It looks much worse than it really is, believe me." Doris must have seen the horrified look on my face. She was still trying to justify her decision. "I'll be up and about in no time, you'll see."

To help with the healing process, Doris asked me to give her a *reiki* session. She settled back on the bed and relaxed as I placed my hands on her knees. It seemed like old times again.

Dinner was served in the boudoir. Doris ate off a tray in bed. I sat nearby in the sitting area. We caught up on things. Doris talked about remodeling her bedroom in Falcon Lair, but because of her surgery, she was going to postpone any renovation or reconstruction.

After eating, Doris and I discussed the agenda for the upcoming year. She confirmed our travel plans: "First, we're going to Hawaii. I'll call and let you know the exact date."

"Great. I just wanted to know whether you remembered what we talked about on the plane."

Doris nodded. "You said the dangerous period starts in February. It's the end of January now. We're definitely getting away."

I thought for a moment. "Uh, Doris, Radha is in town. We'll have to give her a ride back to Hawaii."

Doris frowned when I mentioned my younger daughter. "Yeah, all right."

I calmed Doris' apprehension. The woman disliked children. "Don't worry. She's not a brat or some spoiled kid. Radha is more like an adult than a child. All I have to do is drop her off in Honolulu; her mother can pick her up there. Then we head on to the South Pacific."

Doris cringed a little at the prospect, but the situation was endurable. She consigned herself to the fact that my daughter would have to join us for the first part of our extended journey.

"You know, Doris, when she was much younger, Radha reminded me of you."

"Oh? You're not just saying that?"

"No, honestly. In one of your unauthorized biographies, there's a picture of you with your father. The look on your face is the same as one of Radha's favorite expressions when she was a kid."

Doris smiled.

Since Doris no longer had James Burns to help her with physical therapy, I offered an alternative. "My girlfriend, Susie, was a professional trainer. She could set you up with a routine to get you back on your feet."

"That might be a good idea," she commented. Doris was very interested in this proposal. I wasn't sure what her reaction would be; I remembered how things had gone between Doris and Karina.

Doris surprised me. Her desire to get better outweighed her dislike of having to share me with Susie. Doris hated being an invalid. She wanted to move around. Be independent again.

In her youth, Doris had been extremely athletic. She was the first "white woman" to become a major surfer. She was a natural in the water, whether it was riding the waves or enduring a long-distance swim.

When I met Doris, age and health problems limited her abilities. Surfing was out; she wasn't even really swimming then. Doris was merely doing water therapy exercises. To keep her mobility, she had that pool constructed at Rough Point. Bernard and Johnny gave her assistance, but their main duty was to make sure she didn't become incapacitated while she trained in the water.

Having staff to serve her was one thing, but to require them to physically assist her was abhorrent to Doris. The woman knew what she had to do to prevent such dependency, and she had the will and fortitude to persevere.

"Since you're pretty much in Hawaii the whole winter," I continued, "she can stay there during your rehabilitation. If we need to take Susie with us when you and I leave for the South Pacific, I'm pretty sure she'd be available."

"I tell you what, Nischintya. Why don't you bring Susie to Honolulu for a vacation? Let her see the place. If she likes the Beach House, Susie can move to Hawaii." Doris was thinking and planning out the whole scenario.

"If she has to leave in order to take care of her kids, I'm positive she can come up with an exercise program that you can do on your own."

Doris nodded. I didn't know how long Doris would be able to keep up with Susie's regimen. Some of her sessions could be pretty intense. I kept quiet about that; Doris' initial enthusiasm was a good sign that she would keep up with the physical therapy. I didn't want to scare her off.

We made further travel plans, although none of these were definite, by any means. Doris and I talked story. She asked about the UFO report; I informed her that the book was at the printers and would be out soon. Though she wanted a copy, I knew Doris wouldn't read it.

When I saw that she was weary, I got up to leave. Looking at the clock, I noticed that I had been there six hours. I had spent the whole visit in her room.

"Once you get done with your stuff, and I finish mine, we'll pack up and go, Doris."

She was in agreement. After a hug and kiss, I made for the door.

"You've got a ride, Nischintya?"

"Colin's supposed to drive me back to my place."

"Good."

Doris was always concerned about how I got home. She could get pretty angry and upset if arrangements hadn't already been made in advance for me."

I went up the steps to the living room. I heard Bernard and Colin going at it. I couldn't make out what they were arguing about. The two of them stopped when I entered the room. Bernard went down to attend to Doris.

Colin took me aside, apologizing: "I'd give you a ride, but..."

I could see that he was disturbed about something, so I didn't press the issue. "Don't worry. I took a cab to get here.

I'll just take a cab back. No problem." I was not about to go back down and bother Doris. It wasn't a big deal.

In the taxi, I reflected over what a good time Doris and I had had that day. Despite the surgery and her weariness, she was in great spirits. She was fully conscious of what was going on and what needed to be done. Doris reiterated our travel plans; all we had to do was make the final arrangements. I felt that she could beat the upcoming "dangerous period" without too much trouble.

I did not know it then, but that visit on Superbowl Sunday would be the last time I saw Doris Duke.

CHAPTER 27

Miss Duke Is Not Available

• • • • • • • •

On February 4, Doris called me up and said: "Nischintya, everything is set for tomorrow. We'll be leaving then."

"Well, thanks a lot for the short notice," I replied. "Look, there's no way I'm going to get my business affairs settled by tomorrow."

Having my own independent life was something of a double-edged sword with Doris. I think she appreciated the fact that I wasn't always mooching off her, but at the same time I felt she resented the notion that I couldn't always be there for her. I wasn't at her beck and call twenty-four hours a day like all the others. Doris knew that I appreciated her travel offer, but was also aware that I had several, major dealings to close before I could take off for a whole year.

I thought about my present state of affairs, trying to come up with a compromise. "If you do leave tomorrow," I told Doris, "I'll catch up with you in three or four days. I'll meet you in Hawaii. And if you don't leave tomorrow, I'll go when you go." I was one of the few people who reminded Doris that she changed her mind on a regular basis. "Just let me know, or I'll call you."

"Okay, okay. Fine, Nischintya."

I called her a few days later at Falcon Lair. I was told that "Miss Duke is unavailable." I figured that she had moved to Shangri-La. I phoned there. Same response.

That wasn't unusual. Doris could have been out doing something or seeing someone, whatever. I left a message just as I had done for her at the Los Angeles residence

I tried to reach her on Saturday or Sunday as well as during the following week. Each time I received the same reply: "Miss Duke is not available."

None of the staff at any of the five residences was allowed to tell a caller where Doris was. Standard protocol was to say: "Miss Duke is unavailable." Because of my closeness to Doris and my excellent rapport with the servants, sometimes one of them would let me know: "She's already left," or "Miss Duke is in Newport," etc. The truth of the matter was, the majority of the time, Doris' employees didn't know where she was staying. The woman was always traveling or bopping between estates. With her own jet on constant stand-by, Doris could go anywhere in the world on a moment's notice.

At this point, I was not concerned. I was just merely trying to confirm itinerary plans with Doris, if she had any. Since I needed to check in with her, I called the reliable security people at Duke Farms in New Jersey.

"Please get this message to Miss Duke. I was supposed to travel with her, first to Hawaii, then to the South Pacific. I don't know where she is, but please let her know that I called."

"Sure thing, Mr. Nischintya."

"Thanks." I figured I would be hearing from Doris in no time at all.

No return call. No message. Nothing.

Although there had been times in the past when it proved difficult to get in touch with Doris, I was starting to have misgivings about the present situation. It was now the middle of February. Her "bad time" had begun.

I phoned every estate: Shangri-La in Hawaii, Duke Farms

in New Jersey, Rough Point in Rhode Island, the penthouse in New York, and Falcon Lair in California. I left messages at all five residences.

The days turned into weeks. Soon it was March, and I still had not been able to get a hold of Doris anywhere. Things did not look good.

One day, when I called Falcon Lair, Ann answered. She told me: "Mr. Nischintya, she's not here." The housekeeper's voice had sounded very distraught, almost hysterical. To my dismay, Ann wouldn't—or couldn't—elaborate.

Worried, her tone got me to thinking that perhaps something had gone wrong with her knees or perhaps another health problem had surfaced. I tried the number for her private hospital room, but the phone kept ringing and no one picked it up.

I was distressed and frenzied. Again, I dialed all the estates, only this time I left messages for both Doris and Bernard. After I hung up, it struck me that Bernard had not answered the phone in the almost two months I had been calling. I had talked with Ann, Johnny, Jin, members of Duke Farms Fuzz, the Filipino girl at Newport, and the housekeeper in New York City. But never Bernard.

Not good. Something was up.

Frustrated and frantic, I started leaving messages just for Bernard. If some misfortune had happened to Doris or if she were incapacitated, he would let me know. I thought maybe Doris was pissed at me because I couldn't go with her when she wanted to leave. I wasn't sure. I figured Bernard would get back to me.

I was wrong.

By April I had phoned each of the residences dozens of times. Bernard had not returned any of my calls. Whatever had happened must have been pretty serious.

On Bernard's birthday, April 15, I tried all of the estates again, asking to speak with the butler. It was my last stab at getting in contact with him or Doris. He was unavailable, so I left a final message: "Tell Bernard this is Nischintya. I wanted to wish him a happy birthday. Could he please give me a call?"

No return phone call. Nothing.

Doris was in deep shit now—and Bernard was involved! Things definitely did not look good at all.

I felt helpless and alone.

I pondered over the situation. I thought back to what had happened over the past year-and-a-half. Events that I had dismissed came back to me. The signs had been there, but I had ignored them completely.

In Newport, why had Bernard asked me when I planned on ending my visit? Doris would have done that herself. My leaving had caught her by complete surprise. I remember how hurt she looked when I told her my travel plans. Once I got back to California, the woman called me constantly, saying how much she missed me. Doris had wanted me to stay. It was Bernard who didn't want me there. He made the request seem like it came from Doris. She, in turn, thought I was leaving on my own volition.

I recalled the Thanksgiving Day flight. Had I not been on top of things or Doris had not called me personally, I would have probably missed that flight. Colin had not been informed I was tagging along. He always knew when I was to be a guest. It wasn't Doris' absent-mindedness at all. Bernard was behind that incident, too.

During that flight, Bernard had watched me do Doris' chart. When she and I discussed the reading, he sat in back of us. He was privy to the entire conversation. He knew about the "usual suspects" and the "dangerous period." Then, it hit me! In my vision of the *Clue* game, the butler was one of "the usual suspects."

Bernard had disliked Chandi to the point of hating her. When Dr. Atiga informed Doris that she was being poisoned, he fueled the fire by telling her more bad things about Chandi and James. It had been the perfect opportunity to get rid of her and, at the same time, become closer to Doris.

Before she had called me from the hospital, Doris never received one of my messages. Why? Any information to and from her went through Bernard first. All my inquiries must have been intercepted by him.

Those events took on new meaning as I reflected on the situation. At first, I could not believe Bernard capable of such conduct. I thought he really cared for Doris. He was extremely attentive. The man may have made some serious blunders, but Bernard was always there when he was supposed to be there. Always on call. Always on duty.

But there could be no other explanation. Bernard was part of the plot against Doris. My dear friend Doris had taken his apparent, touching concern hook, line and sinker. I had not suspected him at all. Would she pay for our mistakes with her life?

I recalled all the *pujas* I had done to purge Doris' estates of "bad vibes." I had never done the California residence, nor did I ever perform the rituals in the servants quarters. I prayed that Doris was not at Falcon Lair.

I consulted, unofficially, with friends at the L.A. Police Department as to what course of action was open to me. They listened to my story. Somehow I knew this option would be pointless. I was not disappointed.

Their initial response was: "What can we do about it?"

I had given them suppositions and theories. They gave me the real facts of the case.

"No one is going to believe you, Nischintya. Your credibility isn't that good. First, you're a Hare Krishna. Second, you claim to be a *shaman* and an astrologer. Third, half the time you dress and talk like someone who escaped from the Funny Farm."

Then my friends there had me look at the other side of the coin: "Look, your friend Doris Duke is a multi-billionaire. She

217

has her own special lawyers. Her own private physicians. If something were wrong, they would handle the situation."

"You don't understand—they're in on it!"

"Yeah, right. Suppose we call Miss Duke up and her spokesperson says: 'Yes, Miss Duke is here, but she doesn't want to talk to Mr. Nischintya.' End of case. The police would just assume that Miss Duke is probably ticked off at you or something like that. We're aware of how eccentric the woman is."

"But we were supposed to travel together, starting in February," I volunteered.

"Were they definite plans?"

"No."

"Do you have any documentation? You know, letters or correspondence?"

"No."

"Any others involved in the arrangements?"

"Yes, but I can't get in touch with them either."

"So, you see the problem?"

"Yes, but—"

"I can't take this story to my superiors. I know what they'll say: 'You've got a crazy Hare Krishna priest who tells people's fortunes. This guy says that one of the wealthiest women in the world is in danger. The lady's got access to the best medical care available. She employs the finest legal counsel that money can buy. And your nut case believes the woman is going to be murdered?'"

The cops shook their heads. "We'd get reassigned real fast for wasting the lieutenant's time, Nischintya. Even if he consented to see you, I know what would happen. He'd take one look at you and say: 'Are you on something? Been burning a little too much incense?'"

My detective friends were pretty blunt about the whole matter. I was glad that I hadn't formally pursued the issue. Though somewhat sympathetic, there was nothing they could legally do. They convinced me that no one would take me seriously.

I had cautioned Doris, but my warnings had not been specific. Little did we realize until it was too late that there was a snake in the grass. Neither of us suspected Bernard, the closest person to her.

Maybe my imagination had gotten the better of me. Doris could be angry with me. Look what happened to Chandi. The more I thought about it though, the more I was convinced that Doris was in serious trouble. In the back of my mind, I knew she wasn't going to live through this. They got to her. Perhaps Doris was dead already.

I started drinking. Not to the point of being completely drunk, but in order to go to sleep at night. I'll admit, there were a few times that I got pretty loaded. I was freaked out about the whole situation. Someone I knew and cared for was in serious trouble and I had no way of getting to her.

Susie was concerned about my own health. She offered a suggestion: "Why don't we just drive up to Beverly Hills and bang on the doors?"

"What's that going to do? There are security guards. Attack dogs patrol the place. They're in control. They don't have to let us in. Doris wouldn't even know that we'd been there. It's hopeless."

I wondered if others were trying to contact Doris. Her nephew, Walker Inman, Jr. Her doctor, Harry Demopoulos. Her cousin, Angier Biddle Duke. Were they allowed to see her? I had no way of getting in touch with any of them to find out.

Every few weeks or so, I would make perfunctory calls to each of the estates. I left messages for both Bernard and Doris. I did that from May through September.

I still wasn't sure which residence Doris was at, though I had a hunch it was her Los Angeles home. Nobody was saying anything. No one was returning my messages or phone calls. I had no way of contacting Ann, Nuku, Johnny or Colin. I was cut off from them completely. They, in turn, were probably being kept in the dark. Bernard had assumed total control, and everyone had to comply with his orders. I could just picture him bossing everyone around.

By the time I accepted the fact that Doris was finished, I was a physical and mental wreck. I began putting the pieces of my life back together.

CHAPTER 28

Doris Is Dead!

• • • • • • • •

I came home early one day to find the light blinking on my answering machine. I played back the message. A friend had called and said: "Doris Duke is dead."

I couldn't believe it! I wouldn't believe it. Doris can't be dead!

I phoned a couple of friends who confirmed it. News of her death was being broadcast on television. Her obituary would be printed in the next edition of the *L. A. Times*.

I was heartbroken. Even though I had prepared myself for the inevitable, Doris' demise hit me hard. I cried, bawling like a baby.

Later that day, I drowned my sorrows in margaritas and took out that old passport photograph I had of Doris. Between glasses, I reminisced about the good times we shared.

The phone rang. At first, I was going to let the machine take the call, but I decided to answer it, just in case it was someone who knew more about what happened to Doris.

"Hello."

"Your friend was murdered."

I did not recognize the voice. "I think so, too."

"No. You *don't* understand. Her murder was part of *The*

Program."

"Huh? Who is this?"

Silence on the other end. I was about to hang up when this mysterious person spoke again: "A friend of a friend." I listened as he elaborated about the incident.

"*They* wanted control of her fortune."

I decided to play along. "Why?"

"She was becoming a threat. Miss Duke was no longer minding her own business."

"What do you mean?"

"The Powers That Be were not happy with her—her philanthropic philosophy or her choices for charity. Miss Duke's enormous financial support would have been detrimental to their way of doing business."

I thought back to our discussions about AIDS research, the Anti-Vivisectionists, legalization of marijuana and hemp, the Chair of Astrology at Duke University, and the restoration of Hawaiian sovereignty. Doris had planned on making waves and changing history.

The anonymous informant continued: "*They* target very wealthy people with little or no family. Arrangements are made so that one of their operatives can get in close to these individuals and isolate them. When the order is given, the person is eliminated. What *they* are after is more wealth and complete power."

I thought a moment. "You're saying that Bernard Lafferty is their operative? The man's illiterate, uneducated, and inept."

"Fooled you, didn't he? One of their best."

"If what you say is true, why didn't *they* eliminate Doris a lot sooner?"

"Did you know that Bernard had a diplomatic passport?"

"No."

"Doris Duke was kept alive until Mr. Lafferty received his American citizenship papers."

"Who is this?"

Doris Is Dead!

"Someone who knows." The man hung up. For a minute or so, I held the dead phone in my hand, contemplating what I had just been told.

I broke out in "chicken skin."

I'll admit I'm anti-Establishment. I believe in various conspiracy theories. But this was too much. Yet this mysterious person was confirming suspicions I had about the existence of *them*. I had only discussed my theories with close and personal friends, the last one being Doris.

I dismissed the phone call. I didn't need to become totally paranoid. It was time to get on with my life—without Doris. Little did I know that those "secret" facts about Bernard's citizenship would be revealed in the next few years.

When I finally had my wits about me, I decided to call the estates to find out about the funeral arrangements. I only got an answering machine at Falcon Lair; I left a message. I did the same at Newport and New York.

Somehow Johnny Gomez answered the phone in Shangri-La. It was nice to hear a familiar voice after so long. There was noise in the background, as if the staff was having a party. Johnny didn't sound sad, not like someone who had just lost a dear friend.

He was cordial, neither abrupt nor rude. His manner was totally different from what it used to be. Johnny was no help at all. He evaded my questions.

"Look, Nischintya. I don't know nothing. We're just waiting word from the head office. If you need more information, talk to Bernard. He's in charge."

When I reached the staff at Duke Farms, I became a bit more persistent, but to no avail. "I want to talk with Bernard. I need to speak to him."

"We'll let Mr. Lafferty know that you called."

So, it was Mr. Lafferty now, not Bernard. Interesting. "Do you know when the funeral will be?"

"Miss Duke is going to be cremated."

"What about a memorial service?"

"To our knowledge, there won't be one."

"What? A lot of her friends would like to pay tribute to Doris."

"I'm sorry, but that's all we know at present."

I couldn't believe it. No funeral, no memorial service. Something wasn't right. Bernard had to be behind it all. The press and the tabloids could say ill about Doris Duke, but the lady did have friends and family. I knew several who would have liked to pay their respects.

I kept up with what was printed in the newspapers. Another doctor, Joshua Trabulus—not Charles Kivowitz, who had been the physician in attendance during her last months—signed the death certificate. Within twenty-four hours, Bernard had cremated Doris' body. He spread her ashes out over the Pacific Ocean in Hawaii.

I tried again to contact Bernard. I called up everywhere and left daily messages. No response. I scribbled a few notes and had them delivered to the estates. No reply.

I decided to write one last letter. I used a sheet of stationery and an envelope that Doris had given me from the Rough Point residence. I figured this message would get through. I didn't even use my return address, just in case someone was sorting through the mail before it reached Bernard.

Dear Bernard,

I know you are busy, but please take time to read this letter. I hope I am still your friend. I loved Miss Duke. Please tell me what happened.

In February, Doris invited me to fly with her to Hawaii, but I was not able to go when she left. Since that time, I have called every estate over and over. Throughout these many months, I have left numerous messages, but no one has returned any of my phone calls.

I was very worried about Doris because she was in a very dangerous astrological period. We talked about what could occur during this "bad time."

When I heard about her death, I prayed to the Deities. I even tried to establish a psychic connection, but couldn't make contact. There were so many things I had promised that I would do for her.

I have been broken up for days because I lost a wonderful, dear friend. I have sent you notes and left more messages, but I have not heard from you. I only want to talk. I loved Doris very much. I need to know what happened.

Please call me. If I'm not home, be sure to leave a message so I can reach you directly.

Sincerely,

Nischintya Dasa

I never heard from Bernard. All those bad things I thought him incapable of doing, I now firmly believed. He was guilty. He murdered Doris. I cursed the man.

* * * * *

I read newspaper and magazine articles concerning the circumstances of Doris' death. All of them reported how sad it was that the elderly and reclusive Doris Duke had been all alone in the end. Alone, except for her loyal and devoted butler, Bernard.

I was so angry! They didn't know the truth. He was the culprit who isolated her. He was the one responsible for making Doris so dependent upon him. No one had access to Doris without his approval during her final days. No one knew what had really gone on behind those closed doors.

I could just picture the scene in my mind: *Doris lying in bed, sad and lonely, weak and helpless. Bernard would come in with her light breakfast of juice and toast. She would perk up and make inquiries.*

"Good morning, Miss Duke."

"'Morning, Bernard."

"How are we feeling today?"

"About the same."

Bernard would fluff up her pillow so Doris could sit up in bed and eat.

"Nischintya hasn't called, has he?"

"No, Miss Duke."

"He didn't come by either?"

"No, Miss Duke."

"Has Walker visited yet?"

"No, Miss Duke."

"My cousin... you left him another message, didn't you?"

"Yes, Miss Duke. Several."

"Angier never got back to you?"

"No, Miss Duke."

"Ellie Dawson?"

"Not a word."

"What about Nana Veary's granddaughter, Noelani?"

"Nothing."

"Any cards or personal letters in my mail?"

"None."

"They all know how sick I am?"

"Yes, Miss Duke."

"Then, it's true, isn't it, Bernard?"

"What's that, Miss Duke?"

"Nobody really cared about me. All any of them ever wanted

was my money." Tears would roll down her cheeks.

"Seems that way, Miss Duke. I'm sorry."

"All my friends and family have abandoned me."

"Not all, Miss Duke."

"Oh?"

"I'm still here."

Doris would extend a frail, bony arm. Bernard would take her hand in his, patting it. She would smile, touched by his deep concern.

"Bernard... ever faithful, ever loyal... "

The mental image sickened me. God, how I hated Bernard. Because of him, Doris died believing that nobody loved her. The lady went to her grave thinking that there was no one she could trust—except for Bernard. The man who was responsible for her demise.

* * * * *

I wondered which charities had received bequests from Doris in her Will. I checked the numerous obituaries. Most of them evaluated her estate at $1.2 billion. I laughed. *Forbes* listed her net worth at only $850 million. What a joke.

I had visited each and every residence that Doris Duke owned. The art treasures displayed in those five estates were easily worth close to $3 billion. If you throw in the buildings, real estate, cash, stored collections, gold and jewels, treasury bills, stocks, bonds, and other business assets, I figured her accumulated wealth hovered around $5 billion.

In *Daddy's Duchess*, a book written many years before I knew of Doris' existence, let alone met the woman, Tom Valentine and Patrick Mahn speculated that Doris Duke was the richest person in the world.

The moment Doris was born, she was worth at least $100 million. Almost thirteen years later, when Buck Duke passed away, the girl's total inheritance would come to $300 million.

Despite the stock market crash in 1929, most of the Duke fortune remained intact. Under Nanaline's shrewd investment and management skills, this amount had more than doubled before Doris' social debut in 1930. By the 1950s, the stock she owned in Duke Power Company was valued at $450 million alone. Her net worth was close to the $1 billion mark. According to information in *Trust No One*, a recent biography by Ted Schwartz and former chef Tom Rybak, Doris believed her wealth to be in excess of $7 billion. Knowing her eye for detail and her financial prowess, she would know not only her true worth but also where every penny of that fortune was.

Her wealth had always been underestimated. Doris even contributed to such misinformation. None of her advisors or investors ever saw the entire picture. Each one thought he alone was privy to her true financial status. Every one of them believed he was working with her entire fortune. In truth, they only possessed small pieces of the puzzle.

The only person I believe who had any notion as to Doris' true wealth, other than herself, would have been Chandi. When I first met her, she would always volunteer: "Two or three billion easy." Chandi was not some "little girl" running around the house. The young woman wheeled and dealed for Doris. I bet she was very good at it. Doris had taught her well. Yet I don't think Doris would have trusted anyone enough, including Chandi, to know everything about everything.

While Doris Duke's net worth was being debated, the Probate controversies continued over her estate. Everyone was trying to get a piece of the pie: the Federal Government; the IRS; the State of New Jersey; Chemical Bank, the original Co-Executor; U.S. Trust Company, the newly-appointed one; Katten, Muchin and Zavis (KMZ), the law firm hired by Bernard; and various relatives and individuals, including Chandi.

The lawsuits will probably drag on for years. The only people who will benefit from Doris Duke's estate will be the attorneys. The Twentieth Century will be over before any of the charities see some money. Unless that wealth is disposed of in the manner that Doris requested, the Duke fortune will remain cursed and tainted.

Doris had left most of her vast wealth to charity. Bequests of $10 million each were designated for the Metropolitan Museum of Art and Duke University. The New York Zoological Society was slated to receive a $1 million gift, as was the Elizabeth Taylor AIDS Foundation. Two other foundations had been established: one for the Preservation of Endangered Wildlife and another for the Preservation of New Jersey Farmland and Farm Animals.

Her Will stipulated that none of the money was to go to Chandi Heffner. Doris specified that her disowned, adoptive daughter "not to be deemed to be my child for purposes of disposing of my property." According to a quote in Stephanie Mansfield's book on Doris, that adoption had been one of "the biggest mistakes in her life."

Doris did not forget her staff. She left money for her numerous employees; the amounts they received were based upon their salaries and years of service.

Large sums had been set aside for her family and friends. Her nephew, Walker Inman, Jr., was to benefit from a $350,000 annual annuity. Her dear friend Eleanor Dawson was entitled to $3 million.

Bernard was designated the Executor of the Estate and Chief Trustee for the Doris Duke Charitable Foundation; Doris' physician and former executor, Harry Demopolous, had been relieved of that position years ago. This institution was dedicated to the improvement of humanity. As Executor, Bernard was directed to collect the $5 million owed Miss Duke by Imelda Marcos; the Will stipulated that this loan need not be repaid until the former First Lady and the Philippine government had settled their dispute. Bernard appointed U. S. Trust of New York as Co-Executor to assist him in his duties.

And for those of you wondering—no, I was not mentioned

in Doris Duke's Will. I never planned to be one of her benefi-ciaries, however, I'm sure that Bernard made certain of that.

* * * * *

Through a mutual friend, I made arrangements to meet with James Burns at the Los Angeles Temple. With his help, I hoped to get in touch with Chandi.

No matter what people or the press said about her, I knew Chandi would be broken up about Doris' death. The two of them had been very close. I felt that Chandi would take the news hard, like I had done.

Unfortunately, when I talked with James, I found out that he and Chandi weren't seeing each other anymore. They had been on the outs with one another for quite a while and then split up. James informed me of the latest between them.

"I filed a Palimony Suit against her. If she gets anything from the Duke estate, I want half."

James based his legal action on the common-law marriage statutes. When Chandi had been booted out of Shangri-La, James Burns took care of her. He gave up his plans to go back to school. The ex-bodyguard used whatever money he had saved to get them through their "hard times." James even reno-vated Chandi's farmhouse on the Big Island. The two of them had been together for more than a year. The man was pretty smart; he kept records of all the expenses he incurred from helping Chandi.

Since this connection with Chandi had been severed, I re-solved to write her a letter. In my correspondence, I offered her sympathy. I filled Chandi in on my views and explained the stuff that Doris and I talked about. I informed her that although she came across as vicious and hateful in the Will, Doris had listened to the idea of reconciling with her. I even offered to perform a *puja* on her behalf, so she would get some money. I didn't expect any payment or donation for my services; it was an expression of good will.

Chandi never responded to my letter. I tried calling, but she changed her phone numbers constantly. According to mutual friends, the woman still believed I was responsible for what happened that February. She was convinced that I had been out to take her place. I figured that if Chandi felt that strongly deep in her heart, there was no way I could change matters. I did the *puja*, in remembrance of the good times we shared.

I looked at the situation logically. Chandi was being pragmatic. Her attorneys had probably informed her not to talk with anyone. They were trying to use her adopted daughter status to sue the estate for money. A lawsuit was filed, and she eventually settled for $65 million.

* * * * *

Once I got over Doris' death, I again talked with my cop friends. "Look," I pointed out, "she's dead now. What does that tell you? I was right all along."

"Nischintya, nobody in this country dies without an attending physician or somebody signing the death certificate. Otherwise, an autopsy is performed. Believe us, for a person like Doris Duke, if anything looked funny or wasn't kosher, they'd investigate it."

I tried to convince them: "I told you before that the doctors were in on the plot to kill her."

"Even if that were true, no one's going to believe your story or take you seriously. We told you that before."

After those subsequent conversations with the police, I decided not to make any inquiries or contact myself. The detectives were probably right—my notoriety, or lack thereof, would not carry any weight or lend any credibility to my story.

I figured if the police couldn't or wouldn't help me, I would try other avenues of attack. I asked a couple of friends who were publicists if they could set things in motion. I offered them suggestions.

"Call the radio and television stations. Tell them: 'Doris Duke's astrologer knows that the billionairess was murdered.' That's news."

I gave these people the "facts" as I saw them: One of the world's wealthiest women had died. Her astrologer is claiming that he warned on a Thanksgiving Day flight aboard her private jet that her life was in danger.

I knew the media would love a story like that. The talk show hosts would be stepping over each other to line me up on their programs. Their ratings would boom. Sensational headlines would have increased newspaper circulation. The resulting publicity could have sparked an official investigation. No matter whether my story was true or not, Doris Duke's death would have garnered attention.

I did not receive any phone calls from the talk show hosts. No newspaper or magazine editors sent their reporters to interview me. There was no breaking story on the nightly news. Nothing.

I thought maybe I had approached the wrong people for the job. I checked with them to see if they had made the necessary inquiries. I did not know if these people had talked to the media like they said they did. According to them, no one was interested in my views and opinions.

I settled into my new life style. I made book deals. Did readings for new clients. Paid the bills. I got on with my life. One without Doris.

Deep inside, I was still sad, angry and upset.

CHAPTER 29

The Butler Did It

• • • • • • • •

For the next thirty months or so, the numerous legal battles kept the Duke billions in the spotlight. Chandi settled her initial lawsuit against Doris' estate for $65 million. She then sued the Duke Family Foundation, the trust fund set up by Buck Duke in 1924, for an additional $180 million. The amount was still nothing compared with what she had originally hoped to inherit.

Colin Shanley and Ann Bostich filed Breach of Employment Agreement lawsuits. The now ex-employees alleged that there had been foul play in the death of their employer during her final months.

After extravagant spending sprees and drunken bouts, Bernard's right to administer the Duke Estate was questioned. A lower court ruling relieved him of his duties, but awarded him a settlement, plus an annual, lifetime annuity. A higher court later overruled that decision.

The judges involved were concerned that no money from the foundation had yet been given to charity, yet estate attorneys had charged more than $25 million in legal fees. The probate problems continued.

Two years later, in January of 1996, the story broke to an

astonished public. Bit by bit, the information leaked out. One of the nurses, Tammy Payette, who attended the dying Doris Duke, spoke out about a conspiracy to kill the billionairess. An article appeared in *Vanity Fair*, "A Hostage to Fortune" by Bob Colacello, exposing the possible culprits. Suspicions were raised. An investigation was soon underway.

The tabloids, in the meantime, were having a field day. Chandi was depicted as Doris' lesbian lover, who was disowned because of her affair with a male bodyguard. Tammy Payette had been stealing from all her rich clients. Irwin Bloom was accused of embezzlement. Colin was reported as having been fired because he was an alcoholic. Rumors flew concerning Doris' pets, the dogs and camels, who supposedly lived better than the domestic help. These stories made a mess of the legal system which was trying to sift out the truth.

Out of all the bad publicity and sensational press, one question remained: How did an illiterate lush end up in control of the multi-billion dollar estate after only six years of employment?

I waited for my opportunity to answer that question. But still, no one called. No one asked me. The media completely ignored me. I never got to tell my story. I could never figure out why.

I finally learned my lesson. "That's life." I resigned myself to believing that my voice would never be heard. Bernard and his conspirators had won.

They were definitely in control. The status quo remained unchanged. I was still a lowly pawn in the scheme of things.

* * * * *

Around mid-1996, from out of the blue, I received a phone call from England, of all places. It was from Outpost Films working for Independent Television Network (ITN), the commercial station in Great Britain. Ann had given them my number. They had been told I was the late Miss Duke's astrologer.

The lady who called, Helen Twigge-Molecey, informed me that her staff was working on a biography of Doris. She briefed me on the background of her production unit. Helen wanted to know if I would meet with her when the crew came to America. Their initial trip to the United States was more of a fact-finding mission than a filming expedition.

"First, we'll be checking out locations and doing other investigations. Then we'll return later to shoot actual footage for the documentary."

I was more than happy to talk with her. I could barely conceal my enthusiasm and anticipation, not to mention my gratitude.

Helen, on the other hand, was astonished by my cooperation. "You don't have to check with your agent or solicitor?" she inquired.

"No."

"What a refreshing relief."

"Why's that?"

"Everyone else connected with this case had to. Some would say: 'Well, I don't know. You'll have to contact my agent and see what he says.' Others were more emphatic: 'You'll have to make an appointment with my attorney.' In fact, most of those I previously asked wanted to know how much money they were going to get."

I was quite willing to spill my guts. I had waited years for the chance to tell my side of the story. I would co-operate, no strings attached. I didn't need my lawyer present, nor did I want any money.

Helen thought she had a far-out angle with me as Doris Duke's Hare Krishna astrologer. She filled me in on how the work was progressing. The woman wanted her crew to film in the house where Doris had been born, but had been refused permission. She was told: "Nobody's allowed there." Of course, for a substantial bribe, they would be permitted inside. Helen informed them: "It's a British documentary. We don't have any extra money to spend. You're not dealing with Hollywood. I'm on a very tight, low budget."

Helen made an appointment to come see me in Los Angeles around the end of September or the beginning of October. We met at the Govinda's Restaurant. Miss Twigge-Molecey was a vegetarian, too. She arrived late, around noon. I just happened to walk out toward the entrance at the right time to greet her.

She was impressed. "Wow, how did you know it was me?"

"Well, I'm psychic." Although I said it jokingly, I must have sounded serious to Helen.

"You must be."

"No, not really," I confessed. "All I had to do was look for a woman who didn't know where she was going or who she was meeting."

Originally, we were going to keep our preliminary talk short, about an hour. Instead, we had an extended conversation. Helen stayed until five o'clock. She and I left the restaurant when it closed at three and headed for Susie's apartment. I showed her the pictures I had taken at Duke Farms and Rough Point. I described the opulence of Shangri-La.

I was just what her Doris Duke biography needed. "This is perfect. It's fabulous." Helen had found a gold mine of untapped information. I knew all kinds of stories that no one else was even aware of. I had insight on the woman.

Helen became intrigued with Doris Duke. I showed her a side of Doris that had never been revealed before. We discussed the events that led to the investigation into her death.

"The whole can of worms seems to have been opened up when that nurse came forward."

"Tammy Payette. It's interesting to note that the nurses who took care of Doris during her last months commented that she could have lasted through 1998 or 1999. They figured that under their care and supervision, Doris would have lived that long at least. That's the same estimate I gave her aboard the plane when I first warned her."

"Really?"

I nodded.

"When were you first convinced that Bernard Lafferty was guilty of foul play?"

"I will bluntly admit it, I did not suspect him at all. I was totally taken in by Bernard. I thought he cared about Doris. He made sure that she took her herbs regularly and exercised faithfully. He was always on top of things concerning her health. Bernard may have been a bumbler, but I always felt that he was devoted to Doris.

"But when he would not return my phone calls or letters, I knew Bernard was involved. His true nature came out. I was very cordial in my correspondence. I never threatened. I was very humble. All I wanted to know was what had happened.

"I think Bernard felt guilty. I think he was concerned at first because I was a close friend and maybe I could prevent what they were doing to Doris. Afterward, I believe he was worried that I might expose the whole conspiracy."

"So, you truly believe he killed her?"

"Yes, the butler did it."

Suddenly, I lost it. During our whole meeting, I had been laughing and joking. Our conversation had been casual, informal and friendly. I had a good time reminiscing and sharing anecdotes with Helen. The topic of Bernard brought out the worst in me. The mood in the apartment changed. Now it was dramatic, tense and sinister.

"Bernard is going to die!" I shouted.

My vicious remark took Helen by surprise. I had become very emotional and vehement.

"What do you mean?"

"He's going to die."

"Why do you say that?"

"Because I'm going to curse him! The son of a bitch killed

my friend. He'll pay for that. I want him dead! Dead! Dead!"

Helen thought I was freaking out. My yelling and cursing had been totally out of character.

"The third anniversary of Doris Duke's death comes up in a few weeks. Bernard is going to die within a week of that date, and he's going to hell for what he did."

I cursed the others involved, the doctors and the lawyers. "They're just a bunch of vultures," I told Helen. "They're just hovering about, waiting to pick at her corpse for whatever scraps they can get." Anyone connected with Doris' money, I condemned.

"There's a curse on that money," I concluded.

"Why?"

"All that wealth was made because millions of people suffered and died, smoking tobacco. I don't really have to do anything because there are so many "bad vibes" attached to the Duke fortune."

"Kind of like the evil associated with the Hope Diamond or King Tut's Tomb?"

"Exactly. If anyone uses that wealth for their own personal gain, it will bring about their own downfall. Mark my words."

With that anger off my chest, I began to calm down. I apologized to Helen. We got back to the interview. She and I made arrangements to meet in Hawaii around the beginning of November.

* * * * *

Bernard Lafferty passed away of natural causes on November 4, 1996, only eight days after the third anniversary of Doris Duke's death. The world's richest butler was only fifty-one. I wasn't even aware that he had died, until a friend called me with the news.

One of the first things Helen and her crew asked me was: "Did you really curse him?" All of them were shocked to learn of Bernard's passing. They were concerned and wary of any potential part I may have played in his demise.

"Not really. I prayed to the Lord Nrisinghadeva Deity that Chandi and Doris had given me. I asked only for justice. He struck Bernard down. I did not put an actual curse on him.

"By invoking the wrath of the Deities, you throw out a massive amount of negative energy; some of that malevolence lingers around you." I elaborated: "Had I cursed Bernard enough to kill him, who knows what would have happened to me. I didn't feel that the personal risk was worth it. As it was, a centipede bit me after I got back home. I suffered for a couple of days."

The production staff looked at each other. Some in disbelief, others uncertain.

One of the technicians was curious: "Looking back, was it worth the pain?"

"Definitely."

"You believe his past caught up to him?" Helen asked.

"Yes."

"You were so sure that he would die," she commented. "And now he's dead."

"Bernard wouldn't have lasted that long anyway."

"Oh?" The entire film crew was intrigued.

"Bernard was an alcoholic. While Doris was alive, he had a reason for living. The man was given an important job. Daily tasks and duties to perform. When Doris died, he no longer had a purpose in life. Bernard then had access to enormous amounts of cash and credit. For someone who drinks and goes off on binges, that's a death sentence. Any alcoholic who inherits that kind of money will kill himself."

Before I flew to Hawaii, I had advised Helen as to what days she should come: Friday, Saturday and Sunday. "You'll get good pictures, if you do," I told her. "The weather will be nice." They were originally scheduled to film those three days, however, due to a rescheduling of talks with Pony Duke

(Doris' godson), they showed up on Tuesday, Wednesday and Thursday.

It rained each and every day. I razzed them the whole time. "See what happens when you don't listen to your astrologer," I admonished them. "Look what happened to Doris. Think of where that woman would be if she only had taken my advice."

At the Honolulu Temple offices on Wednesday, I met Helen's producer, Philip Dampier. Philip had been delayed because he attended the memorial service for Bernard Lafferty. For the actual interview, I had brought along my maharaja outfit. The shirt is made of blue silk with a gold trim. I thought it would be appropriate, since Doris always appreciated it when I wore those clothes. Philip was overjoyed at my choice of wardrobe.

"Excellent, excellent. Just the right touch."

On Thursday, the crew set up their equipment in my Spiritual Master's old room. This suite contains a full-size, life-like statue of Srila Prabhupada. The director of photography positioned me and the camera so that his image filled the background during my consultation.

Helen and Philip were in ecstasy. "Brilliant, brilliant."

For the rest of the day, we filmed the interview. Unfortunately, most of this could only be taken indoors. I reminded the group that had they come when I told them to, they would have gotten better pictures.

In the Temple proper, Helen and Philip requested that I recreate the *Nrisinghadeva Puja* ceremony I performed for Doris on behalf of Imelda Marcos. They were extremely interested in this religious ritual.

After giving the temple officials a small donation, I informed the crew that I could only do certain sections of it. "If you want the whole program, we'll have to come up with a few hundred bucks."

"No, no, that's fine."

We did a major production in the temple. I was impressed

with Helen's crew. They respected the place as a house of worship. None of them said anything inappropriate or did anything offensive toward the Deities. They were extremely professional and courteous.

Since I had previous experience with television and film, I was accommodating to their specific needs and problems. Many times, I would ask either Philip or Helen: "Do you want me to do that over again?" The British technicians appreciated my patience. The crew commented about how seldom they encountered an individual who was aware of what they were trying to accomplish.

They enjoyed themselves. All of us had a great time. Fortunately, Helen and Philip were granted an extra day in Hawaii. The two of them had been trying to figure out a way to either stay longer or come back for a return visit.

"Before you leave," I promised them, "I'll come up with an angle. This won't be your only visit."

Friday morning arrived, and it was still raining. Philip was upset that they might not get any decent outdoor shots. The crew got on my case.

"You said today would be a good day for shooting."

"I said Friday, Saturday and Sunday."

"Well, it's Friday—all we see is rain!"

"Don't worry. I'm going to recite some *mantras*. I'll even have my daughter, Radha, pray to the Sun God. You'll have sunshine by afternoon."

"Okay, Nischintya, whatever you say."

I made plans to meet the crew out at Shangri-La, a few hours later. "It's possible to film the estate from the back," I pointed out to Philip. "We can get pretty close to the property without trespassing."

Near mid-afternoon, the clouds parted and the sun came out. I got strange looks from the crew for the rest of the day. They were starting to wonder about me. I predicted that Bernard would die soon—and he did! I told them what days to come, but they arrived earlier—terrible weather! Finally, I promised them sunshine for their last day—sure enough!

Philip got the footage he wanted. In fact, when I had to leave, the crew was still filming.

"Look," one of the camera operators informed me, "we're just going hog-wild here. This has been the only day that we've been able to film outdoors. If you need to go back to the hotel, we'll call you a cab. But we're not finished here. Not by a long shot."

I thought it might be a little difficult to get back, seeing as how we were in the middle of nowhere. Philip volunteered to give me a ride back.

Later, when the ITN production staff had packed up everything and were ready to leave, I caught up with Helen and Philip. Earlier, the two of them had told me that their small film crew produced biographies subcontracted from British television. I had come up with an angle for them.

"David Kalakaua, known as the Merry Monarch of Hawaii, visited England during his reign. This *elected* King was a big hit with the Britons. Do a documentary on him, and you'll get to come back. We'll have some more fun."

"I'll see what I can come up with," Philip said, enthusiastic about a return trip to Hawaii. I could also see the wheels turning in Helen's head. She wanted to come back, too.

Helen promised to keep me abreast of things. "I'll call you when I know the air date." We parted ways. Those two days everyone had a great time. I had the opportunity to get everything off my chest. Helen and Philip came away feeling good about what they had accomplished.

I had a gut feeling that Outpost Films and ITN would do a fantastic job on their biography of Doris Duke. Helen had asked some very intelligent questions about what Doris was like, her spiritual search for The Truth, and her paradoxical nature. She was also intrigued by the many people who were part of her inner circle.

Helen had mentioned to me that her staff had done a film documentary on the Getty family; the family had been impressed with the end result. Having the opportunity to see first hand how thorough and professional her unit was, I could imagine why.

All members of this tight-knit crew, even though none of them had ever met the woman, liked Doris Duke. In the few days we shared, they had developed a kindred spirit with her. They had a real feel for Doris, aware of the various facets of her personality. Helen and Philip were not interested in producing a biography that was superficial or sensationalized. They cared about the project they were working on.

They were into the little things that make the difference between something good and something great. Their documentary was not just going to be a film with people talking about Doris Duke. They wanted and strived for a more in-depth, substantial life story.

Helen and Philip had done their homework. They had conversed with Ann Bostich and Colin Shanley. Interviews with Pony Duke and Nana Veary's daughters, Marie and Emma, were on the agenda in the weeks to come. Ben Reed was also on their list of contacts.

The production staff even attended and filmed the memorial service for Doris held at Duke University. How much more thorough can you get?

Helen called me in California a few weeks later. One of Doris' personal pilots, who agreed to an interview, had missed the film crew. He told Helen that if ITN would fly him to England, he would be happy to answer all their questions.

She could not believe that these people thought they had unlimited funds. "If we had that kind of financial backing," Helen joked with me, "we would have stayed a lot longer in Hawaii, believe me."

* * * * *

Dollars, Diamonds, Destiny & Death

Doris Duke: The Lonely Heiress, the American version of the British ITN biography, aired on August 18, 1997, over the Arts & Entertainment Cable Channel. I was very pleased with the finished product. The original version, *Doris Duke: The Billion Dollar Babe,* was scheduled for broadcast on the fourth anniversary of her death, October 28, 1997. Due to the tragic death of Princess Diana, the documentary air date was postponed until early 1998.

CHAPTER 30

Party of Five

• • • • • • •

I finally got in touch with my friends from the Duke Estates. I needed to discuss what had transpired during those months I tried to reach Doris and Bernard. Before I could start working on this book, I wanted to be able to put everything into perspective. I also needed them to help jog my memory on a few things.

Nuku desired to keep her personal memories of Doris private; I respected her wishes. Trying to coordinate a meeting with Johnny proved impossible; I finally gave up. I did reach Ann and Colin. He was going to be in Los Angeles for a bit, so we made tentative arrangements.

We got together at the home of Danelle Morton, a writer for the Domestic Bureau Department of *People* magazine. Rather than a business affair, this was going to be a private night, a reunion of old friends and a gathering of new ones. Even though she was familiar with the story, whatever Danelle learned during our socializing would be off the record.

I had not seen either Ann or Colin in almost four years. They got a chance to meet my girlfriend, Susie, who came along to party with us.

Ann was still reserved and taciturn. It was painful for her

to talk about anything that had to do with Doris. She had not recovered emotionally from the trauma the incident had caused her. I thanked her for having Helen get in touch with me. I also noticed that the earlier "professional distance" between us was gone.

Colin was his old jovial self; it seemed like only yesterday for us. He was still nervous and high-strung, but a lot calmer than when I last saw him on Superbowl Sunday in 1993.

During the evening, we would talk here and there about what happened to Doris. Ann and Colin told us about Bernard's true feelings regarding me.

"He really didn't like you, Nischintya," Ann said.

"Bernard hated you," Colin agreed. "He hated you because you were a Hare Krishna. He hated Chandi because she was a devotee, too. Every time I fixed Indian food, Bernard and I would have a big fight."

Susie wanted to know some of the things Bernard would say about me behind my back.

Colin elaborated. "He would say stuff like 'I spent five bloody years getting rid of one Hare Krishna'—meaning Chandi—'Am I going to have to spend another bloody five years getting rid of the other one?'—meaning you." Colin cautioned me. "I wouldn't take any of his remarks personally, Nischintya, because he hated everyone."

"Everyone?"

"Anybody that was a friend of Miss Duke. Anyone who was better than he was."

"Colin, you and Bernard had a major fight the last time I visited Doris. What was that argument about?" I asked.

"Bernard did not want me to give you a ride home. He yelled and screamed, 'I don't want him in our cars. He's not going to get a ride from any of us. Tell him to take a damned cab!' Bernard always got on my case whenever I drove you somewhere. 'You're Miss Duke's chef, not his personal chauffeur,' he would complain."

Ann, reflecting back, admitted: "We should have told you what Bernard was like when he wasn't talking to you. All of us would have been in a much happier situation right now."

Colin nodded.

"Neither of us," Ann continued, "felt that ratting on a fellow employee was ethical, even if it was well-intentioned."

Colin gave us a brief description of Bernard's behavior. "While Miss Duke was seriously ill, he started drinking again. He was always belligerent. Bernard even made fun of Miss Duke." He gave me a wary look. "Helen said that you cursed him."

"Oh?" Danelle's journalism instincts perked up. "You put a hex on the butler?"

"Sort of," I said.

"That's not quite how I heard it," Colin joked.

"Me, either." Ann and Colin smirked.

"He cursed Bernard enough to kill him," Susie interjected.

"Everytime I say something," I protested, "it gets blown out of proportion. I merely predicted that a number of people involved were going to die."

"Sure, Nischintya."

Nobody believed me.

Danelle, Ann and Colin glanced at each other. "That's interesting," Colin pointed out, "because somebody else with the case just passed away. One of the Duke Estate attorneys was struck down by an automobile."

A most timely bit of news. Definitely interesting.

"There will be more deaths," I promised. "That money is cursed. Look at all the tragedies in Doris' life. Look how she died. Her demise intensified the evil aura surrounding the Duke fortune."

Both Ann and Colin felt bad about what happened to Doris. I could see in their faces how much they blamed themselves for Doris' death. Over the course of the evening, they repeatedly said: "If only we had said or done something."

Susie and I pointed out that neither of them was really close to Doris. Danelle maintained that they were the hired help; she was their employer.

"True," Colin said. "I just couldn't go up to Miss Duke and say: 'We're having mushroom pate, string beans, and chocolate mousse for dinner. Oh, by the way, Bernard and the doctors are trying to kill you.'"

"And I was scared to death of her. I would be petrified if I had to speak to Miss Duke," Ann asserted.

"You also have to understand," Colin specified, "Miss Duke was a woman of the 1900's. The lady was not approachable like people we know or normal American people. I was her chef. I traveled with her. I never called her anything but 'Miss Duke.' I very rarely spoke to her without Miss Duke speaking to me first. If I had a problem, it was awkward for me to ask her a direct question."

"Everything was formal, right?" Danelle asked. "Proper etiquette was observed at all times?"

Colin and Ann nodded. "We were employees." They glanced at me. "You were Miss Duke's friend and guest."

"She looked to you for guidance," Colin added.

"Did either of you know that Nischintya was trying to get a hold of Doris?" Susie inquired.

Both of them shook their heads. In the beginning, Ann and Colin had figured that I was in constant contact with Bernard. By the time they suspected something was amiss, circumstances had changed.

"Bernard brought in this attorney from Chicago," Colin explained, "Bill Doyle. The staff was instructed—in no uncertain terms—not to answer the phone under any circumstances. We got some personal messages, but I don't think I got all mine." He looked at Ann.

"Same here."

"I got one from Walker Inman," Colin continued. "I know for a fact that he tried to see Miss Duke several times."

"Harry Demopoulos also called, asking to talk with her," Ann volunteered.

"I bet all kinds of people were trying to get through," I mused. Everyone agreed with me.

Ann sighed. "You have to remember, too, we had to be careful of Bernard."

Colin nodded. "He was in control of the situation. All instructions came from him."

"When were you notified of Doris' medical condition?"

"In the Spring of 1993. Her regular staff was made aware that she had suffered a stroke in February on the return trip from Hawaii."

"Did they tell you what the new complications were?"

"Bernard and one of the nurses, Pearl Rosenstein, told us that Miss Duke was dying of leukemia." Colin went on: "We also witnessed the documents that Miss Duke had drafted in March. Bernard and Doyle informed us that by signing the Will and other legal forms, Miss Heffner would be prevented from coming into the picture. As Doris' closest relative, Chandi could have taken charge of any nursing care."

"It was clear to me and Ann what they wanted us to do. We were stating for the record that Miss Duke was all right, when in fact, she was seriously ill. They kept telling us their way was the best of all possible solutions. From past experiences with Chandi, I could rationalize my actions."

Ann concurred.

Though I wanted to learn more, I could see the effect our conversation was having on Colin and Ann. It must have been a harrowing experience for both of them.

After toasting Doris' memory, the group of us started reminiscing about the good times. We shared humorous anecdotes, caught up on things, and partied well into the night.

* * * * *

Ann and I continued our dialogue at a later time. She discussed a few of her confrontations with Bernard. How he got rid of one of the attending nurses, his unauthorized opening of a personal safe in Shangri-La and, after Doris' death, the way he wanted to totally renovate Falcon Lair, making it his home.

According to Ann's testimony in one of her Affidavits, Bernard and Nuku had been shredding documents the month after Doris died. A few had not been destroyed. This evidence consisted of Bernard's hand-written notes and excerpts from a make-shift diary.

I had a chance to view copies of those writings. Unfortunately, none of the scraps of paper had any dates. The sequence of entries was jumbled. Most of the fragments were difficult to read, due to Bernard's lack of a proper school education. A good portion was devoted to Chandi and her lawsuits. I have grouped those passages below:

...Nelson Peltz [Chandi's brother-in-law]. Bad press. Land in Somervill... If I can be of help to Somervill I will tray... No papers for Heffne to file. A undue influce against me. It will be me against her. So I will take to my hands. What to do with her. It is time for some bad press for her. Investgaters like Bart Swortz [Bart Schwartz]. Has he found James Burns. Is Don Egan working on this. Heffners famley. Cladie Peltz [Claudia, Chandi's sister]. I want to be in cort when charges are filed...

Make no dcisions ontil after Heffner depeisison...

My drinkig is not the problem. It is Heffner... My sickness shoud secert in office...

Things to do. Mr. Swarts. sill dose not. wae Burn is. He must goo. But he semes to hange around. Not dowing very much. Bill + I have to talke about the future. Dr. Demoplis has to be destroyed. Him. Heffner. Bloom. Levey, Heffner's mither... It mite b good to Mr. Pelts.

What about Mr Bloom. Miss H depesion to teh press. I nver see reportes. From the invagates. So. I dont know what work ther are doing.

Moore press about Heffner. Good or bad.

I do not want to have my depession take to the last and I dont come Cigago... I will not be nice to C.H. at depesion. I have to call pess. I want to see what Heffne will be delt with her Will it be low prowel file ore a high one. At her depesion.

C.H. I think we shude know whear she is at all times.

Wherr is Heffner getting the money. Bloom. We know notthing about Heffner... [SIC]

There were bits and pieces concerning Doris and the situation at Falcon Lair:

Sucurity just sucks. Back stabin. Cominig in back - north gate. Lising to. Phone call. Phone lines. NY + privat line in to Pine Room. Chage...

New securtry. Boat House to be done... lites camra at all gates. Messagtes takten at Gate House... Tephone calles all houses. It will keep gosip down.

Nefr boos. Miss Duke not boss.

I think Miss Duke is fading fast. Rite now it not much good.

Colin. What to do. Hold. Bodygard + driver. All clear Big hurrey to sell plan. My money... [SIC]

Some of the last sections dealt with Bernard after Doris' death, when he was the Executor of the Estate. Those extracts reveal a little more insight on how overwhelmed Bernard might have been, caught up in the backlash of his actions:

... My owne person... A new image for me. Not the bank. I am the. Will birng. The personal touch to the Foundation...

I think i shoud have my owne bank acounting... Still no credid card...

Finacial proposels to me about Stole in N.J. not NY... I shoud be named head of Foundations. I have to Presend of Foundations...

My money... The time has come to figh. And hard. Nothin is gowin to stope it I will goo to no ends. I do not wan to come out of this - woch I am.

How much mone is spent on this case...

Motion in cort for everyone to get ther money tax free.

Talke to Miss Lee [Lee Ann Watson, colleague of William Doyle]... I must. See acountans.

No bonds sold. Weat proplems cood the bank make...

How much Mr Bloom has to be payed. is some held back to the end of the case... This is a gray arraie I wood like my papers that I sind back.

Called Miss Lee... Vanity Fair Storey. Had nothing good to say: about Miss Duke. Now a letter. To late... [SIC]

After reading Bernard's own words, any lingering doubt I had about his part in the conspiracy was gone. His guilt was evident. But because of the cremation of Doris Duke's body and the butler's subsequent death, there would be no trial to establish legal proof of his culpability.

* * * * *

Getting together with Colin a second time presented difficulties. Our schedules constantly conflicted with one another. In the meantime, Colin had Tom Hoving get in touch with me.

Tom Hoving had been a former director of the Metropolitan Museum of Art. A published author, he was beginning work on another book—this one about the mysterious illness and death of Doris Duke.

I did not envy the man his task. Tom has to sift through hundreds of financial reports, legal documents, court files, deposition transcripts, nurse's notes and medical records. He has to read the thousands and thousands of pages of meticulous research assembled for the project. His investigative findings are going to be most enlightening and highly detailed. He expects the book to be published in 1998. Over the phone, Tom and I exchanged notes; we shared information and stories.

One of the first topics we discussed was Bernard Lafferty. Tom stated to me that several of the people he interviewed thought "Bernard was one of the best actors they ever met." He commented that "the man fooled a lot of people. Bernard was a perfect actor. Maybe he was actually playing at being inept, so nobody would suspect him?"

"I thought he cared about Doris," I confessed. He might have been devoted to her in the beginning. Somewhere along the line, over the years, the idea of being Mr. Doris Duke appealed to him tremendously. The concept of having control over all that money went to his head. But I believed that Bernard was really there for Doris.

Tom informed me what happened between Bernard and Roberto, how the butler made good on his threat to get even. Roberto was invited as a guest on Doris' trip to Vietnam in late 1992. Bernard misled Roberto regarding the departure time, so he missed the plane when they took off for Asia.

We moved on, talking about Doris and Chandi after their falling out. "Doris wasn't afraid that Chandi would come back to kill her," I told him. "Doris was not concerned that the Hare Krishnas might approach her estate in a speedboat and shoot her."

He laughed at that remark. "Yeah, they don't do that."

I shook my head. "Don't be so sure. It's been known to happen. But take my word for it, Doris wasn't worried in the least."

We debated over whether or not Chandi had tried to poison Doris. I believed that Dr. Atiga and Bernard were to blame for that incident. After long talks with Harry Demopoulos, Tom was convinced of his innocence in the matter. He asserted that the physician had been a "knight in shining armor" to Doris.

He read me a footnote from the physician's Preliminary Statement of his Memorandum of Law filed in the Doris Duke probate proceedings to prove his point:

> ... when Miss Duke raised concerns about poisoning (apparently as a result of statements made by others around her), Dr. Demopoulos suggested that an investigation be made to rule out such poisoning. That investigation revealed no evidence of poisoning. Dr. Demopoulos then informed Miss Duke that there was no evidence of poisoning by Heffner.

Despite this testimony, I was not completely satisfied one way or another concerning the doctor's role during what occurred in those years. "Just follow the money trail and the truth will be known," I joked.

"Well, Chandi did get some," Hoving pointed out.

"A mere fraction of what she expected. I did warn her. I told Chandi that she could win a fortune and lose a fortune in the blink of an eye. And that it could happen more than once."

"Your prediction came true. Depending upon the courts, it remains to be seen just how much she actually ends up with."

"But no matter how much wealth she inherits," I insisted, "as much as that money will be a blessing, it's also going to be a curse."

CHAPTER 31

Colin's Close Calls

• • • • • • • •

It wasn't until Spring that I was able to further discuss matters with Colin. In the meantime, I learned about the death of the publicist that Elizabeth Taylor had hired for Bernard Lafferty. The Duke Curse was still potent.

On April 1, 1997, Susie and I had an hour-long phone conversation with Colin. He took up the story at the point after he and Ann had witnessed documents signed by Doris.

"Lafferty was like this control freak. He didn't want anyone to have access to Miss Duke other than himself. Because Miss Duke suffered a stroke in February of 1993, she was completely dependent upon Bernard. A few months later, she was also in a great deal of pain from the second surgery on her knees—"

I interrupted him: "Second surgery?"

"She had the first knee surgery done before you visited her on that Superbowl Sunday. Well, the doctors botched up the operation. They inserted the wrong prosthesis, so it was necessary for the surgeons to open up Miss Duke's knees again."

"The poor woman," Susie lamented.

"The subsequent surgery was scheduled in June of 1993. While the doctors were planning the second operation, I managed to get a hold of Miss Eleanor Dawson. I told her about what had happened and what they intended to do. She agreed with me that it was both unethical and inhumane. Bernard got wind of our conversation; after that, Miss Dawson wasn't allowed at Falcon Lair anymore."

Susie had a question: "As Doris' health failed, Bernard and the doctors still maintained that she was dying of leukemia?"

"Up until the end. However, I started having my doubts."

"How come?"

"In September, I was talking to one of the on-duty nurses. Because I didn't know much about leukemia, I was hoping that she could tell me more about the disease. I said: 'It's terrible. First the knee surgery, then the stroke, and now, terminal leukemia. Poor Miss Duke.' The nurse looked at me weird and replied: 'What are you talking about? This woman doesn't have leukemia.'"

"Can you believe that?" Susie was appalled.

"Bernard was caught in so many lies... "

"Colin," I asked, "what happened on the night that Doris died?"

"A pharmaceutical package was delivered on October 27, 1993, and I signed for it in the kitchen. Bernard was notified. When he picked it up, Bernard said to me: 'Now, Miss Duke will be dying this evening,' and he brought it downstairs."

[I later talked with the delivery man, Bob Das. He informed me as to what Bernard and the doctors were spending on drugs for Doris. Two thousand dollars one week. Three another. One time, it was five thousand.]

"Shortly thereafter," Colin continued, "Pearl Rosenstein called the Saratoga Nurse's Registry. She canceled the nurses scheduled for the late shift, saying that 'they would no longer be needed. Miss Duke is not expected to survive the night.'"

"But Doris lasted until the next day, didn't she?" I pointed out. "She lingered a lot longer than they had expected."

"Yes. Miss Duke passed away around six o'clock in the

morning the following day. Kivowitz did not sign the death certificate, which I thought was unusual, because he was Miss Duke's attending physician at the time. But he authorized the medication in that package."

"Which was Meperidine, more commonly called Demerol."

"Kivowitz also prescribed morphine for Miss Duke."

"What happened after Doris died, Colin?"

"That night, I got pretty smashed. I swore at Bernard and accused him of killing Miss Duke. About a month later, Bernard, me, Nuku, a couple of lawyers, and some bankers journeyed to Duke Farms. While Bernard and his group were touring the estate, I had what I call an 'out of body slip.' I was sober at the time. I watched myself walk over to the pantry and pick up a bottle of scotch. I saw a second me turn the bottle upside down and guzzle it as if the liquor was club soda. Then I went completely bananas. I screamed that Lafferty had killed Miss Duke.

"Bernard was notified by one of the staff. I was immediately abducted by security. They twisted my arm, escorting me from the premises. They beat me up. Security put me in a van and took me to a psychiatric hospital."

"Do you know when this occurred?"

"Most vividly. It happened on November 22, Miss Duke's birthday. I ended up in Long Island, at a place called South Oaks. I was in rehab for a whole month. When I was released, I went back to working at the estate in New Jersey.

"In June of 1994, Bernard and I were in a restaurant in New York with a couple of his friends. I was so miserable, so knotted up inside, I couldn't take it anymore. On the pretext of going to the men's room, I left and went across the street to a bar. After eight double shots, I was off the deep end. Back in the restaurant, I started screaming at Bernard. In public, I accused him of murdering Miss Duke.

"Somehow, I made it back to the apartment on Park Avenue. The next thing I knew, Duke Security showed up. The guards forced me into one of their jeeps. I didn't know where they were driving me, but I knew I was in big trouble. When we got to a toll booth, I kicked the car's window and screamed that I was being held against my will. I managed to get out of the jeep, and they drove on."

"Those men were taking you on a one-way ride, weren't they?"

"Uh-huh. Bernard and the others must have decided that I was too dangerous to keep around."

"We might not have ever seen you again!"

"That whole time, from when Bernard took charge until they wanted me out of the picture, was really unbearable. I don't know how I survived it, mentally and physically. I ended up taking medication for severe depression.

"I was afraid of becoming homicidal. I wanted to kill Bernard. Because of what was happening, the only way Lafferty could influence Miss Duke was through her needing to be dependent upon him. The sicker she got, the more dependent she became on Lafferty.

"I didn't see it at the time. Subconsciously, I recognized it. I was in such anguish about it that I couldn't express my thoughts until I got very drunk. When I got drunk... "

"You poor thing." Susie sympathized with the nightmare that Colin had gone through. I could relate to Colin's feeling of frustration. Having to block it out mentally. Doing whatever it would take not to think about the situation. I could easily picture him having a few drinks and losing control. That behavior easily fit his personality.

"It was even worse for Ann," Colin admitted.

"How so?"

"Ann couldn't walk. She literally was unable to get out of bed. You've seen her. Ann still hasn't fully recovered."

"No, she hasn't," Susie sighed. "The two of you must have been so tortured. You both had mental breakdowns."

"For the rest of my life, I will regret that I didn't do anything."

Susie and I reminded Colin that nothing he might have done would probably have mattered. He and Ann weren't in their right state of mind. If at any time Bernard and the others felt they were a threat, both he and Ann would have been silenced. Permanently. I also pointed out that they didn't even know which staff members could be trusted. I told him about all the problems I had, not being taken seriously by the police.

"Who do you think was the mastermind behind the whole plot to kill Doris?"

"I believe the man responsible to have been Bernard Lafferty, but he really didn't have the guts to do it... "

"You think he was a kind of puppet?"

"He became a puppet—Bernard probably had the original idea to do Miss Duke in, but when he brought in other people to help him, they kind of took over. The sinister one here is Harry Glassman."

"The plastic surgeon?"

"In the autumn of 1991, Bernard called Ann and asked her: 'Would you find out something about Dr. Harry Glassman? Miss Duke is interested in consulting with him.' After two consultations, Miss Duke arranged the plastic surgery in April of 1992."

"For a face lift, right, Colin?" Susie guessed.

"Yes, that's correct."

"What!" I was shocked.

Susie shook her head. "Nischintya, you didn't even know she had that face lift, did you?"

"No!"

"Miss Duke didn't tell anybody, did she, Colin?"

"No. It was top secret."

Eighty years old and still concerned about her looks. That was Doris for you. I can't believe she didn't want me to know.

"So, you believe that Glassman's the one who took advantage once the opportunity presented itself. He probably said to Bernard: 'Now's the time. She's not well. I have a lawyer. He lives across the street from me. Let's get his help. We can do this.'

"Okay, at that point," Susie continued, "Glassman, Kivowitz and Doyle seized the moment, and Bernard was just kind of a big dummy who thought about killing Doris but didn't know how to orchestrate it."

"Exactly. In all fairness," Colin emphasized, "I don't think that Kivowitz, the doctor who overdosed Miss Duke, is as bad as the other two. I think Kivowitz got in over his head—just like Bernard—and he did something he wouldn't have done ordinarily. Kivowitz—unlike Glassman and Doyle, who always seemed to be casing Falcon Lair—was genuinely a decent guy. He was pressured into doing all these things. The man did not get that much money, only his $50,000 monthly retainer for treating Miss Duke. Lafferty gave half-a-million dollars to Glassman."

"Do you think that's why Kivowitz didn't sign the death certificate himself?" I asked.

"Probably."

Colin had arrangements to make; he was taking a vacation in Mexico. We had to cut short our conversation. Susie and I thanked him for his assistance and wished him well on his trip. Before hanging up, he promised to send me copies of his affidavits and court filings. I received those documents a few days later.

Despite how Colin feels about Chandi personally, he said later that he would be willing to bury the hatchet if she was. Colin offered to help in any way to bring about a Wrongful Death Suit against Doyle, Glassman and Kivowitz.

Still no word from Chandi or her attorneys regarding this matter.

* * * * *

In all fairness, Bernard should be able to come to his

defense. Although now dead, he can talk from the grave, so to speak. One of the scribbled notes that survived the shredder contained a statement of how he felt:

Last will.

I have been. Abused. By Miss Heffner for 5 year. it was a nighmare. Miss Duke was very good to me. She told I wood alwas have. and kepp all dogs with me.

it I ever asked her I was nver refuse. This gas amount. Is small. My life Dr. Glassman made shure of that.

I have lost. alott. + and I have very little in return. No bodey but me underste. Doris Duke now I know whie.

My mothe + F wear poor. But I was brough up very. well. Now thers is to meney people invoved. I think Nucku shoud go to Hawae. Colin cwo go and leav. From. But I dont thin it woork.

Harry + Blum traie to Miss Duke away. These home wear our home. I know very well that she did no leve t hose to. Hut Bill when you say that. To me... We are very proud...[SIC]

Bernard believed that he had been persecuted. Perhaps it was true. No matter how deep his involvement in the conspiracy to murder Miss Duke, the man still felt guilt and remorse. His conscience must have caught up with him in the end.

Bernard Lafferty, once the world's richest butler, left all he had to the Doris Duke Charitable Foundation.

CHAPTER 32

Reflections

• • • • • • • •

Biographers have said that Doris Duke was unable to trust people. I won't deny it; I did perceive that in my late friend. What most of those authors failed to focus upon was why she "trusted no one."

Even though her vast wealth allowed Doris to enjoy the best pleasures in life, that money also brought out the worst in many of the people she knew. Because of numerous negative impressions and bitter encounters, Doris would always maintain a distance when dealing with anyone.

She did have a number of close friends. Some of those whom Doris expressed a great fondness for were: Nana Veary, Chandi Heffner (initially, at least), Eleanor Dawson, Walker Inman, Jr., and myself. Perhaps we were the exceptions. I could tell that whenever Doris met someone new, she would be thinking in the back of her mind: "Are they really here for me or my money?" or "If I were somebody else, would they still hang out with me?"

The falling out with Chandi severely hurt Doris. That incident left a permanent scar on her psyche. She had opened up to her adopted daughter. More than she had probably done with anyone since those years spent with her governess, Jenny

Renaud. Doris never again put herself in that type of relationship or so vulnerable a position.

Her rich family upbringing and its lifetime of perennial distrust forced Doris into a social awkwardness. Middle-class and poor people have to get along with each other because we must in order to survive. You and I yield or compromise much more than we would like to. But it's a necessary part of our lives. Not so for Doris. She wasn't dependent upon others to make life bearable. Her outlook on social contact was much different than ours. We would definitely consider her "spoiled."

To a certain degree, that was true. One must remember, though, that Doris Duke was born at the end of America's Gilded Age. During that by-gone era, four percent of the United States population owned ninety-six percent of the country's wealth. Even though a permanent income tax was established in 1913, the year after Doris was born, the rich still took care of the poor. She was a product of that environment: its self-indulgence and its humanitarianism.

Doris would either take an immediate liking or disliking to people. If she couldn't stand someone, Doris was wealthy and powerful enough not to have to deal with that individual. Doris snubbed the Queen of England once; she was supposed to assist in a tour of the Newport Restoration Society. Doris simply failed to show up. No phone call. No explanation. No excuse. Doris could care less whether the British monarch was offended or not.

Doris preferred persons who were "real." More down to earth. Unpretentious. During her lifetime, the woman had been surrounded by snooty-nosed snobs and blue-blooded social-ites who couldn't get enough of themselves. She sought out individuals without an air of arrogance and contempt. It seemed the more outrageous your personality, the better your chances were of Doris noticing you.

Doris felt a bond with the underdog, the outcast, the black sheep. She had a special place in her heart for such unfortunate souls. I fit that bill, as did her nephew, Walker, and her adopted daughter, Chandi.

During our many discussions, I commented to Doris that she and I were from opposite sides of the track. She could not grasp that concept. "What does that mean?" she asked. Doris truly saw people as equals. Servants, staff and employees had their place, but on the basic level everyone was the same.

Doris could not understand why white and black people were so prejudiced against one another. Color of skin didn't matter. As a youngster, Doris accompanied her father and uncle to nightclubs in Harlem. The lady associated with people from all walks of life. Most important to Doris was who you were. All this from a woman who, on so many levels, was no one's equal.

My friend was a very gifted person. She could sing, dance and play the piano. In her younger days, Doris was very athletic, swimming and surfing. She was intelligent, witty and, at times, extremely funny. Her financial fortitude and business investment skills were first-rate and highly respected.

Despite all these hidden talents and amazing abilities, Doris lacked a matching high dose of self-esteem. She constantly worried: "Would I have been able to do anything if I didn't have all this money?"

I tried to explain to her that "It's part of who you are Doris. You have to take the good with the bad."

* * * * *

Doris despised the image the press and public had of her: a lonely, reclusive and wretched person. In *The Richest Girl in the World*, Stephanie Mansfield quoted Doris' cynical response to that false, pathetic portrait: "I'm not a recluse; I'm a loose wreck." Doris was very proud of her witticism.

A story called "Caged by Fortune" appeared in a Newport magazine, a periodical supplement in the Rhode Island Sunday paper. The piece described Doris as a completely isolated, friendless, and paranoid old woman. She and I talked about the article.

"C'mon, Nischintya, you know me. Am I really like that?"

I was always honest and up-front with Doris. She appreciated my candor and expected such bluntness from me.

"Certainly there is *some* truth to the report," I told her. "Obviously, to some degree, you do have some amount of loneliness—but you're not at all like what they say.

"You definitely like to have a good time. You're not this old biddy that nobody loves or cares for. You've got many friends who come to visit. You get around a lot. Not many women your age travel as much as you do. You're not paranoid, Doris, you just want your privacy. And you want others to respect that."

From the moment of her birth, Doris made headlines. For over eighty years, the woman maintained a love/hate relationship with the media. Though she preferred having to deal with the press on her own terms, Doris would read whatever had been written about her, good or bad.

Doris would be offended if reporters took an unflattering photograph of her at some event. She would be angry and upset if the journalists did not acknowledge her presence. Doris would be disappointed if she *failed* to receive publicity. On the other hand, she hated it when the press were in her face with cameras or asking her an endless barrage of questions.

When Mansfield's unauthorized biography hit the stores in 1992, Doris was one of the first people to buy copies of the book. Yet, during the time the author was doing her research, Doris made it clear that none of the staff was to talk to the woman. She also had a couple of first editions of *Daddy's Duchess*. A copy of any tabloid, newspaper or magazine that mentioned her would end up in her sitting room.

* * * * *

Reflections

Doris showed me her soft side. I was allowed to see the vulnerable woman. Most people never knew that Doris Duke.

Her business associates dealt only with a shrewd, female entrepreneur, who was on top of every penny she invested. Servants and staff were aware that if they screwed up enough, they were history. Doris projected her own image to those around her: someone in charge; things have to get done, and I want them done my way.

I was witness to the caring side of Doris. The woman enjoyed helping others. She was a gifted healer. Some of the happiest moments in her life were when she was doing good for others. Whether it was helping friends in need, choosing the most worthy philanthropic causes, or giving *reiki* to someone in pain—she liked performing acts of kindness. To prove her ultimate generosity—after personal bequests to family, friends and staff—Doris left the entire Duke fortune to charity.

She also had a great fondness for animals. She would have had that same bond or attachment for her fellow human beings, except that, unlike her four-legged pets, most of the two-legged animals "bit the hand that fed them." Doris generally wanted to like people and have them like her, but because of all the adversity in her life, she was apprehensive and cautious about entering into any lasting personal relationships.

Doris was not perfect. She had faults like everyone else. She had received the best and worst character flaws of her parents. The diversity and dichotomy of those personality traits gave her a unique identity: Doris Duke was a woman of extremes.

From her father, she acquired an inclination toward life's excesses. She possessed the insatiable Duke sex drive and indulged it frequently until a very advanced age. Buck Duke believed in his daughter. He doted upon her, showering her with expensive gifts and a nurturing love. Buck was both father and friend to Doris. He showed her that all men and women were equals.

Dollars, Diamonds, Destiny & Death

Doris inherited the miserly manners and misanthropic attitude of her mother. Literally held at arm's length, she never received that necessary, formative, maternal care. Nanaline Duke left her daughter a legacy of self-doubt and cynicism. Her blue-blooded overbearance contrasted with the down-to-earth realism of her father. Her mother constantly chastised Doris for behavior inappropriate for someone of her social status.

From both parents, Doris gained business acumen and financial prowess. Her specialized upbringing and education enabled her to increase her net worth by more than two thousand percent.

Doris maintained an $80 million checking account, in case she came across something she wanted to buy. Yet this same woman was concerned about wasting gas on a trade-in car. Doris bought an entire village without batting an eye, but quibbled over the cost of simple repairs at each of her five homes. She could afford to hire the finest domestic help, yet the lady surrounded herself with a personal entourage as unique and outlandish as she was.

In her global travels, Doris encountered the best and worst of humanity. The woman attended soirees for the Rich and Famous; she shared meals with the Poor and Unfortunate.

Doris confided in me that "The Hare Krishnas are the most obnoxious people I have ever met." But she adopted a Hare Krishna as her daughter, and I was also a devotee. Doris chanted Hare Krishna prayers, ate their food and read their books.

Those Dorisisms, which endeared her to me and others, were part of the enigma and paradox of Doris Duke. Being with Doris, I could see she was like a twelve-year-old girl. Doris was almost locked in that age emotionally. The death of her father stunted that part of her psychological maturity. Her behavior reflected this abnormality.

Doris could have been many things in life, but she never had the opportunity nor the confidence to do so. Money changed everything for her. The Duke Fortune was truly a Blessing and a Curse. My friend was proud of the fact that she was who she was and, at the same time, Doris Duke was also never quite sure of who she really was.

THE END

Acknowledgments

• • • • • • • •

For our mother, Marie Higgins, deepest gratitude for her loving thoughts, constant prayers, and financial assistance. We will always cherish her warmth, tenderness, and encouragement. The two of us are truly proud to be her sons. Sincerest thanks to our grandmother, Raffaella "Fiela" Volino, who always found time for her grandchildren. Because of her love, concern, and friendship, she forever holds a special place in our hearts. We are beholden to our great-uncle, Joseph Ventura, who was confident enough to invest his hard-earned money in this business endeavor.

We extend profound appreciation to our sister, Judith Higgins Gilbert, and her husband Lowell, who listened to our problems and frustrations with loving patience. To our relatives for their kindness over the years: Margaret and Eddie Barry, Alice and Frank Cosentino, Elspeth Gilbert, Janet and Joey Guide & family, Debbie and Mike Imundo, Eileen McCormack, Jeanne and Larry Roppolo, Justin Roppolo, Dina and Doug Sweet, Michael Volino, Tony and Mary Volino, Vito and Arlene Volino, and Jennifer and Jeff Wilson.

We would also like to thank dear and close friends: Gour Govinda and Sita, Maureen and Frank Hendron & family, John, John Paul, Patty and Richard Vail, and Noelani and Nana Veary. Their generosity knew no bounds.

We are grateful also to these other good friends that saw us through rough times: Tabitha Bridges, Maryanne Petty, Pat and

271

Nick Ponce, and Marian Smolinski. All of them were rays of sunshine during the darker hours.

Special thanks to Nischintya's Spiritual Master, A. C. Bhaktivedanta Swami Prabhupada, founder of the International Society for Krishna Consciousness and The Bhaktivedanta Book Trust. His teachings continue to sustain and inspire us.

To those individuals that at one time or another encouraged us, inspired creativity, and/or convinced us never to give up our dreams, we are truly grateful: Paul Boundas, Diane Burrell, Georgio Cerquetti, James Dunworth, Larry Flynt, Bonnie Franson, Ian Fukumori, Nancy Gableson, Laura Geyer, Kathryn Hallmark, Nina Hartley, Chandi Duke Heffner, Esther Izaguirre, Janet March, Madonna, David Raiford, Paul Raymond, Mary Lou Reardon, Angie Rodriguez, Peggy Sasamoto, Sara St. James, and Jeanne Wehrheim.

We acknowledge the following persons for their unselfishness and charity: Ann Bostich, Colin Shanley, and all the other employees of Doris Duke; Carmella Cosentino, Tom Cusak, John de Lancie, Marilyn Donko, Andy and Gail Duro, Susie Griffith, Linda Gibb, Jean Hays, Mary Hooker, Clyde Jones, Olivia Kalav, Rita Kellman, Nancy Kirkpatrick, Robert LaBotz, Leland and Emily Lockridge, Tom McDonough, Chet Moskwinski, Dorothy Murray, Clarence Pagano M.D., Tim and Pat Sage, Otha Seals, Joe and Clare Sikora, Mike Sikora, Caroline Smorin, Edward Strenk D.D.S., Norb and Nancy Ulaszek, Barb Upton, Susan K. Vigil D.D.S. and Adam Chen D.D.S.

The authors appreciate the excellent education they received from the nuns, priests and lay teachers at Our Lady of the Snows School, as well as our instructors at Quigley Preparatory Seminary South.

Also former colleagues at LaSalle Copy Services; the attorneys, legal assistants and support staff of Peterson & Ross; the crew at Auto Repair Experts; the kind folks at Thomas M. Mareing D.D.S., Ltd., and Primary Eye Care Associates; Alisha

Acknowledgments

and Tina of Shear Madness, and Reverend George McKenna and the Midway Airport Chapel Workers.

To those professionals involved in various aspects of the entire project, we are indebted: Shawn Laksmi, Vishaka, Joseph Fedorowsky, Tom Hoving, Jayne Iorfida, David Liberman, Danelle Morton, Roy Richard, Julia Shopick; Helen Twigge-Molecey and Philip Dampier of Outpost Films, and Emma Rodgers of Black Images.

Particular mention goes to certain deceased relatives who guided us throughout our lives: our paternal grandparents James E. Higgins, Sr., and Rose Higgins; our maternal grandfather, Vito M. Volino; a great-aunt, Margaret Ventura, a great-uncle, Julius "Gus" Ciasto, and an uncle, Edward Barry.

Proper credit and distinguished merit must be awarded to our late father, Lieutenant Colonel James E. Higgins, Jr. (USAR Retired), who gave us lots of excellent advice, especially: "Son, you're all right; it's the rest of the world that's all wrong."

Special credit goes to Nischintya's former spouses Debra Giles, Alice Trachsel, and Karina Carvajal for service above and beyond the call of duty (basically for putting up with him for as long as they did). Love, hugs, and kisses to his children Lance Corporal Prema Bhakti Higgins, Radha-ramana devi-dasi Higgins, and James E. Higgins IV (aka Hawaiian Narayana).

Last but not least Suzanne Griffith, her son Rama Griffith and Nischintya's goddaughter Isani Griffith.

Since it would be very difficult to thank all the persons behind the scenes or who aided in this literary labor, the authors apologize for missing anyone in particular. To list everyone would probably fill an entire book.

—Nischintya Dasa and Joseph P. Higgins, May, 2000

About the Authors

• • • • • • • •

James E. Higgins III, a.k.a. Nischintya Dasa, is an accomplished astrologer, psychic, and *shaman* with 27 years of practicing experience. He has studied to be a Catholic priest as well as Vedic arts and mysticism in Thailand, India, Japan and Hawaii. Through his extensive travels to many far away lands and imbibing the cultures and ancient teachings therein, he has developed a unique, authoritative and also entertaining approach to metaphysical counseling.

His insights and talents have helped clients from all walks of life. Aside from his association with Doris Duke he has shared his astrological and spiritual understanding with people such as Timothy Leary, Alfred B. Ford, Imelda Marcos, and many others. Nischintya tries to use his knowledge to empower people, and says: "I'm not here to simply predict your future, I'm here to help you CREATE your future!"

Nischintya hasn't only limited himself to astrology. He has been involved in the publication of over 50 volumes of ancient Vedic literatures in several languages. He helped establish food relief programs in Thailand, India, the Philippines, Hawaii and the United States. He was recently featured on A&E's Biography of Doris Duke, "The Lonely Heiress," and ITN's production of "The Billion Dollar Babe" in Great Britain.

He is presently taking groups on healing retreats to the Big Island of Hawaii. These retreats include a life reading, acupuncture, massage, yoga, gourmet vegetarian meals, cultural excursions and plenty of fun in the sun. He has been specializing in inner child card readings and emotional healing. Healings are conducted and fulfilled utilizing Vedic, Hawaiian, or Roman Catholic traditions and techniques. He continues to distribute the profound books of his spiritual master, Bhaktivedanta Swami, as he has been doing for over 27 years. He uses the knowledge that he has learned from his spiritual teacher to continue to assist those in need. His skills and talents are especially sought after by leading business professionals and several law firms. He continues to expand his own learning, by teaching others the arts and sciences of worship, prayer, astrology, and healing. Nischintya has now begun work on his third book *Catholic Prophecies for the New Millenium.*

● ● ● ● ● ● ● ●

Joseph P. Higgins is Nischintya's younger brother. He owns a vast audio/visual collection consisting of more than 3,500 titles on video tape, compact disc, and laserdisc; subjects range from silent classics to recent blockbusters, Gregorian Chant to Heavy Metal. Joseph also boasts a formidable literary library including thousands of comic books, magazines, paperbacks, and hardcovers; his scholastic tastes are just as eclectic as his interests in film and music.

Based in Chicago, Mr. Higgins is a writer with a Television and Film Production background. He has completed half-a-dozen scripts, written several short stories and poems, and drafted the lyrics to more than fifty songs. Joseph is currently at work on an adaptation of this book into a possible mini-series or theatrical movie. He is now the Senior Editor at VCA Publishing as well as the manager of the Chicago office.

LIFE READING

Doris Duke tipped me $3000.00 for her life reading. You don't have to! A face-to-face life reading will give you a more in-depth understanding of your personal strengths and the challenges awaiting you in your life.

You also receive a 6-page astrological natal chart and a highlighted copy of my new book, *How to Read Your Horoscope*. Only **$225.00** (regularly $555.00).

**For a Free Initial Consultation and More Information
on Metaphysical Services Call:
1-310-839-1491
Leave a message and I will call you back**

VEDIC TEXTS

A special edition of my spiritual master's translations of ancient Vedic texts is now available. Every one of the 18 hardcover books contains 16 full-color plates. Each volume averages 1,000 pages.

Order a complete set and you will receive a FREE Life Reading along with your purchase. Only **$555.00** (Suggested retail price is $750.00).

CARD READING AND HEALING

I have been specializing in doing readings using the Inner Child Cards, illustrated by Christopher Guilfoil and authored by Isha and Mark Lerner. Reawaken the unique child in yourself and soothe the emotional pains of your childhood.

Healings are conducted and fulfilled utilizing Vedic, Hawaiian, or Roman Catholic traditions and techniques. Suggested donation is **$225.00.**

ANCIENT VEDIC FIRE SACRIFICE

A fire sacrifice, or *yajna,* is a spiritual ceremony performed to relieve negative *karma* and to enhance good fortune. The ritual is also carried out to promote auspicious beginnings to any major life changes: getting married, making new career choices, buying a house, etc. Suggested donation is **$225.00.**

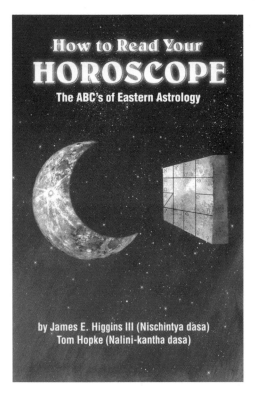

HOW TO READ YOUR HOROSCOPE

The ABC's of Eastern Astrology

By
James E. Higgins III (Nischintya dasa)
and
Tom Hopke (Nalini-kantha dasa)

Trade paperback
168 pages
5-1/2 x 8-1/2
$15.00 plus shipping & handling
Available: NOW

How to Read Your Horoscope is an introduction to the ancient science of Vedic astrology. A book designed especially for the beginner, the easy-to-read guide explores the intricacies of this 5,000-year-old method. Vedic astrology is highly accurate and very specific in its predictive capacity. As a result, Eastern interpretation is becoming more and more popular in the West.

You can look up the traditional delineations for your own chart. The book also outlines calculations unique to Vedic astrology: the star signs (based upon the ancient system of 27 *naksatras*) and the placement of the House rulers. The authors, Higgins and Hopke, give you a basic overview of this fascinating astrological system. (See order form at the back of the book.)

Also Available
THE VIDEO THAT STARTED IT ALL

"Island Astrologer"

60 minutes, VHS (NTSC) only
Only $19.95 plus shipping & handling

After watching this television program, Doris Duke designated Nischintya Dasa as her personal astrologer. The show is a basic introduction to Vedic astrology: how and why it is different from the more well-known Western version, as well as the symbols, instructions, and terminology of a proven system that dates back thousands of years. (See order form at the back of the book.)

PURI: HERITAGE OF AN ANCIENT LAND

By Somanath Khuntia
Photography by Elizabeth Burnett

Hardbound
218 pages with 167 color photographs
8-1/2 x 11
$39.95 plus shipping & handling
Available: NOW

Jagannatha Puri, situated on the Bay of Bengal, India, is a holy and peaceful temple town that has existed since antiquity. *Puri: Heritage of An Ancient Land* makes the culture and traditions of the people and the temple of Jagannatha come alive – their daily life, temple rituals, festivals, holidays, their wisdom and proverbs, and their drama and dance. The lavish photographs transport the reader to this sacred city to experience the life and customs of this ancient holy place. (See order form at the back of the book.)

THE LILAS OF LORD JAGANNATHA

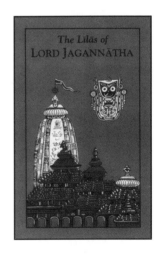

By Somanath Khuntia

Trade paperback
88 pages with 8 color plates
5-1/2 x 8-1/2
$12.95 plus shipping & handling
Available: NOW

This book contains a collection of short stories and miracles from the 2000-year-old Jagannatha Puri Temple. Beautiful original Orissan art, commissioned especially for this edition, is reproduced in full color. An extensive question-and-answer section is included. (See order form at the back of the book.)

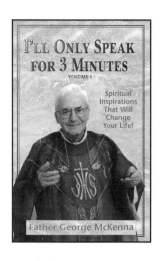

I'LL ONLY SPEAK FOR 3 MINUTES, VOLUME 1

Spiritual Inspirations That Will Change Your Life
By Father George McKenna

Trade paperback
99 pages
5-1/2 x 8-1/2
$10.95 plus shipping & handling
Available: NOW

The first volume in this series of spiritual advice contains an uplifting collection of three dozen, easy-to-read, brief homilies from the founder of Chicago's Midway Airport Chapel. These inspirational messages are for people of all ages, walks of life, and faiths. Father McKenna provides an illuminating keepsake of simple and creative approaches that can make a profound difference in your daily life. (See order form at the back of the book.)

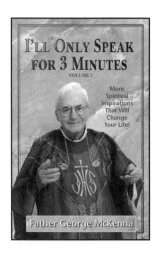

I'LL ONLY SPEAK FOR 3 MINUTES, VOLUME 2

More Spiritual Inspirations That Will Change Your Life
By Father George McKenna

Trade paperback
105 pages
5-1/2 x 8-1/2
$10.95 plus shipping & handling
Available: NOW

Father McKenna shares more of his famous three-minute sermons in this second collection of short life-lessons. His engaging stories and practical insights will bring you spiritual comfort, guidance, humor, and wisdom. You will treasure his timeless gems for many years to come. Allow Father's wisdom and warmth to further brighten your life and enrich your soul. (See order form at the back of the book.)

I'LL ONLY SPEAK FOR 3 MINUTES, VOLUME 3

The Personal Best of Chicago's Midway Airport Chaplain
By Father George McKenna

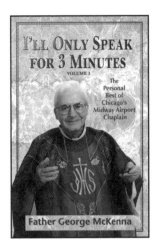

Trade paperback
5-1/2 x 8-1/2
$10.95 plus shipping & handling
Available: HOLIDAY SEASON 2000

Volume Three in this motivational book series offers the reader another collection of thirty-six new, three-minute homilies by a master storyteller. These are Father's favorite parables, special ones that give comfort, offer guidance, and provide inspiration to all. Father George McKenna has brought godliness into our lives and the lives of thousands more. His reflective words have evoked hope and faith.

OUR LADY OF LORETO CHAPEL

Live in the Chicago Area?
Visiting the Windy City?

Mass is offered at the Chicago Midway Airport Chapel on the weekends in the "B" Concourse. Signs are posted and announcements made prior to services.

SATURDAY— 3:00 pm
SUNDAY— 8:30 am

Mass lasts one-half hour ✝ Confessions heard upon request ✝ Communion is available before and after the Mass ✝ Hear one of Father McKenna's famous three-minute homilies in person ✝ Take home a complimentary bulletin ✝ Pick up FREE blessed rosaries (by Father McKenna), traveler prayer cards, Care Notes© and Catholic literature ✝ Purchase autographed copies of Father's books from the Chapel Volunteer Workers or have him personalize ones you have already bought ✝ Come as you are ✝ Everyone is welcome! ✝ Please call Airport Information **(1-773-838-0600)** for any last-minute schedule or gate changes

LIONS IN THE CITY

Missionary to America

A Novel
By Jack Casserly

Deluxe Softbound Edition
French fold-out Triptych covers
6 x 9
$19.95 plus shipping & handling
Available: FALL 2000

An American missionary, after laboring for 33 years in the African bush, returns home to the U.S. in 1998 to die from malaria. Instead, he lives to face the two greatest challenges of his life: the controversial changes in the Catholic Church following the Ecumenical Council of Vatican II and a soul-wrenching, face-to-face confrontation with his older brother, a fellow priest. Penned by best-selling author Jack Casserly, *Lions in the City* is a down-to-earth story of humanity, humility, and hope. His novel reveals today's conflicts between Catholic traditionalists and futurists, not with hair-splitting theological terms, but through all-too-human, riveting drama.

THE WHOLE PARENT

12 Steps to Serenity for Unwed Parents

A Practical Life Guide
By Margot Sheahan

Trade paperback
5-1/2 x 8-1/2
$12.95 plus shipping & handling
Available: FALL /WINTER 2000

Margot Sheahan, the founder of *Unwed Parents Anonymous, Inc.,* has written a life guide for helping families deal with the problems of out-of-wedlock parenting. Her twelve-step program offers change for these persons, a chance to feel serene, happy, and in control of their lives. This book will teach them acceptance of their situation, along with a forgiving, non-judgmental attitude toward others. Her practical guide cannot provide all the answers to their problems—no single book can—but it does offer a promise of understanding and the hope of serenity by following its precepts.

COP TALES! Volume 1

Stories from the Street

A Collection of Police Stories
By Thomas J. Cline

Trade paperback
5-1/2 x 8-1/2
$11.95 plus shipping & handling
Available: HOLIDAY SEASON 2000

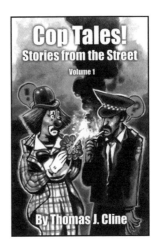

Told in gritty, street vernacular with a dose of dry humor and a dollop of veteran hindsight, *Cop Tales!* is a unique, empathetic peek into the harsh realities and aberrant adventures of a police officer. Whether as a recruit training at the academy, a rookie going through his baptism of fire, or a cop with years under his belt, Cline paints a vivid picture of his emotions, thoughts, and opinions. Also included is an excerpt from "Surviving Storms," a four-hour seminar taught by the author at Chicago's Timothy J. O'Connor Training Academy for Police.

CATHOLIC PROPHECIES FOR THE NEW MILLENNIUM

*Astrological Interpretations
of Saintly Predictions*

A Commentary by
James E. Higgins III (Nischintya dasa)

Trade paperback
5-1/2 x 8-1/2
$10.95 plus shipping & handling
Available: SPRING/SUMMER 2001

Famous Vedic astrologer James E. Higgins III (aka Nischintya Dasa) examines the prophecies and predictions of Catholic saints, the Bible, and apparitions of the Blessed Mother. He claims, as we start the new millennium, that the Apocalypse is upon us. The Last Judgment, foretold by the prophets, martyrs, and mystics since antiquity, will come to pass—unless we get down on our knees and pray! Is it the end of civilization as we know it? Provocative, shocking, ominous.

How VCA Publishing Was Born

Originally, my brother and I submitted our book proposal for *Dollars, Diamonds, Destiny & Death* to a number of literary agents. To our amazement, several of them contacted us. We were wined and dined, promised a six-figure advance, and informed that a deal would be made within a few months. However, within weeks the two of us were reading rejection letters from all of the top publishers. Later, we realized that our representatives had envisioned a book much different than the simple story we wanted to write. Oh well, so much for being rich *and* in print.

Around this time we attended a seminar held at Book Expo '97. It was a self-publishing lecture hosted by Emma Rogers of *Black Images.* Ms. Rogers and her panel of black authors fired up the assembly. They instilled in us a desire to publish the book *our* way, no matter the cost or the hardships ahead. I said to my brother and co-author: "Look, I've been helping the Hare Krishnas for twenty-four years—if there's one thing I know how to do, it's how to print, publish, and sell books." He agreed, having worked in the printing industry for twenty-two years himself. This book is a testament to our perseverance.

VCA Publishing is based upon co-operative efforts. We split the overall expenses 50/50 with our authors. Because we know from personal experience how hard it is to get a literary work published, we are making this special offer: if you have written something spiritual, socially uplifting, cosmic in significance, or just good reading material, send us a query letter. Who knows, the next book we advertise might be yours . . .

VCA Publishing
P.O. Box 388352 • Chicago, IL 60638-8352
Attn: Senior Editor, New Projects

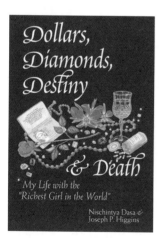

VCA PUBLISHING

VCA Publishing is a division of the **Vedic Cultural Association**. Its mission is one of enlightenment—to convey spiritual knowledge to all peoples in order to check the imbalance of values in life and achieve real unity and peace in the world. VCA Publishing offers an eclectic mix of titles in a variety of subjects:

Spiritual Inspiration

- I'LL ONLY SPEAK FOR 3 MINUTES, VOLUME 1 ($10.95)
  By Father George McKenna
- I'LL ONLY SPEAK FOR 3 MINUTES, VOLUME 2 ($10.95)
  By Father George McKenna

Vedic Astrology

- HOW TO READ YOUR HOROSCOPE ($15.00)
  By James E. Higgins III (aka Nischintya dasa) and Tom Hopke
- DOLLARS, DIAMONDS, DESTINY & DEATH:
  My Life With the Richest Girl in the World ($35.00)
  By Nischintya Dasa and Joseph P. Higgins

Sacred and Mystic Places of the World

- PURI: HERITAGE OF AN ANCIENT LAND ($39.95)
  By Somanath Khuntia with photography by Elizabeth Burnett
- THE LILAS OF LORD JAGANNATH ($12.95)
  By Somanath Khuntia

Forthcoming Titles

- LIONS IN THE CITY: Missionary to America (Fall 2000)
  By Jack Casserly
- THE WHOLE PARENT: 12 Steps to Serenity for Unwed Parents
  (Fall/Winter 2000) By Margot Sheahan
- I'LL ONLY SPEAK FOR 3 MINUTES, VOLUME 3 (Holidays 2000)
  By Father George McKenna
- COP TALES! Volume 1 (Holidays 2000)
  By Thomas J. Cline
- CATHOLIC PROPHECIES FOR THE NEW MILLENNIUM:
  Astrological Interpretations of Saintly Predictions
  (Spring/Summer 2001)
  By James E. Higgins III (Nischintya Dasa)

Order Form

Name _____

Address _____

City _____ ST _____ Zip _____

Quantity	Description	Product Code	Price	Subtotal
	Dollars, Diamonds, Destiny, & Death	DDDD	$35.00	
	How to Read Your Horoscope (book only)	READ	$15.00	
	Healing Others	WW1	$11.95	
	Healing Yourself	WW2	$11.95	
	How Prayer Heals	WW3	$12.95	
	Healing Others, Healing Yourself, How Prayer Heals (3 volume set)	WW4	$35.00	
	PURI: Heritage of an Ancient Land	PURI	$39.95	
	The Lilas of Lord Jagannatha	LILA	$12.95	
	I'll Only Speak for 3 Minutes, Vol. 1	MCK1	$10.95	
	I'll Only Speak for 3 Minutes, Vol. 2	MCK2	$10.95	
	Island Astrologer (video)	VHS1	$19.95	

Shipping Chart	Merchandise Subtotal	
Please add $1.00 for each of these items: READ, WW1, WW2, WW3, LILA, MCK1, MCK2	Shipping Charges (see chart at left) (Maximum $7.00)	
Please add $2.00 for each of these items: WW4, VHS1		
Please add $3.00 for each of these items: DDDD, PURI	Handling Charge	$3.00
	Illinois residents add 8.75% Sales Tax	
Maximum of $7.00 for shipping charges	**TOTAL ORDER**	

**All U.S. orders are shipped via Priority Mail, usually within 24 hours.
You never pay more than $10.00 for shipping & handling combined.**

Please send check or money order to:
VCA Publishing • P.O. Box 388352 • Chicago, IL 60638-8352

**Credit card customers (AMEX, VISA, MC, DISCOVER)
may order by visiting our website or calling our toll-free number**
www.govedic.com

ORDER TOLL FREE 1-888-468-3342